ECONOMIC ASPECTS OF THE WAR

ECONOMIC ASPECTS
OF THE WAR

NEUTRAL RIGHTS, BELLIGERENT CLAIMS
AND AMERICAN COMMERCE IN
THE YEARS 1914-1915

By

EDWIN J. CLAPP

Professor of Economics, New York University

NEW HAVEN: YALE UNIVERSITY PRESS
LONDON: HUMPHREY MILFORD
OXFORD UNIVERSITY PRESS
MDCCCCXV

PREFACE

This story of international lawlessness in the first year of the Great War is the outgrowth of a public lecture given at New York University in March, 1915.

The book was written because it seemed to me that we Americans were paying too much attention to the affairs of belligerents and too little to our own.

After all, we are by no means untouched by the war. It imperils not only our present material interests but also neutral rights upon which the material interests of all peaceful nations in the future depend.

The neutral world is watching for us to realize and assert its rights and ours. Hence this statement of what those rights are and this record of what seems to have occurred to threaten them.

EDWIN J. CLAPP.

University Heights,
   New York,
      August, 1915.

CONTENTS

CONTENTS

x CONTENTS

CONTENTS

CONTENTS

ECONOMIC ASPECTS OF THE WAR

CHAPTER I

Rights of Neutrals under International Law

Before this war had been long in progress most of us learned for the first time the real nature of international law. The word "law" had tricked us into thinking of something clearly defined and accepted by those to whom it applied, and something backed by force to compel obedience.

Now we learn that what we considered international law consists mainly of a great body of precedents of different nations, some of them conflicting. These precedents represent certain immunities granted by belligerents to the commerce of neutrals in time of war. To be sure, the immunities are an advance over the days when a belligerent proceeded like a pirate against lives and property on ships trading with the enemy. But the advance, when we consider it closely, is seen in no way to have kept pace with the growth of the vast interests it was designed to protect. International law at the best is an inadequate recognition of the rights of those who keep the peace at the hands of those who break it.

Yet even such law as there was has been disregarded. Blinded by self-interest, the belligerents have inaugurated a return to the practices of piracy

from which this law has been designed to save us.
When we turn to a power sufficient to compel obedience to the law, we find that behind it there is nothing
but international morality, the public opinion of the
world.

Especially in the last fifteen years this public
opinion has been enlightened as to the great interests
dependent upon an uninterrupted flow of peaceful
commerce in war times. True, in the process of public enlightenment there has been more emphasis upon
the horrors of war in general. The strongest of
the forces forming public opinion on international
matters has been the peace movement. Today we can
say that more good might have been accomplished if
the greater emphasis had been not upon preventing
all war but upon confining its damage to those who
fight. But a valuable by-product of the peace movement has been the spread of information on the rights
of peaceful nations compared with belligerents and
the need to extend those rights, not restrict them.

It was hoped that in time of war this international
public opinion as to the rights of neutrals would
exercise a strong moral force upon the belligerents
to stay within the limits of law. That is, it was expected that the conscience of belligerents, fearing the
disapproval of neutrals, would compel respect for
the established order of things.

We were doomed to disappointment. The disapproval of neutrals has not been lacking, expressed
most clearly in the protests of their governments
directed to both belligerents. But a belligerent con-

science, that is, fear of this disapproval or even any large respect for it, is lacking in the parties to the war.

Perhaps it was too much to expect that international morality alone would suffice to give sanction to international law. Within national boundaries we do not trust to morality alone. The prime interests of life and property are safeguarded by definite, clearly understood laws, accepted by all, and backed by force. Morality supplements force and does not supplant it. Withdraw the force of the law in any nation and its observance would disappear. Could we expect international morality alone to be any more able to supplant force in compelling observance of international law?

Whatever our expectations were, regarding the binding force of morality upon warring nations, we can have them no more. It is necessary to find some form of peaceable compulsion that will bring the belligerents back to the limits of law. Everyone recognizes the necessity of doing this at the end of the war. As a sequel to the peace, men are planning a new sort of international law with sharp power to enforce it. But the return to legal limits must be now, in the midst of the war. For neutrals to forfeit their rights will be a victory for the forces of international immorality and disorder. Respect for international law will be permanently weakened.

Moreover, no one can with certainty say that the end of the war will see established the formal system of international law of which we dream. It may be that this law will still be largely a matter of precedents, enforced by nothing stronger than the morality of nations. What security will there be in our relations if those precedents, hard won in the past, are now effaced and if that international morality notoriously proves unequal to its task?

Apart from this matter of principle, the great interests of trading nations, injured by the actions of belligerents, and the constant peril to innocent lives upon the high seas, both call for a return to freedom of neutral trade and travel now, before the end of the war, whose end we cannot foresee. Now is the time to put an end to the sacrifices of life and property demanded of those who choose to remain aloof from the conflict.

From the very beginning this war went beyond the limit of military and naval actions. It became an "economic war"; namely, a process of interrupting the flow of commerce between neutrals and belligerents and even between neutrals themselves. The purpose was to deprive the interrupted belligerent of necessities of military, industrial and civil life and so bring upon the enemy nation "pressure" sufficient to end the war.

But an economic war of this sort is also an economic war against neutrals, for the same pressure is brought to bear upon them as upon the belligerent attacked, perhaps even greater pressure. It may be that the belligerent can find or develop a substitute for the neutral's product more easily than the neutral can find a substitute for the belligerent's market.

There are two parties to all trade. It is impossible to interrupt the trade without striking them both.

The economic war began in August, 1914. Soon after the outbreak of the military war England's sea power drove German naval vessels from the ocean. Since then, Germany's navy upon the high seas has been unable to do more than carry on a sort of guerrilla warfare beneath the waves. England, after driving German cruisers from the Atlantic, proceeded to inaugurate measures designed to withhold from Germany the importation of most commodities that come to her by sea. Germany retaliated by a submarine campaign that endangered not only neutral property but also neutral lives on vessels sailing to or from England.

Through this policy of action, retaliation and counter-retaliation the seas have become a battlefield where the commerce and citizens of neutral countries venture at peril of capture or sudden destruction.

This book, dealing with the effect of belligerent violations of neutral trade rights upon the agriculture, industries and commerce of the United States, could be written about any nation now at peace. Our wrongs and losses are merely types of what has been forced on other neutrals as well. The sum of these wrongs and losses is an argument demanding that nations which plan to work and trade be led to dismiss now, and for all time, the aggressions of those that plan to devastate and slay.

It happens that the United States is the only great power remaining neutral, the only force today that is able to assert the rights of the world of peace. If we fail in the objects we seek, in the negotiations we carry on with both belligerents, the hope of all neutral nations is gone.

It is worth while briefly to review that body of neutral rights which we called international law and the successive measures by which those rights were abolished.

By common consent the seas are the public highways of nations; outside a zone three miles from shore they are not the domain of any one nation. They belong to peaceful commerce, not to belligerents who roam their surface seeking to destroy each other. As a remnant of marine barbarism, a belligerent has the right, if it has the power, to capture or drive from the ocean the merchant vessels of its foe. To the extent of its command over the sea, a belligerent may prevent contraband of war from reaching an enemy in any vessels; and, if capable of blockading the enemy's seacoast, may put a stop to all ocean commerce of the blockaded country. Under international law, these were the limits and conditions of interfering with commerce between neutrals and a country at war.

Only within much narrower limits, according to modern conceptions of international law, can a belligerent interfere with commerce between neutrals themselves. This commerce may be interrupted only when it consists of contraband of war—the actual tools of fighting—demonstrably in transit to enemy territory.

These are the rights of commerce on the seas. The rights of travel are as well understood. Though a belligerent may capture and in certain cases destroy a merchant vessel of the enemy, this may not be done without providing for the safety of crew and passengers. All passengers on neutral vessels, wherever bound, are immune from interference, excepting members of the armed forces of the enemy traveling home.

The laying of mines at sea is not permitted except for defensive purposes and then only in the territorial waters of the warring power that lays them.

With these main exceptions, which are burdensome enough, the sea must be free for the uses of commerce.

While this is international law as generally understood, it has not been in form to give nations a sense of security. The law is mainly in the form of precedents, such as proclamations of belligerents in previous wars, decisions of the prize courts of captors, and treaties between individual nations. Some of the precedents of different countries are conflicting. Therefore civilized powers have made several attempts to reduce the law of the sea to a form acceptable to all and accepted by all.

One such attempt resulted in the brief Declaration of Paris, adopted as a sequel to the peace negotiations following the Crimean War. More recently in the Hague Conferences efforts were made to form treaties which all nations were to sign. Most important for our present purposes is the Declaration of London. The British Government in 1909 called the London Conference to codify the law of the sea. All the leading nations took part. The result was the Declaration of London, signed by all national representatives who attended the Conference.

It is true that not all the Hague Conference agreements, called Conventions, were accepted by all civilized nations. It is true that for reasons partly selfish and partly technical the Declaration of London was not *ratified* by many home governments and so did not become officially binding upon them. But it was signed by the representatives of all great powers. The Preliminary Provision reads:

"The Signatory Powers are agreed that the rules contained in the following Chapters correspond in substance with the generally recognized principles of international law."

Hence it is that neutrals felt that the Declaration of London was morally binding. Hence it is that nations at peace looked forward to seeing the judgment of civilized nations as to the rights of neutrals upon the sea, expressed particularly in the Declaration of London, proclaimed as sea law by all belligerents at the outbreak of the war. We were disappointed.

The disregarding of legal limits was first in evidence when either Germany or England began laying floating mines upon the high seas, forbidden in a Hague Convention. Each took the alleged action of the other as the excuse for retaliation. Because of these floating mines in the North Sea, literally scores of vessels were lost, mostly belonging to the Scandinavian countries or Holland. Three American vessels were included, the Greenbriar, Carib and Evelyn. Because of the danger of mines, ocean freights and war risk insurance rates became a heavy burden on shippers and buyers and, in the case of some commodities, became prohibitive of commerce. A pall of uncertainty and fear was thrown over the commercial world.

Unfortunately, as it would seem in the light of later events, America refused to join the North Sea neutral countries in a protest against the mining of the North Sea. Such action might have made more effective the protest of all neutrals against the later German War Zone about the British Isles.

Yet the effect of mines upon the high seas was small compared with the paralysis of trade effected by a practical abolition of the rights of neutrals to trade with Germany and a severe restriction of their right to trade with each other. England brought this about by certain amendments to international law through its Orders in Council. Germany, with her retaliatory submarine warfare, designed the same paralysis of English trade. That the object was not attained is due solely to the fact that German submarines are less omnipresent and less able to intercept all trade than British cruisers are.

The exact process of this abolition of the freedom of commerce is easy to follow.

At the very opening of the war the American Secretary of State, with a view to protecting neutral rights while allowing the belligerents all lawful free-

dom of action, suggested to them that they adopt
during this conflict the unratified Declaration of
London as their code of action towards neutrals.
Germany and Austria agreed. Russia and France
delayed their answer until they could hear from
Great Britain, and then joined that country in its
policy announced by the Order in Council of August
20, 1914, accepting the Declaration of London with
modifications.

The modifications were subversive of the principles
of the Declaration to which they were attached.
These modifications, supplemented by an unexampled
extension of the British contraband list, and finally
by what our government calls an illegal blockade,
have been England's method of exercising economic
pressure upon Germany and, necessarily, upon all
neutral nations that trade with her.

In the Declaration of London the articles classed
as *absolute contraband* of war—that is, articles which
Great Britain might properly shut out of Germany
altogether—were restricted to the actual tools and
equipment of fighting nations. *Conditional contraband* was a more comprehensive list, including such
merchandise as food, clothing, coal, harness and
saddlery, horseshoes and barbed wire. These articles,
capable of direct use by the armed forces of the
enemy, might be stopped only if the interfering belligerent could prove that they were destined for those
forces. Finally, the Declaration specified a list of
free goods, articles which might not be molested because only distantly related to warfare, necessary

to the civilian population, and contributing a very important portion of the commerce of peaceful neutrals. Such articles were cotton, wool, hides and skins, and rubber.

This was law as codified in the Declaration of London. The British Order in Council of August 20 had the effect of adding the conditional contraband list (food, clothing, etc.) to the absolute list, by decreeing that conditional contraband would be presumed to be moving to the German military, and hence subject to capture, if the goods were "consigned to or for an agent of the enemy state or to or for a merchant or other person under control of the authorities of the enemy state." That is, goods could be consigned to no one in Germany; they could not be shipped to Germany at all. It is obvious that after this action any addition to the British conditional contraband list was as complete a ban on commerce as an addition to the absolute contraband list. The two henceforth were identical.

This action stopped our direct trade with Germany. It might appear that goods on the free list could still move. Some of them did move, from free to contraband. People feared to ship the others lest they should be so listed while ships were on the ocean, and the goods made subject to seizure. Practically nothing has been shipped to Germany from this country but cotton, and it was not shipped until December. In belated response to the insistence of southern senators and of American business interests which had found themselves gravely embarrassed by the cessation of cotton shipments, Great Britain finally made a clear statement that this particular commodity would not be considered contraband.

So much for direct trade with Germany.   There was still a method by which we should have been able to export our goods and discharge our neutral obligations to trade with Germany as with England. We might have carried on this trade via neutral ports like Rotterdam or Copenhagen, from which the goods might have been shipped to Germany.   The Declaration of London allows a belligerent to interfere with a shipment between two neutral ports only when it consists of absolute contraband for enemy territory. Conditional contraband so moving may not even be suspected.   The Order in Council changed this.   It extended the new intention of capturing conditional contraband to goods moving to Germany even through a neutral port.   And, as explained, conditional contraband was seizable if destined to anyone in Germany; it was not conditional but absolute.

The British action, besides stopping our trade with Germany, barring only a certain amount of indirect trade carried on with much difficulty and danger, subjected to grave peril our commerce with other neutrals.   The British contraband lists were extended so rapidly that soon almost no important article of commerce with neutrals was free from seizure by England, who suspected everything on these lists as being of possible German destination.   The shipper to a neutral country then had the prospect of a British prize court passing judgment as to whether shipments were destined for Germany and, in the case of an affirmative judgment, whether any compensation should be paid the shipper, or his cargo simply confiscated. The uncertainty was a risk against which no one could insure.

As for the British contraband lists, a few instances will illustrate how they grew. On September 21, copper, lead, rubber, hides and skins were added; on October 29, motor vehicles, motor tires, mineral oil and leather. On December 23, naval stores and cottonseed oil went on the list. On March 11, raw wool was banned. The Germans have retaliated and published a contraband list containing articles that have nothing to do with war, like lumber and flax.

Our protests against the British August 20 Order in Council resulted in the substitution of an Order dated October 29. But when we came to observe the operation of the October 29 Order, we found that it did not lift the ban on our trade with Germany either direct or via neutrals, and that it added to the existing difficulties of our trade with neutrals a prohibition of shipments "to order." This prohibition dislocated the ordinary methods of foreign trade. Our protest to England of December 26 against interference with our trade with Europe failed to secure any modification of that interference.

At last a real test was made of the possibility of provisioning Germany. In January a St. Louis firm tried to get a cargo of foodstuffs to Germany on the American steamer Wilhelmina. The provisions were consigned to no one in Germany but to a member of the American firm who went to Hamburg to receive the cargo and distribute it to the civilian population. The British stopped the vessel.   Unable to find any law for continuing the detention, they made law through a new Order in Council, enabling England to requisition, without trial, the cargo of any neutral ship brought into port.   The Wilhelmina's cargo was so requisitioned.

On February 4 Germany, claiming that its act was a reprisal against an unlawful British attempt to starve a civilian population, declared the waters around the British Isles a War Zone where British merchant ships would be destroyed by German submarines—if necessary, without search—and where the submarines might endanger neutral vessels by mistake.   Neutrals were warned to keep away.   It was stated that it might be impossible to provide for the safety of passengers or crews of the British steamers destroyed.

When the War Zone was announced, our government recognized the danger, and addressed a sharp note to Germany, warning that country to be careful not to strike at American vessels or American lives. At the same time, we seemed to recognize in a degree the German point of view; so we sent a joint note to Britain and Germany suggesting that Britain give up its policy of stopping foodstuffs for German civilians, that Germany abandon its submarine warfare, and that both belligerents desist from mining the high seas.

With certain reservations Germany accepted the

proposal. Great Britain rejected it and, indeed, instead of accepting, proceeded to more radical measures than before. On March 1, stating its action to be a retaliation against the submarine war and other alleged breaches of international law by the Germans, England instituted a "blockade" of Germany. The authorities at London announced that all vessels carrying cargoes to or from Germany, whether direct or via neutral ports, would be subject to seizure. This was the culmination of the British lawlessness. The culmination of the German lawlessness was the Lusitania horror.

The British "blockade" terminated our cotton trade with Germany, virtually the only trade that had moved. Whatever even of cotton thereafter found its way to Germany was involved in a smuggling operation. The third largest buyer from America became as distant from us as another world, barring some dangerous, indirect trade. Moreover, all our shipments to European neutrals adjacent to Germany now became tainted with suspicion and detention. Scores of cotton cargoes bound for neutrals have been held up in British ports.

For the first time American importers of German goods saw their supplies endangered; until March 1, the flow of commerce *from* Germany had been unhindered. Our Federal Government faced a loss of $20,000,000 per year in customs revenues levied on German goods.

The most striking circumstances in this extraordinary situation is the fact that Great Britain has at no time maintained a genuine blockade. British warships, fearing submarines, dare not undertake a close blockade of German ports. The Admiralty merely intercepts all traffic passing by Scotland or through the English Channel. Thus the blockade does not bear equally on all neutrals, for Scandinavian countries ship undisturbed to German Baltic ports, from which American products are barred.

This whole process of gradually damming the currents of trade to and from one of the members of the comity of nations has been attended with huge financial loss to the neutrals. More important than this, these neutrals, because the British operations have been contrary to the accepted interpretations of international law, have been put in a position where they ask themselves seriously whether, without violating their neutrality, they may lawfully continue to trade with one belligerent which unlawfully prevents them from trading with another. Above all, they question the possibility of silent acquiescence in the policy of both belligerents in abandoning decent restraints in their treatment of the lives and property of neutrals.

The time has arrived to revive the restraints and reassert international law and morals.

The lifting of the British "blockade" will not suffice, for we neutrals should then find many of the products of peaceful industry each burdened with an individual blockade. That is, these products would be found included in the British contraband lists, with all that that means in the hindrance of

trade between neutrals as well as between a neutral
and a belligerent. If the "blockade" were lifted and
the October 29 Order in Council and the British contraband lists kept in force, the relief to neutrals
would be small.

What we need is a code of law and morals so
simple in its terms that the self-interest of neither
belligerent can evolve a quibbling interpretation of
it different from that which neutrals hold. In this
code must be determined what may be contraband
and what may not; and it must define the entire
method of procedure against merchant ships at sea.

There is no time now, in the midst of the war, for
neutral nations to meet and devise such a code. The
best we can do is to point to one already in existence: the Declaration of London. Formed by the
best legal talent of all nations, it is fair and it is
clear.

Along with the removal of England's illegal practices against the goods of neutrals must go the
removal of Germany's illegal practices against their
goods and lives. Germany must restrict her swollen
contraband list and likewise return to the Declaration of London. She must not use submarines
against unresisting merchant vessels except to stop
and search them in the approved legal way. Nor
may English merchant vessels under any conditions
be sunk until the safety of crew and passengers has
been provided for.

Floating mine fields must be removed by those who
laid them.

The following chapters are a review of the successive measures that led up to the present situation, and the effect of those measures upon leading articles of our foreign trade and upon our neutrality. It will be shown that it is in America's power, as it is her duty, to restore international law on behalf of the neutral world.

CHAPTER II

The British August Order in Council and Its Effect on the Export of Foodstuffs

The various measures taken to restrict the trade of neutrals are best reviewed in connection with a consideration of their effect upon the trade in foodstuffs, for it was foodstuffs against which most of these measures were aimed.

For a belligerent to interfere with food moving over the sea to the civilian population of the enemy is contrary to our conceptions of international law—and contrary to the conception formerly insisted upon by Great Britain—unless such interference is accomplished by means of an effective blockade.

Violation of the rights of trade means violation of the rights of both parties trading. In this particular case, one party was Germany and one party was the United States. We are less directly interested in the infringement of the right of German civilians to receive food than in the infringement of our right to ship it. Thomas Jefferson even tells us that to send food to one combatant and forego our right to send food to the other is a clear breach of neutrality.*

* For his letter to Pinckney, see Appendix, p. 318.

From the early days of August, 1914, England attempted by means lacking all legal recognition to shut off the movement of grain, flour and provisions to Germany. The frank object of the action was to bring such pressure to bear upon the entire people of Germany that it would sue for peace. In March the "attrition" campaign was given an outer appearance of legitimate practice by what is generally described as a blockade of the German coast, but what is in reality nothing more than an indefinite extension of the law of contraband.

The control of England over the food supply of the nations of the world was exercised at once after the declaration of war. Britain ordered to her own ports every British steamer on the seas then carrying foodstuffs to Europe. Their cargoes were unloaded and sold in the British market, which became glutted with grain. English vessels were carrying most of the world's trade. The diversions not only threw into the British market all German-bound grain, but also all neutral-bound grain in British steamers, and assisted the government materially in exercising pressure upon the neutral countries to comply with certain policies of the British Ministry which will require later attention.

After this initial measure to get control of grain that might be moving to Germany even via neutral countries, the British Government, in its August 20 Order in Council, altered the status of foodstuffs in international trade in war time. This alteration took the form of a modification of the Declaration of London, which England by that Order "accepted" as its code of naval warfare, and with whose terms we are already familiar.

It is recalled that the Declaration classified articles of commerce as *absolute contraband, conditional contraband* or *free.* Absolute contraband might be captured if moving to an enemy either in direct trade or via neutral countries. Conditional contraband might be captured if moving direct to the enemy's country, provided it could be proven destined to the enemy's armed forces. The destination of conditional contraband might not be questioned if it were moving to the enemy via a neutral; that is, conditional contraband so moving would be immune. Goods on the free list could move unhindered to the enemy's country in either direct or indirect trade. Goods *from* the enemy's country might not be stopped except by an effective blockade.—Foodstuffs were conditional contraband.

Translated into terms of the present war, the Declaration prescribed that no interference should occur in trade between the United States and Holland, or Scandinavia, except in the case of ships which could be proven to carry absolute contraband, like arms and ammunition—with ultimate German destination.

There could be no interference with the movement into Germany of such goods on the Declaration's free list as cotton, rubber and hides. There could be no hindrance of our export to Germany of conditional contraband like grain, flour and provisions, unless it could be proved by England that such shipments were destined for the German state or its armed forces. All foodstuffs moving to the civilian population of Germany were immune from capture. This question of army or civilian destination could not be raised if the food were moving to Germany via Holland or Scandinavia.

The Declaration prescribed that there could be no interference in the movement of any goods from Germany to the United States unless in the event of an effective blockade of Germany.

The things which by the Declaration of London Great Britain was obligated not to do gradually came to constitute a fairly good record of what she actually did. Step by step, the British Admiralty interfered with the shipment to neutral countries of the most innocent goods, like cotton, requisitioning the cargoes for British purposes. Rubber was haled into the absolute contraband list; hides were eventually made absolute contraband. Neither food nor other conditional contraband was allowed to get to Germany, either by direct sailing or via neutral ports. Without the maintenance of a genuine blockade, the export of all goods from Germany to the United States was finally made impossible.

The first of these serious "modifications" of the Declaration of London, appearing in the British August 20 Order in Council, was a change in the Declaration's contraband lists. Aeroplanes were made absolute contraband; they were conditional in the Declaration. The change was unimportant in itself but it introduced a policy that led to the greatest abuses.

The second and more dangerous change was in the treatment of conditional contraband, which was lawfully liable to capture only if it could be *shown* destined to the enemy state or its armed forces. The obligation of proof, as always under international law, lay upon the captor. Such hostile destination, the Declaration specified, might be presumed if the foodstuffs were consigned to the enemy authorities or to a contractor in enemy country publicly known to supply the enemy; or if the foodstuffs were sailing to a fortified place or base serving the armed enemy forces. That is, food ships consigned to ordinary merchants, not army purveyors, and sailing to commercial ports, were to be immune. As the Declaration says, "In cases where the above presumptions do not arise, the destination is presumed to be innocent."

So much for the law regarding conditional contraband. What did its British "modification" provide? It provided that destination for the hostile forces might be "inferred *from any sufficient evidence*" and experience proved that a mere suspicion in the mind of the British naval captain was sufficient evidence to detain ships. Moreover, in the new British-made law, destination for enemy forces was to be presumed *if the goods were consigned to or for an agent of the enemy state or to or for a merchant or other person under control of the authorities of the enemy state."*

This "modification" made direct shipment of foods to Germany impossible. It abolished the difference between absolute and conditional contraband; henceforth neither could move. The prize court judges who must administer this new sort of international law were thereby prevented from allowing the civilian population of Germany to get foodstuffs from America. Such foodstuffs must obviously be shipped to someone. There is no one in Germany or any other land who is not either "an agent of the enemy state *or a merchant or other person in control of the authorities of the enemy state.*"

To be sure, the shipment might be consigned "to order," but events showed that the "evidence" would then be "sufficient" to "infer" destination to the enemy's forces.

Yet this did not exhaust the sweep of the British change in international law as brought forth in the Order in Council of August 20. There still remained the possibility of provisioning Germany by shipping to Rotterdam, Copenhagen, Gothenburg or Genoa, and thence forwarding into Germany. Against interference with conditional contraband so moving, stood the clear and unmistakable provisions of the Declaration of London. It read:

"Conditional contraband is not liable to capture except when on board a vessel bound for territory belonging to or occupied by the enemy . . . and when it is not to be discharged in an intervening neutral port."

If food is to be discharged in a neutral port, its destination is not subject to suspicion.

That is, applying the Declaration to the geography of the war, food bound for Germany, even if destined for military consumption, might lawfully be stopped only if shipped directly to Germany or Belgium, not if shipped to Germany through Dutch or Scandinavian ports.

The reason for this last provision is simple. It would be a disturbance of trade sufficiently serious if doubtful foodstuffs moving from America direct to Germany were to be subject to the review of English judges on the often debatable question whether their destination were civil or military. It would become insufferable if international law should enable the British authorities to halt food consigned to Scandinavian merchants and pass upon the dual question, first, the possibility of German destination, and next, the possibility of German army destination.

Such power would enable the British judges to ruin trade between America and Scandinavia, upon the mere suspicion that some of the goods might be leaking through to Germany. Great Britain might use this annoying power over Scandinavia and Holland to force them to refuse to trade with Germany in articles of their own growth and manufacture. Therefore international law forbids England the right to suspect that shipments to neutral countries have German military destination. International law forbids England the right to guard against such indirect shipment, in the interest of the higher right of neutral trade which would thereby be exposed to the constant peril of a prejudiced interpretation.

Experience has demonstrated the justice of these principles. And yet Great Britain in its August 20 Order proceeded to disregard them. That Order provided that conditional contraband, if destination to enemy forces could be shown, was

"liable to capture at whatever port the cargo is to be discharged."

But, as we already know, destination to enemy forces was assumed if the goods were moving to Germany at all. Conditional contraband, such as foodstuffs, could not move to Germany via a neutral country just as they could not move direct.

After barring neutral trade with Germany in all goods on the absolute and conditional contraband lists, England then increased these lists by adding to them articles that were either free or unclassified in the Declaration of London; such as rubber, copper, wool, hides and leather. Shippers feared to ship most goods not on the contraband lists, for fear they might be added to those lists. The result of all this was so severe that when the British began their "blockade," on March 1, the effect of it was not severely felt so far as traffic from America was concerned, excepting for cotton. Trade in most of our other important exports had already been stopped.

It is necessary to bear these facts in mind because, six months after hostilities began, we find England solemnly declaring that, as a retaliation against the barbarities of German warfare, it may find itself obliged to institute reprisals and shut off the oversea supplies of Germany, particularly food. Germany, in the light of history, has a better right to call her acts reprisals, for the British policy began on August 20, 1914.

Yet the action of England went further than the measures described. There was still a possibility that Germany might be supplied with food or other commodities via neutral countries. This trade could move from America to merchants in Holland or Scandinavia, who would take delivery and later resell into Germany, attracted by the magnet of high prices prevailing there.

Two means were taken to prevent this resale trade. In the first place pressure was brought to bear upon steamship lines, plying from the United States to European neutral countries, not to accept shipments of articles on the British contraband lists unless each such shipment were accompanied by a sworn statement by the shipper to the effect that the goods were, to the best of his knowledge and belief, for bona fide consumption in the neutral country. The steamship companies required such an affidavit because without it the vessel faced detention by England while the uncertified shipment was being taken off. The fact that the neutral shipment was uncertified might then in the British prize court be "sufficient evidence" to prove it destined to the German military.

In spite of this, there was a chance that some merchant in neutral Europe might deceive the American shipper who, after all, could give no guarantee of the ultimate destination of his goods, once they were delivered abroad. This contingency Great Britain met by inducing the European neutral governments to lay re-exportation embargoes upon articles in the British absolute and conditional contraband lists. That is, the neutrals were brought to pass laws penalizing any citizen for reselling into another country these articles when imported. A neutral government which did not take this precaution might find that the absence of a re-export embargo upon goods was "sufficient evidence" to presume their destination to the German military and the neutral's own supplies from America would then be detained in England.

The working of this system may be illustrated by the case of Holland. It is recalled that at the outbreak of the war Great Britain at once summoned to home ports all British steamers carrying foodstuffs to Europe, and that the cargoes were sold in the English markets. For example, 770,000 bushels of wheat moving to Rotterdam were so diverted to English ports. This wheat was needed by the Dutch millers.

Holland was allowed to import no foodstuffs for herself, and before the end of August the government of that country was willing to enact any embargo and give any guarantees that Great Britain wanted. On August 23 a Dutch Minister of State announced this, in an interview published in London. On the following day the London Corn Exchange asked Sir Edward Grey for permission to export grain to Holland, since the people of that country were suffering from a food shortage and would not be in a position to export any of the wheat to Germany. Sir Edward felt compelled to refuse their request, so the London despatches said, on the ground that the strength of the German army on the Dutch frontier might be so great that Holland could not guard its own food supply.

No doubt the strength of the German army was a factor that influenced Sir Edward's attitude. The strength of the Germany army on the borders of Holland did not decrease, yet he eventually did let food into Holland. If he had not, the Dutch would have starved as the Belgians did. But he waited not only until the Dutch Government laid an export embargo on foodstuffs but also until the Dutch Government agreed to act as the sole consignee of all contraband and conditional contraband moving into Holland. Merchants importing grain, flour and provisions had to transmit to the government their demands and furnish it with funds and guarantees. The government in turn guaranteed to England that all of these imports would be consumed within Dutch borders.

In the course of time the work of handling all imports for Holland became too heavy for the Dutch Government. Its departments were not equipped for commercial operations. Therefore under government auspices the Netherlands Oversea Trust was formed, composed of prominent Dutch business men. To it were henceforth consigned all goods on Britain's contraband lists except grain, flour, petroleum and copper, which still could be sent only to the government direct. The Holland-American Line, the only regular steamers between America and Holland, bound itself to accept contraband goods only when consigned to the government or the trust.*

Before this arrangement had been worked out in Holland and before the other European neutrals had taken measures satisfactory to Great Britain, they had all fallen into real want because of a restriction of their food imports. Throughout October the newspapers of Denmark, Norway and Sweden contained complaints about the detention of grain and food shipments by England. Under such conditions it is not strange that by early November those countries had placed the most stringent embargoes on the export of food. It appears from our note to Great Britain of December 26 that the British Government had consented, in November, to be satisfied with the guarantees offered by the Norwegian, Swedish and Danish Governments as to non-exportation of "contraband goods" when consigned to named persons in the territory of those governments, and that orders had been given to restrict interference with neutral vessels, so consigned, to verification of ship's papers and cargoes.

---

* American exporters have never been enthusiastic about this arrangement. In the fall of 1914 they protested against the Dutch Government assuming a monopoly of flour purchases for Holland. It was claimed that this monopoly, in supplanting the normal competition of Dutch dealers, prevented Americans from getting a competitive price for their flour.

No one in this country worried about the restriction of our grain and provisions trade with Germany and the adjacent neutrals. We shall see that, because of the distress of the cotton planters, largely due to the impossibility of getting cotton started for Germany, there was a successful agitation in October to have the British ban taken off cotton. But no one was in distress about grain.

It is true that in the first weeks of the war grain did not move out of this country, for reasons concerned with the general maritime situation. The uncertainty of the North Atlantic lanes, until Great Britain had cleared them of German cruisers, forbade vessels to venture out. As soon as England was alone in the North Atlantic, neutral and British vessels were safe from capture. Then there were initial difficulties of insurance and especially of finance to be overcome. Bills drawn on forcign buyers were unsalable; for the London discount market, through which these would ordinarily be turned into funds by the American bankers, had temporarily broken down. Requisitioning of British vessels by the Admiralty served to reduce the tonnage available for carrying grain or any other commercial cargo.

Large purchases of our grain were made by foreign buyers in the last week of July and the first week in August. But at that time the goods could not be moved out of this country. Grain left interior centers for the seaboard, filled elevators at the ports and intermediary points like Buffalo, and lay in cars that choked the Atlantic terminal yards of the railroads.   Railroads to New Orleans and Galveston stopped receiving grain for export until the situation at the ports should clear up.

Yet all this caused little worry to the farmer. The purchases of exporters and their continual bidding for grain drove up the prices paid on the farm.   The world began to see that we were to feed Europe, especially when it considered Russia's participation in the war and the stoppage of her exports.

Every day the farmer saw his property in wheat grow more valuable.   On July 18, 1914, cash wheat (No. 2 Red Winter) was selling in New York for 88 cents per bushel.   On July 24 it was 92, on July 29 it was 98½.   Wheat sold from 95 cents to $1 during the first half of August.   On August 17 it touched 102½ and was never again below $1.   On September 1, cash wheat sold for 120½.   Until December, when the next rapid advance took place, wheat sold in New York for prices varying between 115 and 125.   With the cereal selling at 125, the farmer who still held his wheat was being paid 37 cents per bushel more than on July 18, when the New York price was 88 cents.   The capital of the man who owned wheat had increased over 44 per cent.

On December 18, the price reached 130¾.   It rose almost without interruption to 138 on January 2, to 145½ on January 7, to 153¼ on January 14.   On January 27 the price touched 160. On February 4 it was 176¾.   From then until the last of May it fluctuated often violently between 160 and 175. This averaged fully 100 per cent higher than the 88 cents which was being paid for wheat in New York in the middle of July, 1914. Early in July, 1915, spot wheat still sold for 130, though the September option, due to the expectation of a large American crop, was below 110.

Once the financial and shipping difficulties had been removed, wheat was exported at the rate of 1,000,000 bushels per day. Countries like Italy and Greece, which had always bought heavily from the Black Sea, had to buy in America. Scandinavia, which had secured rye from Russia and East Germany, had to substitute rye and wheat from America. France found part of its harvest appropriated by the invading Germans, who also occupied all of Belgium. The various relief funds for Belgium, notably the Rockefeller Commission, began purchasing food, largely grain and flour, at the rate of $7,000,000 per month.

Obviously no one was needed to come to the rescue of the wheat farmer. His constant interest has been in the continuance of the war, just as the constant interest of the cotton farmer has been in its conclusion. Peace rumors send the grain market down. They send the cotton market up. The Turk, in closing and holding the Dardanelles, thus interning the Russian wheat supply, has been the American farmer's best hired man. The price of wheat on our markets would be reduced along with the forts at Kilid Bahr.—While Wall Street prayed for peace, the Produce Exchange, a few blocks away, prayed for the war to go on.

As with wheat, so with flour. Winter patents sold in the third week in July for $5 per barrel. On August 11 the same flour was $5.25. On August 25 it was $5.75; on September 25, $6. Here the price remained until the last week in December, when it sold at $6.50. The next week the price was $6.75. Then the rise was rapid, reaching $8.25 on February 1. This about corresponded with the summit of the wheat prices. From February 1 on, the price long averaged $7.50. Compared with the price of $5 in July, 1914, the advance was very perceptible. To be sure, it did not represent clear profit, such as the wheat advance represented to the farmer or the middleman. The miller had to pay more for some of the wheat in his 1915 flour than for the wheat in his 1914 flour. Nevertheless, even the millers, who chronically complain, confessed to some degree of prosperity because of the war.

From August 1, 1913, to May 31, 1914, we exported 75,600,000 bushels of wheat, receiving therefor $71,800,000. In the August-May months of 1914-1915, the war year, we sent abroad 224,000,000 bushels and were paid $297,000,000. In these months of 1913-1914 we exported 10,200,000 barrels of wheat flour, for which we were paid $46,750,000. In the August-May period just past we were paid $85,000,000 for 14,400,000 barrels. On the other hand, high prices which foreigners paid to farmers were matched by the equally high prices paid for grain and flour by domestic users. This was one of the less cheerful sides of the boom in the export food trade.

Indeed, the concern of the government was not to see that the miller and the farmer got their rights, but to see that the miller and the grain speculator did not rob the public. On August 18, 1914, an agent of the department of justice was a visitor at Minneapolis flour mills, inquiring as to the sudden rise in the price of flour. At the beginning of 1915 both New York and the Federal Government were investigating the sensational rise in the price of wheat, and trying to discover in it the machinations of speculators. It was found that the old law of supply and demand was operating. The usual Russian supplies were cut off from neutral countries. The Allies were consuming more heavily than ever, and their own crops were short. With everyone bidding for American wheat and flour, prices naturally advanced.

It is clear, therefore, that the American farmers and millers did not suffer because they did not ship to Germany. Had they been able to do this, wheat and flour would have been higher than they were and our citizens would have made still more money than they did, for Germany's demand would have been added to that of the rest of belligerent and neutral Europe. But our grain and flour people did fairly well.

Under these circumstances, naturally, no great agricultural interests went to Washington to clamor for freedom of foodstuffs shipments to Germany.

Yet the principle at issue was no less vital than if large losses had been involved. The historian of the future will find it difficult to reconcile our insistence on the movement of cotton because we needed the cotton money, with our acquiescence in the stoppage of the grain and provisions movement because we did not need the grain and provisions money.

Nor will it suffice to say that Germany, by self-denial, did pull through, in spite of stoppage of food from America. Our rights and our duty were neglected, even if neglect of our rights did not mean distress to any of our citizens and even if neglect of our duty did not result in the starvation of Germany.

Moreover, the farmer will perhaps not find himself untouched. September wheat at less than $1.10 in New York in July, 1915, meant well under $1 per bushel on the farm. The contrast with the price the farmer received for his last year's crop will be striking. The contrast will be intensified if the Dardanelles fall and Russian wheat is let loose.

Above all, the final British measure, the "blockade" of Germany, has established a new practice, a new definition of blockade which may in the future be of the very greatest harm to the farmer. This feature of the question is reserved for Chapter V.

CHAPTER III

Foodstuffs Under International Law. The October Order in Council

What we considered our rights in the matter of trading with belligerents was early in the war set forth in an announcement of our State Department declaring that such trade, except in contraband of war, was lawful and might go forward. On August 15, 1914, the State Department published the following:

"The existence of war between foreign governments does not suspend trade or commerce between this country and those at war. The right to continue to trade with belligerents is upheld by the well-recognized principles of international law.

"Conditional contraband consists, generally speaking, of articles which are susceptible of use in war as well as for purposes of peace; in consequence, their destination determines whether they are contraband or non-contraband.

"Articles of the character stated are considered contraband if destined to the army, navy or department of government of one of the belligerents or to a place occupied and held by military forces; if not so destined, they are not contraband, as, for example, when bound to an individual or a private concern."

This theoretical right of America to ship food to Germany, asserted August 15, was cancelled five days later by the British Order in Council whose provisions we already know. In August and September of 1913 we shipped 4,700,000 bushels of wheat to Germany; in August and September, 1914, we shipped none. In August and September, 1913, we sent to Germany 20,500 barrels of flour; in August and September, 1914, only 65 barrels. In August and September, 1913, we sent to Germany $4,100,000 of lard; in August and September, 1914, not a dollar's worth. The comparatively small sales even in 1913 are of course no measure of what Germany would have taken in the war year 1914.

Noting the disappearance of shipments from oversea, Berlin protested in early October. In a note handed to foreign diplomats in Berlin on October 10, Germany called attention to the violations of the Declaration of London by the August Order in Council and the British September 21 contraband list. The protest was directed partly against Britain's absolute disregard of the contraband list established in the Declaration, especially against making rubber, hides, skins and certain kinds of iron ore contraband. However, the chief complaint was against the British "modification" which abolished the meaning and the privileges of conditional contraband and made it as impossible for food to move into Germany as for cartridges. Finally, the protest asked neutral nations what they were going to do about these attacks upon their rights, and intimated that Germany would not engage to abide longer by the Declaration of London if Great Britain persisted in violating it.

The German protest was cabled to our government on October 22. Our answer was sent shortly after. We replied that the United States had withdrawn its suggestion, made early in the war, that for the sake of uniformity the Declaration of London should be adopted as a temporary code of warfare. We withdrew the suggestion because certain belligerents refused to adopt the Declaration without changes and modifications. Thenceforth, our reply continued, during the war, the United States and its citizens would rely for protection upon the existing rules of international law.

None of the rights of trade with belligerents is more firmly established by the well-recognized principles of international law than is the right to trade in food for the civilian population. This is a principle upheld by us in the past, and upheld with especial stress by the English Government, when Great Britain was a neutral. Continuously since the eighteenth century Britain has asserted that food was not contraband unless destined to a belligerent government or its military forces.

In 1885 China was at war with France. France declared rice contraband of war, with the purpose of starving China into submission. The declaration met with immediate, sharp and successful opposition from Great Britain. Lord Granville, British Minister for Foreign Affairs, wrote the French Government that regarding foodstuffs "there must be circumstances relative to any particular cargo, or its destination, to displace the presumption that articles of this kind are intended for the ordinary use of life."

Is there any distinction between the French act of declaring foodstuffs contraband of war, and the British instituting of measures that made it impossible to ship them to a belligerent even though they were left on the conditional contraband list?

America also interested itself in the French case of 1885. The American Minister at Berlin wrote our Secretary of State regarding it. He called attention to the fact that an immense portion of our exports consisted of foodstuffs. Every European war, he added, produced an increased demand for these exports. The French doctrine attempted to stop food even when bound for civilians. If food, he went on, can thus be captured, clothing, the instruments of industry and all less vital supplies can be cut off, *on the ground that they tend to support the efforts of the belligerent nation.*

"Indeed, the real principle involved goes to this extent, that everything the want of which will increase the distress of the civil population of the belligerent country may be declared contraband of war.

"The entire trade of neutrals with belligerents may thus be destroyed, irrespective of an effective blockade of ports. *War itself would become more fatal to neutral states than to belligerent interests.*"

This letter might have been written in the same words regarding the manipulation of the British contraband list in the present war.

The next instance to the point arose in the Boer War. Lord Salisbury was asked to state the position of the British Government regarding the movement of foodstuffs to the Boers. He said:

"Foodstuffs with a hostile destination can be considered contraband of war only if they are supplies for the enemy's forces. It is not sufficient that they are capable of being so used; it must be *shown* that this was in fact their destination at the time of the seizure."

Yet the same British Government in 1914 chose to cancel its own clearly expressed interpretation of international law, by decreeing that provisions should not move to Germany "if consigned to a merchant or other person in control of the authorities of the enemy state."

Again, in 1904, Great Britain and the United States, acting in co-operation, opposed successfully the action of Russia in seizing a cargo of flour and railway material consigned to private concerns in Japan. In describing the representations of the British Government to Russia, regarding food shipments, Lord Lansdowne wrote Mr. Choate, then our Ambassador to England:

"The test appeared to be whether there are circumstances relating to any particular cargo to *show* that it is destined for military or naval use."

Further than that, Lord Lansdowne clearly stated that Great Britain did not propose to be bound by the decision of a Russian prize court, if the court did not abide by the principle already stated.

"His Majesty's Government further pointed out that the decision of the prize court of the captor in such matters, in order to be binding on neutral states, must be in accordance with the recognized rules and principles of international law and procedure."

The words of Lord Lansdowne might have been quoted in our first note of protest to England, on December 26.

In this same Russo-Japanese War in 1904, our Secretary of State, John Hay, instructed our Ambassador at St. Petersburg to make representations to the Imperial Russian Government in no uncertain terms. He was to communicate, in part, as follows:

"When war exists between powerful states it is vital to the legitimate maritime commerce of neutral states that there be no relaxation of the rule—no deviation from the criterion for determining what constitutes contraband of war, lawfully subject to belligerent capture, namely: warlike nature, use and destination. Articles which, like arms and ammunition, are by their nature of self-evident warlike use, are contraband of war if destined to enemy territory; but articles which, like coal, cotton and provisions, though if ordinarily innocent are capable of warlike use, are not subject to capture and confiscation unless shown by evidence to be actually destined for the military or naval forces of a belligerent.

"If the principle which appears to have been declared by the Vladivostok prize court and which has not so far been disavowed or explained by His Imperial Majesty's Government is acquiesced in, it means, if carried into full execution, the complete destruction of all neutral commerce with the non-combatant population of Japan; it obviates the necessity of blockades; it renders meaningless the principle of the Declaration of Paris set forth in the Imperial Order of February 29 last that a blockade in order to be obligatory must be effective; it obliterates all distinction between commerce in contraband and non-contraband goods, *and is in effect a declaration of war against commerce of every description between the people of a neutral and those of a belligerent state.*"

What of the British treatment of our foodstuffs under the Order in Council of August 20? Was it in any respect different from the action which John Hay so resolutely opposed in 1904? It was not. England as a belligerent has followed the mischievous precedent of Russia in the same attempt which John Hay and Lord Lansdowne defeated in 1904. His Majesty's Government in 1914-1915 proceeded to a "complete destruction of all neutral commerce with the non-combatant population" of Germany, excepting what might fortuitously be smuggled via adjacent neutrals. It can be said of the English policy as well as of Russia's that it "obliterates all distinction between contraband and non-contraband goods"; and that it "is in effect a declaration of war against commerce of every description between the people of a neutral and those of a belligerent state."

It is clear, therefore, not only that the partially abandoned Declaration of London gave to this country the right to send foodstuffs to Germany, but that the common law of nations to which our government reverted, the law established by precedent and by the opinion of high authority, endorsed our right with equal emphasis.

It is not to be assumed that the problem thus presented to our government was wholly overlooked. In October of 1914 the State Department made certain representations, never published, to Great Britain. It cannot be said that this action failed of result. A new Order in Council was called forth. The Order in Council of October 29—superseding that of August 20—contained, together with some apparent modifications of terms, a variety of provisions that made the new regulations in reality more severe upon neutral trade and more subversive of established legal principles than the rulings which had called forth our protest. As in August, so in October, the Order in Council "accepted" the Declaration of London subject to the modifications in the Order.

To be sure, Great Britain has contended that the October Order in Council was an amelioration of the severity of that of August 20. In his February 10 note to us, Sir Edward Grey thus refers to the October Order:

"Your Excellency will remember the prolonged discussions that took place between us throughout the month of October with a view to finding some new formulæ which would enable us to restrict supplies to the enemy forces and to prevent the supply to the enemy of materials essential for the making of munitions of war, while inflicting the minimum of injury and interference with neutral commerce. It was with this object that the Order in Council of the 29th of October was issued, under the provisions of which a far greater measure of immunity was conferred upon neutral commerce."

But the greater measure of immunity, upon closer examination, did not appear.

So far as direct shipment to Germany was concerned, the new Order provided that hostile and forbidden destination of food and other conditional contraband—that is, destination for enemy forces—should be presumed in all cases allowed by the Declaration of London, and that the presumption should further be made,

"if the goods were consigned to or for an agent of the enemy state." (Paragraph II.)

This appeared in terms to be a material modification of the August ruling which had included among forbidden destinations not merely "an agent of the enemy state" but also "a merchant or other person under control of the authorities of the enemy state," which evidently meant anyone within the enemy's boundaries.

But unfortunately everyone within the enemy's boundaries was construed as an *agent* of the enemy state. That is, any consignee in Germany would have to prove before a British prize court that he was not an agent of the state. He would have the impossible task of proving this before the prize courts of a country which officially identified the civil with the military population of Germany. In his February 10 note, Sir Edward Grey clearly states this identity as the British Government's reason for putting the burden of proof upon the captured instead of upon the captor:

"In the peculiar circumstances of the present struggle, where the forces of the enemy comprise so large a proportion of the population, and where there is so little evidence of shipments on private as distinguished from government account, it is most reasonable that the burden of proof should rest on the claimant."

In view of the small English army in the early months of the war it may have seemed to Sir Edward that the forces of the enemy comprised a large proportion of the population. But, adhering to the facts, there were not 6,000,000 Germans under arms when he wrote the February note. The population of Germany being nearly 70,000,000, the chances were eleven and one-half to one that foodstuffs for Germany were destined for the civil rather than the military population.

By its perversion of the law of evidence the October Order in Council was as effective as that of August 20 in preventing any direct trade in food with Germany. We know this better than we should know it if food shipments had been sent and held up in England. We know it because no one even dared to send a shipment—until the case of the Wilhelmina in January, considered in the next chapter.

Having thus kept the ban on direct trade with Germany in conditional contraband, the Order then proceeded to make more difficult than ever the conduct of trade with Germany via neutrals and even the trade between America and neutrals themselves.

Paragraph 35 of the Declaration of London, if observed, provides that the German destination of conditional contraband, like food, shall not be the concern of England if the food is to be discharged in an intervening neutral port. The October Order replaced this with the following:

III. "Notwithstanding the provisions of Article 35 of said Declaration, conditional contraband shall be liable to capture on board a vessel bound for a neutral port if the goods are consigned 'to order,' or if the ship's papers do not show who is the consignee of the goods, or if they show a consignee of the goods in territory belonging to or occupied by the enemy."

IV. "In the cases covered by the preceding paragraph (III) it shall lie upon the owners of the goods to prove that their destination was innocent."

That is, goods moving from us to European neutrals were subject to capture if consigned to anyone in Germany, if the neutral consignee was not named, or if the shipment was "to order" of a neutral. If the goods were going to Germany the owner himself must prove that they were not for the German military. The proof, as we have seen, was impossible.

Therefore nothing was so shipped. It cannot be too strongly emphasized that the *lawful* procedure is for *England,* the captor, to prove that the German destination of conditional contraband is a guilty one; that is, a destination to the military.

We now come to strictly neutral commerce, between America and Scandinavia, for example, to which England, according to Sir Edward Grey, had conferred "a far greater measure of immunity" through the October Order in Council. The reverse is true. Every burden put upon that commerce by the August Order remained, and there was added the prohibition of shipments "to order." Shipments "to order" were not formally prohibited but they were declared subject to capture, and in the ensuing prize court the owner must then prove their innocent destination. Even if a shipper felt certain of his ability to prove this, he would be mad to ship "to order," for this would mean a delay of his goods in England for several months, until they reached their place on the calendar of the prize court. Shipments "to order" ceased as soon as the British action was known.

The ruling against neutral shipments consigned "to order" disarranged the established method of financing our exports of foodstuffs. Ordinarily the exporter draws on a Swedish buyer, for example, and sells the draft to an American bank. The bank buys the draft on condition of being allowed to retain possession of the shipping documents until the purchaser pays. The goods are then forwarded, but are consigned, not to the Swedish buyer, but "to the order" of the American bank. The bank sends the draft and the documents representing the goods to its Swedish correspondent, with instructions to deliver them to the buyer upon payment being made or assured. This general practice was prohibited by the British Order. In a large number of instances neutral buyers were put to the great inconvenience—for some an impossibility—of providing money in New York before the goods were shipped.

A pertinent case, illustrating the operation of this part of the Order, was that of five steamers, under charter to an American line and containing American packing house products consigned to Scandinavia "to order." Three of the ships sailed from New York before the October Order was announced and the other two before it was known in this country. In spite of this the steamers were forced to call at Kirkwall and were then ordered to proceed to Hull and other British east coast ports, where their long period of detention began.

These steamers were the Alfred Nobel, the Björnstjerne Björnson, the Kim, the Fridland, and the Arkansas. They were Norwegian steamers which the Gans Steamship Company of New York had taken over on a long term charter. Months went by and, in spite of all protests from the Americans interested and from the State Department, the steamers and their cargoes lay in the British ports. They were held there, inactive, at a time when they might have been earning $12 per bale carrying cotton to Rotterdam. This would have been equivalent to net earnings of $13,000 per day for the four steamers: $13,000 clear after paying charter money and operating expenses.

November, December, January, February and March passed, without it being possible to get any action on the vessels. The money of the American provision exporters was in the meantime tied up. Their drafts had been returned to them, as the goods had never been delivered. The shippers were of course co-operating with the shipowners in pressing the matter in London and in attempting to get the State Department to do something for them.

Finally, a hearing was set for April 13. On that day the attorneys of the shipowners and shippers appeared in a prize court in London. The British Attorney General moved for a delay in the case, in behalf of the British Government. He said that these cases were very complicated because of the large number of individual shipments on each boat. He said that each shipment must be investigated in America, and this took time. He said that the American shippers should have gotten in touch with the British Government before they made these shipments "to order." He pleaded for delay.

Sir Samuel Evans, who was presiding over the prize court, granted the contention of the Attorney General. He exonerated the Attorney General of all charges of unnecessary delay and insisted that the cases were too complicated to be rushed. The judge of the prize court, following the October 29 Order in Council, which was his law, had to consider that prisoners at the bar were guilty until they could prove themselves innocent. Since the vessels sailed before the Order was known in America, the British prize court procedure established that British laws are retroactive. Eventually a hearing was set for June 7, seven months after these cargoes, destined to neutral ports, had been seized. There were more postponements and at the end of July, 1915, the cases were still unsettled.

Such was the effect of the prohibition of neutral shipments "to order."

The last feature of the October Order which we need consider is one designed to force European neutrals not to send supplies to Germany even of their home growth and manufacture. This measure is one of the most extraordinary occurrences of the war. The October Order read:

(IV. 2) "Where it is shown to the satisfaction of one of His Majesty's principal secretaries of state that the enemy government is drawing supplies for its armed forces *from or through a neutral country*, he may direct that in respect of ships bound for a port in that country, Article 35 of the said Declaration shall not apply. Such direction shall be notified in the London *Gazette* and shall operate until the same is withdrawn. So long as such a direction is in force, a vessel which is carrying conditional contraband to a port in that country shall not be immune from capture."

In plain language, if a British agent reported that Holland or Sweden was feeding Germany either with American or Swedish food, one of His Majesty's

principal secretaries of state could direct British
cruisers to capture food shipments from America to
the offending neutral. It is no restriction of the
omnipotence of these secretaries to say they might
proceed to capture if it is shown to their "satisfaction
that the enemy government is drawing supplies for
its *armed forces* from or through a neutral country."
Anything for Germany was presumed to be for the
armed forces; for, according to British naval practice and to the public contentions. of British Ministers, the German military and the German· civilian
population are regarded as one. Since October 29
our commerce with European neutrals. has been
carried on with permission of the British authorities
who in the October Order were given charge of that
commerce.

Neither Sweden nor any other neutral was to be
allowed to send to Germany food which it raised and
supply the deficiency by abnormal importations
from America. After the October 29 Order *re-
exportation* embargoes on goods in the British contraband lists did not suffice to keep European
neutrals innocent in the eyes of England. It was
necessary for them to lay simple embargoes on the
exportation of these goods, including food, even if
the trade was in the neutral country's own product.

Nor did the export embargoes, when laid, suffice.
Nothing did. Even after neutral governments ad-
justed themselves to the British August and October
Orders, there occurred incessant detentions and seizures of food ships, especially those bound for Holland

and the Scandinavian countries. Under conceptions of law with which no one could learn how to comply, cargoes of perishable goods were held up for months in British harbors.

Our Department of State has finally published a list of the seizures of our vessels. In the first eleven months of the war Britain seized 2,000 vessels with American cargoes destined for Europe. In his note of January 7, Sir Edward Grey stated that 773 vessels left our shores between August 4 and January 3 for Holland, Scandinavia and Italy. Of these 773 vessels, he said, there were 45 from which part or all of the cargo was thrown into prize court. Eight of the ships themselves were so treated. This gives no indication of the loss, borne entirely by neutral shippers and shipowners, due to the detention, unloading and annoyance of the many vessels about which nothing suspicious even to the English mind could be found. It gives no indication of the injury to neutral commerce through discouragement and intimidation, through the well-grounded fear that while a perfectly innocent shipment was on the high seas, His Majesty's Council might legislate some new "international" law which would make the shipment subject to capture.

In the meantime the patience of the United States Government had become exhausted. On December 26 the Secretary of State addressed a note to our Ambassador at London, to be handed to Sir Edward Grey. The note admitted the propriety of Britain stopping contraband for the enemy. It states that, in case of conditional contraband, the policy of Great Britain was unjustified by the established rules of international conduct.   It claimed that the seizure of cargoes consigned "to order" to neutral countries was not legal.   It quoted Lord Salisbury to show that even if our foodstuffs were destined for hostile territory, they could not be lawfully seized unless it could be proven that they were for the enemy forces. The Government of the United States admitted the right to search and detain ships bound from America

"when there is sufficient evidence to justify a belief that contraband articles are in their cargoes; but His Majesty's Government, judging by their own experience in the past, must realize that this government cannot without protest permit American ships or American cargoes to be taken into British ports and there detained for the purpose of searching generally for evidence of contraband; or *upon the presumption created by special municipal enactments which are clearly at variance with international law and practice.*"

Finally, our note stated that American shippers and producers, deprived of established markets, were calling for relief; and that unless this were obtained, there might arise in this country a feeling contrary to that which had so long existed between the American and the British people.

Great Britain sent two answers to this protest; a preliminary answer dated January 7, and a final one dated February 10.   The January 7 reply is a not uninteresting document, though neither this communication nor the one which followed it conceded in the slightest degree the American demands.

The first declared purpose of the British note of January 7 was to "clear the ground and remove some misconceptions that seem to exist." The author, Sir Edward Grey, then accepted the principle that a belligerent should not interfere with trade between neutrals unless such interference were necessary to protect the belligerent's national safety.* Great Britain, he continued, was ready to keep its action within these limits on the understanding that it retained the right to interfere in what was not "bona fide" trade between neutrals but really contraband destined for the enemy's country. Whenever its action unintentionally exceeded this principle, Great Britain, he said, was ready to make redress.

Sir Edward then told us that we were wrong in assuming that our industries were suffering from the loss of their usual market. As conclusive proof he cited the figures of export from New York to Italy, Holland and Scandinavia. In November, 1914, we exported to Denmark $7,100,000 of goods, compared with $560,000 in November, 1913. We sent $2,860,-000 to Sweden, compared with $380,000. We sent $2,320,000 to Norway, compared with $480,000. We sent $4,780,000 to Italy, compared with $2,980,-000. We sent $3,960,000 to Holland, compared with $4,390,000.

* The "necessity of protecting the belligerent's national safety" is the excuse offered for every wrong committed in this war.

The note passed over, naturally, the fact that our November exports to Germany were only $40,000, compared with $48,000,000 in 1913, or that our exports to Austria fell from $1,970,000 in November, 1913, to nothing in 1914. It did not inform its readers that the figures he gave were those of our exports that started for European neutrals. How much got past His Majesty's cruisers was another story.

Moreover, the note implied that our larger exports to the Scandinavian countries consisted solely of articles destined for Germany, and hence subject to British interference. But, according to another part of the same note, Great Britain was interfering only with "*contraband* destined for the enemy's country." By that test Britain could lawfully have interfered with only such of the excess exports to European neutrals as represented absolute contraband—since the Declaration of London allows neutrals to receive conditional contraband unmolested—and even such a course would have assumed that all such merchandise had a German destination.

As a matter of fact, the excess of exports to European neutrals was to some degree destined for Germany. The point is that free goods and conditional contraband had a right so to move. However, much of the excess was for the neutrals themselves. They had need of larger imports from us than ever before. For example, they had formerly bought from Germany their copper products. Germany was keeping her copper at home. Therefore the neutrals needed to import raw copper in larger quantities than before, in order to make their own copper products. Our copper exports to neutrals were the most suspicious thing Sir Edward Grey found. Similarly, we exported more cotton to the neutrals because their own mills were making cotton piece goods that had been coming from Germany, and supplying foreign markets to which Germany was denied access.

Above all, the neutrals needed more foodstuffs. East Germany usually exports large quantities of wheat flour and of rye to Scandinavia. Not only was this cut off, but the ordinary shipments of wheat and rye from Russia dropped, first because of Russia's export embargo (finally lifted) and later, to a degree, because of Germany's control of the Baltic Sea. The closed Dardanelles kept Russian Black Sea supplies locked up. Both Russian and German supplies had to be replaced by supplies from the United States.

The British note has only the following brief reference to foodstuffs:

"With regard to the seizure of foodstuffs to which your Excellency refers, His Majesty's Government are prepared to admit that foodstuffs should not be detained and put into a prize court without presumption that they are intended for the armed forces of the enemy or the enemy government. *We believe that this rule has been adhered to in practice hitherto*, but, if the United States Government has instances to the contrary, we are prepared to examine them, and it is our present intention to adhere to the rule

though *we cannot give an unlimited and unconditional undertaking in view of the departure by those
against whom we are fighting from hitherto accepted
rules of civilization and humanity and the uncertainty as to the extent to which rules may be violated
by them in future.*"

In the face of the conditions which we have reviewed, we are touched by the simple "belief" of His
Majesty's Government that they had adhered to
international law hitherto.

However, Britain was preparing the way to institute severer measures, should the need arise.   The
italicized clauses can be translated into ordinary
English.   They mean: "We cannot unconditionally
agree to continue to adhere to the limits of law.
Our enemy has departed from the rules of civilization: therefore we may insist upon having a free
hand in the future."

Here was the theory that England was fighting
our battle, and that of the civilized world.   To
assume that the United States would calmly agree
to this proposition was a clear imputation that this
country was not genuinely neutral and would be
willing so to confess.

The obstructive tactics of the British Government
were to be put to a severe test by the case of the
American steamship Wilhelmina, with which we shall
now deal.

CHAPTER IV

THE WILHELMINA—A TEST CASE

Early in 1915 the question whether our merchants could send foodstuffs to Germany, when not intended for the government or for the armed forces of that country, was sharply tested in a case which merits its own corner in history. This was the case of the steamship Wilhelmina. America lost the case.

The Wilhelmina was of American registry, and was under charter to the W. T. Green Commission Company of St. Louis, a concern engaged previously to the war in exporting provisions to Germany. Noting the statement of Sir Edward Grey in his January 7 note, that Great Britain was not considering foodstuffs contraband unless destined for the government or armed forces of the enemy, the St. Louis merchants determined to take advantage of this expression in an effort toward the resumption of their trade. Accordingly they loaded on the Wilhelmina a cargo of grain, flour and provisions to the value of $200,000, and despatched the vessel from Brooklyn on January 22, with sailing papers for Hamburg and under conditions such as to put the British policy very clearly to the test.

The goods were not consigned "to or for an agent of the enemy state," or even, recalling the wording of the August Order in Council, "to or for a merchant or other person under the control of the authorities of the enemy state," at least in any reasonable interpretation. Nor were they consigned "to order." Instead, the consignment was made to Mr. Brooking, manager of the W. T. Green Company, who sailed in advance for Hamburg to receive the cargo on arrival. The food was going to an American citizen.

There was nothing in any British Order in Council making shipments so consigned subject to seizure. Further, the cargo went forward with the endorsement of the State Department, Mr. Bryan having stated that he saw no reason for action against the vessel by His Majesty's authorities. It was evident that if Great Britain were to seize the Wilhelmina, some new excuse must be found for such action.

The manner in which the British public looked upon the voyage of the Wilhelmina was apparent from the tone of British newspapers from the day the vessel sailed. A single instance, typical of many, will illustrate. On January 26 the London *Morning Post* discussed the case in an editorial, saying that this was another test prepared by the friends of Germany in America for the injury of British interests. The editorial proceeded:

"This is a more plausible and more insidious experiment than the Dacia, and if it is allowed, will be more injurious to the cause of the Allies.

"At present German food prices are but little, if at all, higher than British food prices, but the Allies hope that if the blockade continues, in time it will become extremely irksome for the German people to continue at war, owing to the increasing scarcity of food, and that they will desire their government to discontinue the war.

"If Americans will fairly consider it, this is the most merciful way of ending such a conflict, which otherwise may continue to rage until the manhood of Europe is destroyed.

"There is a right and wrong in this war, and the United States by their public opinion have already shown where they believe the right to lie. Will they now say that interest is more important than right, and money than justice and liberty? We cannot believe it of a nation which has the tradition and the origin of the United States."

Nothing could be plainer. The voyage of the Wilhelmina was an attempt to thwart England's starvation campaign. In view of Great Britain's fight for civilization, America should stand aside, should waive its legal rights and its commercial interests. Evidently the British press was not of the impression that their government had been allowing food for civilians to proceed to Germany, as implied in Grey's January 7 note, where he said no foodstuffs had been seized except upon presumption of destination for enemy forces. The Wilhelmina was recognized as an insidious attempt to get in motion a shipment for civilians, for the first time.

On January 25 the German authorities, on behalf of the imperial government, confiscated all supplies of grain and flour in the empire. Such action was to be followed by government distribution of these foodstuffs, with the purpose of diminishing the consumption and thereby assuring the sufficiency of the existing stock until the harvest in July. Mere appeals to the Germans to reduce their use of bread had apparently not sufficed to conserve the supply. The confiscation specifically did not affect all foods, but only those for which shortage threatened; namely, grain and flour.

This Decree was announced on the evening of January 25. It was known outside of Germany on the 26th. On the 27th the London press announced that *all* food in and for Germany was now subject to seizure; that it was therefore to be considered from that time as government property, and hence contraband. Therefore, London concluded, the Wilhelmina must be stopped.

To meet this situation the attorney for the W. T. Green Commission Company requested the German Ambassador at Washington to guarantee that the food on the Wilhelmina would not reach the military forces of Germany. Count von Bernstorff replied as follows:

"I, as representative of the German Government, guarantee to you that the foodstuffs will not reach the German Government, its agents or contractors, nor the military and naval forces. I will further take the necessary steps which will insure that the German Government will not make use of its right of pre-emption.

"I shall at once communicate in this matter with the State Department and advise you later."

On the following day, January 29, the German Ambassador communicated this guarantee to the State Department at Washington, on behalf of his home government.

To be sure, the original German Decree specifically stated: "The provisions of this ordinance do not apply to grain or flour imported from foreign countries." But the importer had to operate through the War Grain Company, the Central Purchasing Company, or the German community officials. This did not mean the armed forces of the government or the government's military agents. The agencies named were created to direct *imported* grain solely into channels of private consumption. But the matter was easily misunderstood abroad; and hence, on February 5, the German Federal Council rescinded the requirement for the importer to operate through the companies or the community officials, and the enactment was made to read simply:

"The provisions of this ordinance do not apply to grain and flour which are imported from foreign countries."

This modification of the German Decree was made known to our government by the German Government in a note never published in full but quoted in part in ours to Great Britain of February 15.

In England the German Decree was taken generally as a confession that Germany was in desperate straits. And if the supplies of food in Germany were, in truth, running short, then the last thing that His Majesty's Government wanted was to see its "economic pressure" relaxed. The censored press despatches from London daily told of a firmer and firmer intention on Britain's part to stop the Wilhelmina. A reported offer of the American Relief Commission to buy the cargo of the Wilhelmina was hailed in London as a happy solution of "the Wilhelmina incident, which threatens to arouse the resentment of the British public." The offer of the Relief Commission was finally made, and rejected, on February 7. The president of the W. T. Green Commission Company said the food would be sold at Hamburg for the civilian population, and in no other way.

On February 1 officials of the British Foreign Office stated to the press that they were unable to understand the value of Ambassador Bernstorff's guarantee that the Wilhelmina's cargo would not reach the German military, in view of the German Decree placing all foodstuffs under government control. They omitted the detail that imported foodstuffs were not affected by the Decree.

The German Decree was apparently the excuse England had sought for putting upon a formal basis the stoppage of food for Germany which had been practiced since the opening of the war. On February 2, Ambassador Page cabled our State Department that the British fleet had been ordered to consider grain and flour for Germany as contraband, subject to seizure and confiscation. This included the cargo of the Wilhelmina, it was added, but as a special dispensation this particular consignment, having been forwarded before the confiscation order, would be paid for. Other seizures would be without compensation.

Meantime the Wilhelmina was nearing the English Channel. On February 4 the German Government gave forth its War Zone announcement—a warning that after February 18 all British merchant vessels found in the waters around Great Britain would be torpedoed, without regard to the safety of crews or passengers. As a justification of this unprecedented method of warfare, it was declared that England was attempting to starve a nation of 70,000,000 people by means not recognized by international law. Therefore the Germans proposed to use what means they could to shut off the British food supply.

On the same February 4, the British Foreign Office issued a statement that it would stop the Wilhelmina and throw her cargo into a prize court. The statement said that under the Decree of January 25 all grain imported into Germany must pass through semi-official hands. Therefore it could be considered as destined to the government and hence contraband. (No attention was paid to Count von Bernstorff's guarantee to Washington from his government that the grain would reach only civilians.) If the cargo were seized, the British authorities said they would pay for it, and they would pay the owners of the vessel for any delay caused by the British action. Finally, the statement announced that because of Germany's intention to sink merchant vessels with their crews, England might be compelled to "adopt in retaliation more stringent measures against German trade."

Also on February 4, the German Ambassador at Washington further complicated the case by formally suggesting that the distribution of the food of the Wilhelmina should be supervised by American consular officers in Germany, who could give assurances that none of it would get into the hands of armed forces. The British Embassy intimated, according to Washington despatches, that this would not be acceptable. Even if it were assured, the Embassy said, that the imported food would reach only German civilians, that would make it possible for the military to live on the home supplies while the civilians lived on imports.

Reduced to the last extremity, the British always fell back upon the contention in one or another form, that if the Wilhelmina and such ships got through with food to Germany, this would frustrate the starvation plan.

It so happened that the Wilhelmina, a small steamer, was caught in severe gales on the North Atlantic, and on February 9 put in at Falmouth for refuge. Two days later, the British authorities formally seized the cargo.

The owners of the goods urged thereupon that by the most extreme constructions of international law on the part of England, that country was not justified in seizing more than the grain and flour on

board the Wilhelmina, for only these articles had
been included in Germany's confiscation Decree. It
was claimed that the ship should be free to proceed to
Germany after the British had taken off the grain
and flour, constituting only 15 per cent of a cargo
of foodstuffs.

This contention was communicated to the British
Government, in a note which our State Department
sent to Britain on February 15. The note implied
that the British stoppage of the cargo because of the
German Decree was invalidated by the modification
of that Decree, which exempted from its operation
imported foodstuffs. A communication of the German Government was quoted, citing this modification
and offering to allow American consular officers to
supervise the distribution of such imports to German
civilians. The hope was expressed that unless Britain had in its possession facts not in the hands of the
United States, the Wilhelmina might be allowed to
proceed.

Before the British answer to this note was forthcoming, important events occurred in parliament.
On February 16, the day after our note was sent,
Winston Churchill, Lord of the Admiralty, announced in the following words the forthcoming
"blockade" of Germany:

"We have not yet stopped the importation of food
into Germany, but the time has come to consider the
situation. The Allied Governments will probably
make declaration of action, the effect of which will be
to bring the full pressure of the English naval power

to bear on Germany. The pressure of the navy itself could decide the issue of this war."

It is amazing how thoroughly American public opinion was misinformed as to the facts of the case, and how generally the public accepted as truth the absurd statement of Churchill that "we have not yet stopped the importation of food into Germany *but the time has come to consider the situation.*" And no one seemed to grasp the fact that foods imported into Germany were not lawfully subject to British seizure.

Even in so well-informed a paper as the New York *Evening Post* there appeared on February 18 an editorial which ignored the basic facts that England never had let food go by, and that the German Decree excluded imported food. The *Post* said:

"The historic British position has been that foodstuffs not destined for use of the army must be allowed to pass. That, in general, has been the practice of the English cruisers and courts during the early months of this war. But now that Germany has abolished all private buying and selling of foodstuffs within the empire, the old distinctions are obliterated. The presumption today is that all foodstuffs entering Germany are for military use, or may be immediately requisitioned for military use."

On February 19, Sir Edward Grey answered our note regarding the Wilhelmina. He said that the steamer had been seized after the German Decree of January 25. He added that the February 6 modification excepting imported foodstuffs was not known to Britain at the time of the Wilhelmina seizure, and declared that this modification had *just become known*. A prize court must pass on the question whether the modification changed the status of the vessel.

However, he continued, there were other grounds for detaining the Wilhelmina. The Germans had justified the bombarding of Hartlepool and Scarborough on the ground that these placed were fortified, or were serving as bases for military operations. Therefore England might stop foodstuffs for Hamburg on the ground that Hamburg was fortified and that food so destined was, according to the Declaration of London, presumably destined to military forces. "Hamburg . . . is in part protected by fortifications at the mouth of the Elbe" and is "a fortified town and a base of operations and supply."

The owners of the Wilhelmina's cargo, the note observed, would have a right to establish their innocence, if they could, in a British prize court. It was suggested that diplomatic action by the United States be avoided until full advantage had been taken of the appeal to the courts.

It was protested further that Britain had not yet interfered with food moving to Germany:

"His Majesty's Government have not, so far, declared foodstuffs to be absolute contraband. They have not interfered with any neutral vessels on account of their carrying foodstuffs, except on the basis of such foodstuffs being liable to capture if destined for the enemy's forces or government."

Finally, the British note averred that Germany had violated international law by bombarding British coast towns, laying mines, mistreating Belgians and Frenchmen and torpedoing British merchant vessels. Therefore Britain could not be expected to remain bound by old laws. Neutrals would be expected to stand aside while England declared food contraband, or adopted such other measures of retaliation as should be thought fitting.

It is impossible to pass over this note without commenting upon certain of its features. For example, Sir Edward Grey informed us that England did not know of the modification of the German Decree when the Wilhelmina was seized on February 9. That modification passed the Bundesrat on February 6. The news was cabled to the United States *via London*. At the head of this despatch to American papers, published February 8, we read, "Berlin, February 6; via London, February 7." This means that on February 7 this important news passed through the hands of the British censor. That it was not known to the Foreign Office on February 9 was, to say the least, extraordinary.

The fortifications by which Hamburg is "protected" are at the mouth of the Elbe, over seventy-five miles from the port. Hamburg is fortified about to the same extent as Albany is fortified by the protections about New York City, and on such a theory, Peekskill, Tarrytown and Yonkers are military establishments far more perilous.

The British statement that it "might be obliged" *to consider* interfering with food moving to Germany needs no comment.

It is necessary to say a word about Britain's contention that it should have a free hand because Germany was overstepping international morality in its manner of making war on England. That of course is no excuse for England taking action against Germany which violates the rights of neutrals. When Germany's novel conception of international law infringes upon *our* rights, we protest and take care of ourselves. We do not invite or allow England to defend us against Germany's aggressions any more than we allow Germany to defend us against England's aggressions. Once admit this altruistic policy of reprisals by belligerents and all our neutral rights vanish.

It was evident, however, from the developments in the Wilhelmina case, that no criticisms were likely to change the course of events or to alter the determined policy of His Majesty's Government.

On February 27, the writ was issued putting the Wilhelmina's cargo into the prize court. The attorneys for the cargo, who were in London, hoped for a speedy trial. They expected that the vessel would get to Hamburg, for the "blockade" of Germany was not announced until March 1, three weeks after the Wilhelmina was detained. On March 19, and again on March 23, the American attorneys in New York and London protested against the delay in trying the case in the prize court.

On March 26 the British Solicitor of the Treasury suggested to the attorney of the vessel that in view of the loss of $1,000 per day as a result of the detention, the cargo should be unloaded, and that such part of the merchandise as was deteriorating should be sold through the prize court. The suggestion was refused on the ground that the parties who had chartered the vessel preferred to keep the cargo aboard, ready to sail for Hamburg when the prize court declared it free.

The Wilhelmina case was finally set for March 31. It was evident, however, that the English ministry did not want the case to come before the prize court; and the reason for their attitude becomes clear after a little reflection. As shown in the previous chapter, Great Britain as a neutral has constantly denied that foodstuffs destined for civilians in a belligerent country are seizable as contraband. Any action of a prize court condemning the cargo of the Wilhelmina would have been an absolute reversal of this attitude by her judiciary and would have promised a very possible future embarrassment. The vessel could not be held on any charge of attempted blockade-running, for it had sailed and had been detained before the blockade was declared. Yet it was not safe to let America get a food ship through to Germany. More might follow if such a precedent were established.

The problem was solved by the familiar British method of a new Order in Council, which, if it cannot be called a substitute for international law, served at least to give a legal formula to what was done. This Order was passed on March 23, but was not divulged until the trial, on March 31. Then, to the surprise of the American attorneys, the crown lawyers produced an Order in Council which authorized the crown to requisition any neutral ship and cargo which for any reason whatever had been brought before the prize court. The new Order read:

"Where it is made to appear to the judge, on the application of the proper officers of the court, that it is desired to requisition on behalf of His Majesty a ship in respect of which no final decree of condemnation has been made, he shall order that the ship shall be appraised, and that, upon an undertaking being given in accordance with rule 5 of this Order, the ship shall be released and delivered to the crown."

The counsel for the Wilhelmina's cargo were taken aback, and asked for a continuation of the case until April 13, so that they could revise their argument to meet the new law that was to apply. They found there was no argument. The power of Britain, under her self-made international law, to requisition the cargo of the Wilhelmina, made a trial of that cargo's right to proceed to Germany practically out of the question.

The American shippers were therefore compelled to submit to the purchase of the goods by the British government. The offer was made by Great Britain in a note to Ambassador Page, published April 13, to be transmitted to the W. T. Green Company.

The British note stated that the sailing of the Wilhelmina was designed as a test case to see whether American food could be sent to Germany. Since the Blockade Order, however, the case was academic. That Order would prevent any more food being sent, no matter how the case of the Wilhelmina might be decided. Hence there was no longer any object in continuing the proceedings. The British Government therefore offered to buy the cargo at Hamburg prices, the compensation to be determined by a referee appointed by Sir Edward Grey and Ambassador Page. As to the vessel itself, Great Britain offered to compensate for loss due to the detention so far as that was caused by the action of the British authorities; but it had been contended by London from the first that the ship might have discharged cargo and proceeded immediately after February 9.

Lord Mersey was appointed referee. Early in May, London despatches reported that he had decreed $430,000 as a settlement for the Wilhelmina case. The London *Daily Mail* quoted the Wilhelmina owners as "highly pleased with the handsome and generous settlement made by the government for the steamship's cargo." The W. T. Green Commission Company, through their lawyers, deny any such satisfaction. The profit on that one $200,000 cargo was large, but in their attempt to re-establish their German business they had failed. Had they succeeded, they would have made a large profit not on one, but on a hundred cargoes.

Neither they nor the country was satisfied by this single "handsome and generous settlement" for the enforced surrender of our neutral rights and interests.

CHAPTER V

THE BLOCKADE

Shortly before the arrival of the British Government's note of February 10, containing the final reply to our protest of December 26, the situation with respect to our export trade, and especially as to the question of foodstuffs for Germany, had been given a new phase by the appearance of Germany's War Zone announcement. The British February 10 note was a communication of no epoch-making brilliancy. Its most striking feature was the delicate irony, already remarked, with which Sir Edward Grey informed the American public that the Order in Council of October 29 was an amelioration of the severe conditions of the August 20 Order.

The authorities at London, it appeared in this February note, were considering whether they should not regard all food for Germany as absolute contraband,* because of the alleged identity of the civil and military population of that country. And in view of the recent War Zone proclamation from Berlin, it was intimated that still stricter measures might be necessary to protect the interests of Great

* Grain and flour were already so considered. On February 2 Ambassador Page cabled from London that the British navy had been instructed to treat these commodities as absolute contraband.

Britain. Thus the note furnished a record of the
ending of one episode and the beginning of another,
and for purely historical purposes it had a certain
value; but as to meeting the causes of the complaint
in our December note, or the question of their
removal, it contributed nothing.

Germany's War Zone Decree, growing out of the
actions of Great Britain in obstructing food supplies,
had been issued by the German Admiralty on February 4. It was a warning addressed to the commercial world, stating that from February 18—two
weeks after the issuance of the warning—the waters
around Great Britain, including the whole of the
English Channel, would be a danger zone. In this
area, it was announced, all British merchant vessels
caught by the German submarines would be destroyed
without obligation respecting the safety of crews or
passengers, and neutral vessels would be in danger.
In explanation of the latter portion of the Decree,
reference was made to a secret order of the British
Admiralty authorizing the vessels of that country
to use neutral flags to deceive German submarines.
In a separate statement the German Chancellor declared that neutrals were not protecting their rights
to trade with Germany, and that the Germans could
not sit still and die of famine but must retaliate with
the same weapons that England used.

The danger to our interests involved in this note
was quickly recognized at Washington. Our answer
was dated February 10. It reminded the Germans
that the prerogatives of belligerent war vessels, with

respect to neutral shipping, were limited to the right of visit and search. Our government denied that the United States had been unneutral in failing to protest against violations of its neutral rights. We denied that the British misuse of our flag cast a suspicion on all neutral shipping warranting its destruction. Should a German commander destroy on the high seas an American vessel and the lives of American citizens, it was added, we should hold Germany to a strict accountability. Finally, we stated for Berlin's information that we had made representations to Britain against using our flag indiscriminately to protect its vessels.

Regarding our brief correspondence with England as to the use of the American flag on British vessels, it may be noted merely that Great Britain's reply to our communication was not responsive. The same must be said of the German reply of February 16 to our protest against the War Zone Decree. Germany declared that she had abided by the Declaration of London, as suggested by America early in the war, and had even let food ships go from Denmark to England, though her warships could have stopped such trade any time. In the meantime England had torn up the Declaration of London and was trying to starve her opponent. Neutrals had protested, Germany said, but without avail.

Since neutrals—the note continued—had merely protested, and had taken no action when England was abridging their right to trade with Germany, it was now expected that they would show no less tolerance to Germany. It was stated that both mines and submarines would make the War Zone unsafe. The best thing for neutrals would be to avoid the Zone; or for neutral merchant ships to be convoyed by neutral war vessels. Danger to neutral merchant vessels was doubled by the British insistence on the right to adopt neutral flags, Germany declared.

We were given, further, the well-worn assurance that Germany was fighting for her life. Finally— the hopeful thing about the note—Germany implied that she would give up her submarine warfare if England would abandon her unlawful attempt at starvation, and would allow foodstuffs and raw materials to move into Germany without interference. On the following day, February 17, the German Embassy at Washington, as already noted in connection with the Wilhelmina case, made the statement that the German Government would consent to have American consular officers supervise the distribution to civilians of foodstuffs imported from America.

The American Government believed it saw in the German proposal the basis for a successful negotiation with both belligerents with regard to the rights of neutrals. It saw the possibility of recalling the belligerents to the limits of international law, as that law was known before the opening of the war. We had suffered through the British interference with our exports to Germany and adjacent neutrals. Still greater loss threatened us from the blockade that Britain was obviously about to declare. We had reason to fear serious consequences from the prospective submarine warfare of Germany. It was to the interest of all neutrals to have these evils averted, along with other practices, in violation of international law, which had grown up in the course of the struggle, such as the laying of floating mines on the high seas.

Therefore, we sent Germany and England an identical note, dated February 20, containing certain suggestions. Both nations were to cease the use of all mines on the high seas. Floating mines were to be discontinued. Anchored contact mines, used defensively, and not out beyond the cannon range of harbors, were to be constructed with the stamp of the government that made them and were to be so constructed as to be harmless if they went adrift.

Submarines were to be used against merchant ships only for the purpose of exercising the right to visit and search.

Great Britain was to desist from its interference with the movement of foodstuffs into Germany. Foodstuffs to Germany from the United States or other neutrals were to be consigned to agencies designated by the United States Government, and the German Government was to undertake not to requisition such supplies.

Nearly a month passed before this note was answered. The German answer was dated March 1. It accepted the American proposition in principle and in most of its details. Germany agreed to cease the use of floating mines, and to construct anchored mines only as indicated, though not consenting to forego wholly the use of anchored mines for offensive purposes. Submarines were to be used in accordance with the recognized rules of international law. But these concessions were dependent upon reciprocal conduct by Great Britain, the note apparently demanding that Germany should be allowed to receive not only foodstuffs but also other goods on the free list and conditional contraband list of the Declaration of London. Moreover, British merchant vessels must engage not to go armed or to resist search by the submarines, and must cease the deceptive use of neutral flags.

In contrast to this attitude, Great Britain, on March 15—after the announcement of that country's blockade policy—sent us a flat rejection of our proposal. First, the British note stated that

"The reply of the German Government . . . has been published and it is not understood that the German Government is prepared to abandon the practice of sinking British merchant vessels by submarines. . . ."

The note then referred to the doubts expressed by Germany of the feasibility of foregoing the use of anchored mines on the high seas for offensive purposes. It was denied that so far the British forces, "either naval or military, can have laid to their charge any improper proceedings."

Then followed a recital of alleged German illegal acts in the war: the treatment of civilians in Belgium and France and of British prisoners in Germany;

the laying of mines on the high seas; the sinking of food vessels like the Frye, destined for Britain; the bombardment from the sea of British coast towns and the dropping of bombs from air craft on unfortified places; and the sinking of British merchant vessels by torpedoes without warning.

The British note then stated that considerations of humanity regarding food for the civilian population of a belligerent were inoperative when that belligerent was blockaded. Apart from Great Britain's rights due to the blockade, it continued, such German authorities as Bismarck and Caprivi had stated, in contradiction to the British and American attitude, that pressure on a civil population was a proper means to bring war to an end.

Moreover, there was a blockade, the note added, "effectively controlling by cruiser 'cordon' all passage to and from Germany by sea."

Again a few words of comment. Sir Edward Grey held that the published German note did not propose to stop the sinking of British merchant vessels by submarines. What the German note had said, six days before—and Sir Edward Grey could not have been ignorant of it—was this:

"The German Government would undertake not to use their submarines to attack mercantile (vessels) of any flag, except when necessary to enforce the right of visit and search. Should the enemy nationality of the vessel or the presence of contraband be ascertained, the submarine would proceed in accordance with the general rules of international law."

As for mines on the high seas, both belligerents had used them, and America had not protested. With one exception Germany in her note offered to forego using such mines, and that exception might have been eliminated by negotiation.

As for the atrocity charges, they were matched by countercharges. But whatever their merits, they were entirely beside the point. And further, we had no interest in what Bismarck wrote to the Kiel Chamber of Commerce or what Caprivi said in the Reichstag. Our conception of the rights of the civilian population of a belligerent to buy food from us coincided with the view that Britain had enforced when she was a neutral, with our own previous position, and with the view of civilized nations as set down in the Declaration of London. As to the blockade, the situation to which Great Britain applied that term was not a blockade in any proper conception, and everyone knew that the so-called cordon was not "controlling all passage to and from Germany by sea." All this was made clear to Britain in our note of March 30.

The blockade had been originated two weeks before Great Britain delivered this answer to our note. It was not originally called a blockade, but a measure to stop all movement of goods to or from Germany, or virtually an application of the law of contraband to all forms of merchandise, not only to goods moving to Germany but also to those leaving Germany. By a coincidence the British announcement of this measure bore the same date—March 1—as the German

acceptance of our suggestion made jointly to the
belligerents to modify their war on neutral trade.

So on March 1 the blockade came into sight. On
that date Sir Cecil Spring-Rice handed our Secretary
of State a memorandum referring to the German
submarine warfare, and announcing Great Britain's
proposal for retaliation as follows:

"Her (Germany's) opponents are therefore driven
to frame retaliatory measures in order in their turn
to prevent commodities of any kind from reaching or
leaving Germany. The British and French Governments will therefore hold themselves free to detain
and take into port ships carrying goods of *presumed*
enemy destination, ownership and origin. It is not
intended to confiscate such vessels or cargoes unless
they would otherwise be liable to condemnation."

In the memorandum the word *blockade* was not
used. On March 5 our State Department sent an
answer to the communication. Our answer was less
a protest than an inquiry as to the meaning of
Spring-Rice's note. It was urged that Great Britain
could not lawfully detain all vessels destined for Germany, except in the case of a blockade. If there was
none, neutral ships should not be detained unless
carrying contraband. We asked the British authorities whether they considered that a blockade existed
or not. If there was none, how could Great Britain
detain any goods from Germany to us on neutral
ships? We admitted that the old-time "close-in"
blockade might be impracticable by reason of the
enemy's use of submarines and air craft but held
that Great Britain should state some limit to the

radius of blockading activity and not, for example, seize ships with German cargo when nearing New York.

London answered in a note of March 15, the same date on which she rejected our proposition that both she and Germany return to international law. Our attention was directed to the March 11 Order in Council, enclosed with the March 15 note, this Order giving effect to the blockade policy announced in the Spring-Rice notification on March 1. The note further explained that Britain would interfere with no cargoes outside of European and Mediterranean waters. It was added that there would be no confiscating of neutral cargoes for trying to pass the blockade, out of consideration for neutrals.*

As the March 11 Order in Council provided the substitute for international law under which neutral countries have carried on up to the time of this writing a sort of business with each other, and under which they are stopped from trading with Germany, the document must be considered with some care.

It began by stating its purpose as a reprisal on the part of Britain and its Allies. No vessels sailing to Germany after the first of March, it declared, would be allowed to proceed to a German port. Unless such a vessel received a pass to proceed to some neutral or Allied port, the cargo must be discharged in a

* However, neutral cargoes for Germany were to be confiscated if they consisted of anything on the swollen British contraband lists. That is, shipments to Germany were treated under the provisions of the October 29 Order in Council.

British port and turned over to the marshal of the prize court. If the goods were not contraband of war, and were not requisitioned for the use of His Majesty, they should be restored by the prize court, on such terms as were deemed just, to the persons concerned.

Any vessel sailing after March 1 for a neutral European port, having aboard goods of German ownership or destination, might be required to discharge such goods in a British or Allied port. After being discharged in a British port, if neither contraband nor requisitioned by His Majesty's Government, they should "be restored by order of the court, upon such terms as the court may in the circumstances deem to be just, to the person entitled thereto."

The Order then specified how a neutral might proceed to get justice in the British prize court. It stated that nothing which it contained should be deemed to affect the liability of any vessel or goods "to capture or condemnation independently of this Order." That is, the Order in Council of October 29 was not repealed.

Finally, the last and most novel paragraph of the British Order was a bid for the support of neutral nations in facilitating the measures thus taken against Germany. This paragraph offered to relax the interference of Britain with commerce between America and European neutrals, if the European neutrals would persuade or force the steamship lines under their flags not to carry goods of German ownership or origin. The provision read as follows:

"Nothing in this Order shall prevent the relaxation of the provisions of this Order in respect of the merchant vessels of any country which declares that no commerce intended for or originating in Germany or belonging to German subjects shall enjoy the protection of its flag."

Referring to this March 11 Order in Council, the British note which accompanied it reassured our Ambassador in these words:

"I apprehend that the perplexities to which your Excellency refers will for the most part be dissipated by the perusal of this document."

Far from "dissipating" American perplexities, the March Order in Council, like those that had gone before, infinitely increased them.

Our protest was voiced in our note to Britain of March 30. We said in this communication that the Order in Council of March 11 would constitute a practical assertion of unlimited belligerent rights over neutral commerce, and an almost unqualified denial of sovereign rights of nations at peace. Belligerent rights over neutral commerce, we urged, are limited. The belligerent has the right to visit and search these vessels, and to capture and condemn them if it is found that they are on unneutral service or carrying contraband of war. The belligerent may blockade the enemy's ports and coast, and capture and condemn any vessel trying to break the blockade. It was even conceded that a belligerent may take into its ports for examination suspected vessels engaged in trade between neutrals.—But this, it was claimed, is the end of the rights of belligerents over neutral commerce.

Moreover, even though a blockade should exist, all but absolute contraband shipments, it was maintained, might be freely transported from the United States to Germany, through neutral countries. For the United States to forego this right *would be inconsistent with the solemn obligations of our government, and would be assuming an attitude of unneutrality* towards Germany.

We protested against the announced blockade as including not only all the coast and ports of Germany, but also a great number of neutral ports. No matter if the "close" blockade could no longer be maintained, international law could still be followed. Ships should be allowed free passage through the blockading cordon, if destined to neutral ports. Absolute freedom from interference should be accorded to all trade *from* neutral ports to America, and to all trade from America to neutral ports excepting in absolute contraband in transit to the enemy.

We denied that, whatever might be the illegal acts of Germany in the present war, there was any excuse for similar action on Great Britain's part, so far as such action affected neutral rights.

Our note called attention to the fact that Scandinavian and Danish ports could trade over the high seas with German Baltic ports, access to which Great Britain could not bar. We pointed out the serious interruption of American trade that might result from the enforcement of the Order in Council. We counted on Great Britain to modify its severity, and we reserved the right to exact reparation for every act of that country in contravention of international law.

The issue between London and Washington was thus sharply drawn. We contended for the freedom of commerce, for equal sovereignty with Britain on the high seas with the exception of certain rights which a belligerent might exercise under international law.

Great Britain delayed until July 23 its answer to the March 30 note, and then made no concession to our demands.

This July 23 communication contended that the British blockade measures were reasonable, necessary and "adaptations" of the old principles of blockade. In view of the shocking methods of German warfare, it continued, the Allies felt the obligation to take every means in their power to overcome their common enemy. Further, the British understanding of our March 30 note was that we admitted the necessity of Britain taking all steps to cripple the enemy's trade, though we criticised the methods employed.

It was insisted that the blockade would be ineffective if not extended to enemy commerce moving via neutral ports. It was denied that the United States could expect Britain to make such a modification of its blockade practices. The Bermuda cases of Civil War time (reviewed in Chapter IX) were cited as illustrating an extensive application of the law of blockade by the United States itself.* It was insisted that England had the right to extend the law of blockade to fit the peculiar situation of Germany, surrounded and served as it was by neutral ports. The sole obligation of Britain in the matter was said to be the obligation not to molest bona fide neutral trade. The reason why the British action was not directly supported by written authority was, it was declared, because it was the business of writers on international law to formulate existing rules and not suggest adaptations to meet altered circumstances.

The note insisted that the British adaptations of old rules were in accordance with the general principles of law and that "unnecessary injury to neutrals" was being avoided. It was asserted that our March 30 note exaggerated the degree of British interference with our trade with neutrals. It was denied that there are "certain now clearly determined rights" of belligerents which belligerents may not overstep. These rights were stated to have been variously exercised in the past. The method of exercising the right of blockade, the note went on, might vary with the circumstances of the case. The right itself was by effective means to shut off the commerce of an enemy. So with the principle of contraband and its applications, which must change to meet conditions.

---

* In this July 23 note, England did not again (as in its February 10 note) cite the Matamoros cases, the real Civil War parallels to the British blockade situation. As we shall see, these cases are directly opposed to the British contention.

As for the reminder in the March 30 note that according to the Declaration of Paris "free ships make free goods," the British reply said that England was interfering with goods because of German destination or origin, not because of German ownership (which according to the Declaration of Paris was insufficient to justify seizure).

His Majesty's Government then expressed its satisfaction that the measures being enforced had had no detrimental effect on the commerce of the United States.

"Figures of recent months show that the increased opportunities afforded by the war for American commerce have more than compensated for the loss of the German and Austrian markets."

The note was a clear rejection of all our demands. A few of its points call for comment. No shocking methods of German warfare are a reason for a belligerent abridging the clear trade rights of neutrals. As for our use of the principle of continuous voyage in the Bermuda cases, we did not invent the principle but took it over from British practice. Our Supreme Court in the Matamoros cases specifically halted us from such a distortion of the principle as Britain now makes: namely, the blockading of a neutral port to prevent even non-contraband from moving overland to the enemy.

The British plea of necessity and altered circumstances sounds like the German justification of the terrors of their submarine warfare, or of their march through Belgium. The reference to the flourishing condition of our export trade did not impress us. The total figures of our exports were indeed large, but the presence of a large volume of mushroom trade like war orders did not compensate for the enormous loss sustained by such great interests as cotton. Above all, large exports to the Allies did not soothe our feeling that the principle of neutrality was being violated when we supplied the Allies and yet allowed them unlawfully to prevent us from trading with the Central Empires.

CHAPTER VI

Some Effects and Aspects of the Blockade

Since the blockade was instituted, there has been a continuous series of seizures, detentions, confiscations or purchases. To further "legalize" its actions the British Government adopted on March 23 a new development in "international" law—as usual an Order in Council—already described in connection with the Wilhelmina case. This Order provided that the cargo of any neutral ship in a British port, which had not yet been condemned, might be requisitioned. Any vessel bound from the United States to any port in Europe might be brought into a British harbor in accordance with the terms of the March 11 or October 29 Orders in Council. If Great Britain could find no ground for condemning a cargo from the United States to a neutral country, it could now purchase that cargo and prevent it from reaching its destination.

After March 30 all seizures by the British Admiralty of neutral vessels sailing from America for neutral ports were in defiance of the attitude of our government, excepting as the seizures were made for the purpose of discovering absolute contraband for Germany whose presence might be justly suspected.

A few instances will illustrate the policy of deten-

tion. On March 30 the Danish steamer Louisiana
left New York for Copenhagen. On April 16 she
was taken to Kirkwall. On April 26 she was ordered
to proceed to Hull, where the foodstuffs in her cargo
were to be passed on by a prize court. On March 24
the Lapland sailed for Copenhagen. On April 9
she was seized and taken to Kirkwall; on April 14
she was transferred to Barrow, where her provisions
were unloaded and thrown into court.

It is recalled that five ships of the American Gans
Steamship Company were detained in November, and
after many adventures succeeded finally in getting
their case set for June 7. By the middle of May
twelve other steamers, with provisions for Scandinavia to the value of $11,000,000, lay in British
ports. All the expenses of delay rested upon American packers. Those in this country who knew the
facts were indignant.

We have already reviewed the April 13 proceedings in the British prize court regarding the
detained meat cargoes. Though they were detained
in November, the British Government was not ready
to go on with the cases in April. The scandal of
those proceedings reached this country in the letter
correspondence of the Associated Press, though the
British censors prevented cable news of it from
crossing the Atlantic.

In May the British Government was disturbed at
the growing discontent in America because of the
detention policy, and also because Mr. Urion, who
had been in England representing the packers and

who had failed to get satisfactory action, was departing for America to see what could be done in Washington. With the double purpose of discounting what Mr. Urion might say and forestalling an American note on detention, on May 21 the British Foreign Office issued a statement to the American press correspondents in London, which was promptly cabled to this country. The cabled account reached the United States two days before Mr. Urion did.

The British statement began by saying that only three American-owned ships were detained in England. The first of these was the Joseph W. Fordney, captured off the coast of Norway. This vessel was detained, it was stated, because she apparently tried to evade the patrols of His Majesty's Government. It was declared that the consignments of the Joseph W. Fordney were addressed to a person in Sweden who was suspected by the British Government of supplying food to Germany.

It was then stated that of thirty-six detained ships with American cargoes aboard, twenty-three had cotton cargoes. The announcement said that none of the cargoes had been stopped excepting when destined directly to Germany, or when there was suspicion that the cotton was moving to Germany via a neutral country. "It was never suggested," the author of the statement continued, "that vessels or cargoes with an enemy destination should be allowed to proceed."

With regard to provisions, Great Britain, it appeared from this British statement, had been carrying on negotiations with American packers for the purpose of getting them to limit their shipments into neutral European countries to the amounts actually required in those countries for home consumption. It was added, however, that the packers made their acceptance of these terms conditional upon the purchase by the British Government of the detained Scandinavian cargoes, at the prices for which they would have sold in Scandinavia. The demand was considered exorbitant. Therefore it was proposed to send these cases through the prize court.

The familiar British argument was then adduced, that according to trade statistics America could not be suffering in the matter of its exports of foodstuffs. It was stated that in February, 1915, our exports to European neutrals increased more than our exports to Germany and Austria decreased, and note was taken especially of a large increase in the export of lard and bacon to Scandinavian and Dutch ports, the intimation being that some of this merchandise was reaching Germany.

In all British procedure regarding us there is nothing more annoying than the apparent assumption that we can be silenced by the money argument. It is the argument that appeals to those who have no principles. But our whole contention in the foodstuffs matter is a question of principle. That was the basis of our March 30 note. Moreover, our March 30 note insisted on the right without hindrance to send foodstuffs, provisions, into Germany via Scandinavia. Therefore how were we to be influenced by an argument that the large quantities of lard moving to Scandinavia caused suspicion that lard might be trickling through to Germany? We had expressly denied that this was cause for lawful suspicion or detention.

After this utterance of the British Foreign Office, the packers promptly explained their side of the matter. The British Government, they said, wanted the provisions auctioned in England and the proceeds handed to the shippers. The latter objected to this. First, the provisions were packed for the Scandinavian market, not the British. This meant, for example, that the bacon contained far more fat than England would wish for. To sell Scandinavian provisions in the British open market would mean certain loss to the American packers, under the best conditions. The dumping of $11,000,000 of meat products on any market would depress its prices to abnormal levels. The packers thought that Britain should pay them the contract price of the cargoes.

Surely Great Britain could not have been counting on a supposed American sentiment against the Chicago packers, which was expected to influence this country against any intervention on their behalf. This would explain the difference in treatment afforded by Great Britain with reference to cotton and to cargoes of provisions destined for European neutrals. England promised to purchase cotton cargoes at the price contracted for in Europe, while with regard to provisions this treatment was refused.

—But the British Government must have recognized that, after all, our packers are the selling agents abroad for the meat products of American farms.

On May 24, representatives of the Chicago packers met in Washington. Their agent had returned from London with the story of his months of fruitless effort to get provision ships through the prize court. On the evening of the 24th they met the Secretary of State, and a meeting was arranged for the following day between representatives of the meat men, of the State Department and of the British Embassy.

This meeting, however, did not solve the problem. A public statement was prepared, but the packers decided not to issue it. So far as we have information of the May 25 proceedings, the British representatives would not consent to the purchase of the provisions by their government at the Scandinavian contract prices, while the packers would not consent to limit their exports of provisions to Scandinavia to the amounts which Britain deemed normal. However, a tentative agreement was reached regarding future shipments. The packers consented to notify British officials in this country a reasonable time before they shipped their goods. The British were to be given a fair opportunity to ascertain the bona fide neutral destination of these shipments. This being ascertained, the British officials here were to certify the shipments, and they were to be free of detention. But the British home government never accepted this arrangement.

By the month of July, 1915, there were $14,000,-

000 of provisions for neutral Europe held up in England. Their cases in the prize court had been repeatedly postponed at the request of the British Attorney General. Settlement looked as remote as in November, 1914. Since the Washington conference in May, the British Government had made another unacceptable proposition to the packers; namely, the government offered to withdraw the cases if the goods would be sold in England and if the packers would guarantee the British Government both against claims for detention of the ships and claims on the part of neutral European buyers who had never received goods which they had paid for.

Therefore on July 14, 1915, representatives of the packers again called on the State Department at Washington. On July 16 the long postponed hearing of the provisions cases was to be resumed in the London prize court. Both the April 13 hearing and later events gave clear indication that the prize court would treat the cargoes under the Orders in Council, in disregard of what we considered our rights under international law. So on July 15 our government sent the so-called "caveat" note to England, intended partly for the information of the prize court.

In view of the difference of opinion apparently existing between England and America regarding the principles of international law governing prize court procedure, Ambassador Page was asked to inform England that we should recognize no action of its prize courts proceeding under British munici-

pal enactments (Orders in Council) and not under
the recognized principles of international law.

The answer to this warning came on July 31.
The British Government declared itself unaware of
any differences between America and England as
to the principles of law applicable to prize courts.
It was asserted that in both countries these courts
were subject to the instruction of their sovereign
and, in the absence of such instruction, to the general rules of international law. A decision of Lord
Stowell was cited stating that there is no inconsis-
tency in the duty of the court to enforce at the same
time the King's Orders in Council and the established
rules of law, because the Orders are never in conflict
with that law. The judge said he could not "without extreme indecency" contemplate or discuss his
course in the impossible emergency that a conflict
between the old and the proposed law should arise.

It was pointed out that United States citizens,
if dissatisfied with the decision of a British prize
court, might appeal to His Majesty's Council. If
retrial were there denied, recourse might be had
to an international tribunal. The hope was expressed that this note might relieve the misappre-
hensions under which the American Government
seemed to be laboring with regard to the principles
of law applied in British prize courts.

At present the packers will sell to neutral Europe
only on terms of cash before shipment. The buyer
must take the risk of British detention and perhaps
confiscation. It is a risk no one dares to assume.

No regular steamship line to Scandinavia will accept meat products unless certified as to Scandinavian destination by a representative in America of the Scandinavian country, *and also by a British consul.**

It should be noted also that the British notification on March 1, that shipments to and from Germany would be seized, resulted at once in a modification of insurance contracts—even those of our own Government War Risk Insurance Bureau—declaring the insurance void in the case of goods proving to be of German destination, ownership or origin; and insurance on such goods is still unavailable.

With respect to the consular certificates demanded on meat shipments to neutral countries, it must be observed that these certificates, with the further evidence even of the seal of Great Britain placed by a British consul on the hatches of vessels, are regarded by the English naval officers only as collateral evidence; they do not exempt from search. Moreover, British pressure has forced Scandinavian consignees to give the most stringent guarantees as to the home consumption of American shipments, before these shipments may be delivered at the Scandinavian port.

Denmark, for example, has two lines from the United States: the Interocean Transportation Company and Det Forenede Dampskibs Selskab (the Scandinavian-American Line).

---

* On May 3 the British Embassy at Washington issued a statement of instructions to American exporters as to how to ship to neutral Europe. It is printed in Appendix, p. 325.

The Interocean makes the American shipper attach to his bill of lading a sworn affidavit to the effect that his statement of the merchandise shipped is true, and that it has positively no other destination than the named consignee. The Scandinavian-American Line has the following in its bill of lading, printed in red:

"Consignees of the within goods are under the obligation to furnish Det Forenede Dampskibs Selskab at Copenhagen promptly and on demand a written declaration that the within goods are for consumption in country of destination shown in this bill of lading, and will not be re-exported. A failure to provide such a declaration gives the shipowner the right to withhold delivery of the goods or discharge them at any place, whereupon each and every liability of the shipowner shall cease."

Yet this is not the end. Britain has forced the Danish lines to deliver only to those Danish consignees who submit to having their books examined and approved by an accountant appointed by a British official in Denmark. This accountant is to be paid by the Danish merchant. His purpose is to see where the goods of the merchant go. Before the merchant gets American goods from the steamer he must deposit in a bank money equal to the value of the goods. This money is forfeited to the British consulate if the merchant fails to see that the accountant certifies the disposition of the shipment.

The official British ruling on this point, enforced by the steamship lines, is of interest. The merchant, it is ordered, must agree to the appointment by the British consulate of a chartered accountant

"to examine books and business in order to satisfy itself (the consulate) as to the actual disposal of the consignment; and deposit of a bank guarantee of full value of the consignment, to be forfeited to His Majesty's consulate in case of non-fulfillment of declaration. Expenses of chartered accountant to be borne by the company."

There is only one way out of this labyrinth into which our legitimate commerce has been forced to wander. No one but the United States Government knows the way. No European neutral is strong enough to resist whatever use Britain may choose to make of her sea power, for every European neutral is dependent upon imports of our food which must pass by British warships. No European neutral has said that it would resist Britain or dared to say it. We have dared to say this. In our March 30 note we have declared as subversive of international law interference with our commerce with neutrals; and we have said we cannot stop shipping food to Germany via neutrals without violating the neutrality we choose to observe.

This matter of the right to ship food and other non-contraband to Germany is the crux of the whole situation. Once insist upon that and the whole structure of interference with our neutral commerce tumbles like a house of cards. Once admit, even tacitly, the right to interfere with food to Germany and the whole British structure of interference is the logical law of the sea.

If Britain may lawfully stop our food for Germany via neutrals, it may, if it can, force those neutrals to place export embargoes on the food for Germany.

If food from the United States may not go through Denmark to Germany, it is virtually contraband.

Then Britain cannot be blamed for detaining, searching and annoying our shipments to Denmark; for they then carry contraband and by law Britain may use every means to prevent contraband from moving into Germany. To prevent the losses to steamers due to such detentions, steamship lines are bound to protect themselves against the possibility of carrying shipments that will be viewed suspiciously by Britain. In order to be allowed to get goods, Scandinavian merchants naturally submit to any procedure that will make them personæ gratæ to Britain. In order to be allowed to ship goods, American exporters naturally turn to His Majesty's Government for guidance as to the conditions under which they may ship to neutral countries.

For many reasons the United States should act. It should force Great Britain to allow our foodstuffs to reach Germany, and thus remove the intolerable suspicion that adheres to our shipments to European neutrals. Great material interests are involved. The genuineness of our neutrality is at stake. And apart from the questions of neutrality and interest in the present crisis, we must remember the constant menace in the future of such precedents as Great Britain has sought to establish, all tending toward the one conclusion that the nation dominant in sea power may adopt in restraint of commerce any measure it sees fit.

It is perhaps worth while to picture a situation where, with sea power differently distributed and other belligerents engaged, the latent danger of the precedent now being established would come to light.

Suppose in a future war that Japan's fleet rules the high seas and that Japan is at war with England. Japan decides to starve England, since that is simpler and less strenuous than defeating England by military force. Japan therefore declares a blockade of England. Its blockading cordon, however, because of the efficiency of the British submarines, is not able to invest the British ports, operate around the British Isles or even hold the North Sea. Great Britain undisturbed trades oversea in that direction. However, the Japanese squadrons, a thousand miles off the British coast or even across the seas, intercept Argentine grain and meat as it leaves Buenos Ayres. Japanese ships stop and confiscate Australian mutton and Indian wheat long before they reach England.

These ships also hold up and appropriate all American exports of wheat, flour and provisions, on their way to England across the Atlantic Ocean. They stop not only the exports destined for England but also those destined for the rest of Europe, on

the ground that they might in some way get to
England. All during these hold-ups of American
commerce, Russian grain would move unhindered to
Great Britain, for Japan could not hold the North
Sea. Danish provisions would supply the market
which once Americans held. England would not
starve. It would be American citizens dependent on
the British market who would starve.

If the British blockade of Germany be admitted
as valid, the entire law of blockade as evolved from
centuries of experience will be abolished, and the
possibilities of the future contain endless menace.
England does not invest the German coast. She does
not invest anything. The blockade does not affect
all neutrals. Some are quite free from it. Norway
and Sweden trade with the Baltic ports of Germany
as if there were no war, for Germany, not England,
holds the Baltic. A Swedish exporter of lumber can
send it unmolested over the high seas from Gothenburg to Stettin, a German Baltic port. But if a
Mobile exporter shipped a cargo to Stettin it would
never arrive. England would seize it as it passed
the British Isles.

England blockades, not all commerce with the
German Baltic ports, but only such commerce as
can be reached by British cruisers without too intimate association with German mines and torpedoes.
That is, the precedent is being established that it is
right and lawful for a belligerent with some degree
of sea power to ban our trade if it can intercept our
trade, whether it can so intercept the trade of other

neutral nations or not. This is a new definition of blockade. The word *blockade* means nothing under such circumstances. Instead of a blockade, such action means an intolerable interference.

Were Japan or any other country so to shut off our food exports to England, the wheat farmers would feel the same distress that has come upon the cotton planters in the struggle of the Allies with Germany.

Nor is our acquiescence in the present order of things in accordance with our precedents, especially with our profession of the obligation to supply food to both belligerents if our neutrality is to be unimpaired.

In 1793, England, then, as now, without maintaining a legal blockade, undertook to capture all food products bound for France. The instructions of our then Secretary of State, Thomas Jefferson, to Thomas Pinckney, our Minister to Great Britain, are illuminating today. Asserting that "no nation can agree, at the mere will or interest of another, to have its peaceable industry suspended and its citizens reduced to idleness and want," Jefferson continued:

"Were we to withhold from France supplies of provisions, we should in like manner be bound to withhold them from her enemies also, and thus shut to ourselves all the ports of Europe where corn is in demand, or make ourselves parties in the war. This is a dilemma which Great Britain has no right to force upon us, and for which no pretext can be found in

any part of our conduct. *She may, indeed, feel the desire of starving an enemy nation, but she can have no right of doing it at our loss nor of making us the instruments of it.*"*

It is of interest to note that from September of 1914 to May, 1915, inclusive, we exported foodstuffs to the values of $395,700,000, or $241,600,000 more than during the same period of the year preceding. The larger part of these exports went to England. What if we should decide today that an abandonment of our right to send foodstuffs to Germany means that *we should in like manner be bound to withhold them from her enemies also?*

In the reorganization of the British Cabinet in May, 1915, two members were added who, to be consistent, must support America's contention regarding the illegality of the present form of the British blockade. These new members are Mr. Balfour, head of the Admiralty, and Lord Lansdowne.

In our March 30 note to Great Britain, we declared our right to trade with Germany via neutral countries even if a blockade of German ports were maintained. To renounce this right, we declared, would be to renounce our neutrality. But we denied that Britain was maintaining a legal blockade. We stated its weakness in these words:

"The Scandinavian and Danish ports, for example, . . . are free, so far as the actual enforcement of the Order in Council is concerned, to carry on trade with

* For the full text of Jefferson's letter, see Appendix, p. 318.

German Baltic ports, although it is an essential element of blockade that it bear with equal severity upon all neutrals."

In other words, we declared that England had no right to bar our commerce with German Baltic ports.

Mr. Balfour, before he joined the Cabinet, publicly admitted the truth of this contention. We must, therefore, support our case in the new Cabinet. In an interview cabled from London to the *New York Times* on March 27, discussing this novel feature of the British blockade, he ably explained the rule that a blockade must bar the commerce of *all* neutrals with a belligerent:

"It (this rule) is designed to prevent the blockading power using its privileges in order to mete out different treatment to different countries, as, for instance, by letting the ships of one nationality pass the blockading cordon while it captures the ships of another. Such a procedure is on the face of it unfair. It could have no object but to assist the trade of one neutral as against the trade of another and arbitrarily to redistribute the burden which war unhappily inflicts on neutrals as well as on belligerents."

Mr. Balfour, while agreeing that England's present blockade violates this principle, offered the excuse that "the discrimination, if it may be so designated, is not the result of deliberate policy but of a geographical accident."

But this defense did not even convince Mr. Balfour. He finally admitted:

"But, after all, it is the equity of the Allies' case rather than the law which mainly interests the thinking public of America and elsewhere."

Again, this is the assumption that Britain is fighting our battle and we must therefore let her do as she pleases in destroying our commerce as a means to attain her end.

If, then, there is no blockade which we can, as neutrals, admit, and none which the first Lord of the Admiralty in the British Cabinet can defend, we turn to another distinguished British statesman to learn what our rights are. It is recalled that, at the time of the Boer War, Lord Salisbury stated that conditional contraband could not be stopped by a belligerent unless *shown* to be destined to the military of the enemy.

At this point the second member of the British Cabinet, Lord Lansdowne, tells us our further rights in the matter. He tells us that we must not recognize the action of a belligerent (an English) prize court which stops our foodstuffs (to Germany) in violation of the principle Lord Salisbury laid down.

It is remembered that in 1904 Russia seized food destined to the civil population of Japan. Lord Lansdowne, we recall, then Foreign Secretary, wrote a letter to Joseph Choate describing the warning issued to Russia.

"His Majesty's Government further pointed out that the decision of the prize court of the captor in such matters, in order to be binding on neutral states, must be in accordance with the recognized rules and principles of international law and procedure."

That is, Lansdowne seems to say that every one of the hundreds of British seizures of vessels with American cargoes would have been illegal even if they had been destined for Germany. In the Cabinet he must contend that the British seizures of our exports to neutral ports were doubly beyond the pale of all law.

CHAPTER VII

STARTING THE COTTON MOVEMENT

In the production, ginning and warehousing of the annual cotton crop, direct employment is given to more than four millions of people, and a livelihood to many more. Upon the successful growth and upon the prompt and satisfactory marketing of cotton are dependent all other business interests of the South, and the earning power of thousands of miles of railway. Moreover, since the South depends upon cotton for its ability to purchase other goods, any deficiency in growth, depression of values or interference with marketing means an immediate adverse affect upon agricultural, mercantile and manufacturing activities in the rest of the country.

It happens that successful marketing of the cotton crop depends primarily upon getting it into the export trade. In recent years two-thirds of the cotton crop has been exported and only one-third consumed in this country.

Interference with the foreign movement is thus the most serious evil that can befall the South, far worse than a partial crop failure due, for example, to the boll weevil. If the foreign market is open, high prices are paid for the cotton that escapes a crop failure. The total cotton value is thus often as large in years of partial crop failure as in years of heavy yield. The twelve million bales of 1910 were worth $100,000,000 more than the 16,250,000 bales of 1911. But if the foreign market or any essential part of it is closed, ruinously low prices greet every participant in the crop. In the midst of apparent plenty, everyone is in want.

Such a result in the South was brought about in the fall of 1914, because of the European War. England, the largest consumer of our cotton, normally takes 3,500,000 bales per year, over one-third of our total cotton exports. Germany and Austria come next and normally take from 2,500,000 to 3,000,000 bales of cotton, nearly one-third of our exports. The war would inevitably have affected the cotton trade adversely. But the effect was accentuated by the threatening attitude of England towards our commerce, which kept the German market for cotton closed until the winter months.

The pressure in the South of those 3,000,000 bales, for which exit was long denied, helped force the price of cotton down to 6 cents per pound. The cost of producing is supposed to average about 8 cents. At this low price of 6 cents, thousands of the little cotton farmers, the rank and file of the South, were forced to part with their product. They had not the financial power to hold the cotton until, along in the spring of 1915, its price rose to 10 cents, owing to a temporary reopening of the path to Germany, the broadening demand of other countries and the activities of our own mills. It was the large planters, dealers and English importers who were able to hold the cotton and profit from the advance. The farmers were hard hit.

The cotton year starts August 1. About that date begins the export movement of the new crop. In the second half of July, 1914, "spot cotton"— that is, cotton for immediate, not future delivery— was selling in New York for $13\frac{1}{4}$ cents per pound; on July 27, with war threatening, it was $12\frac{1}{4}$ cents. Two days later, with war certain, this price had dropped to $11\frac{3}{4}$ cents. On July 31 the New York and New Orleans Cotton Exchanges closed.

With the entrance of England into the war on August 4, shipping was paralyzed. Most of our commerce has been carried in British and German ships and no such ship dared venture out to sea because both English and German cruisers were on the North Atlantic. The ordinary marine insurance carried on the hulls and cargoes of these ships did not protect them against the danger of capture or destruction. Against this new peril, war risk insurance was necessary.

The German ships never sailed again, but kept their American ports, being so much tonnage withdrawn from the carrying trade. Some British ships were chartered by their government for war services. The remainder were in a position to sail when, a short time after August 1, the British Government insured against war risk British vessels carrying for the United Kingdom; and when, two weeks after the outbreak of the war, the British Admiralty announced that the North Atlantic route was free of German cruisers. This partially solved the problem of getting American cotton exported to England. But the method of financing such shipments also had broken down. A cotton exporter gets his money by selling to his bank a draft drawn on the English buyer or the latter's bank. Owing to the disturbance of international finance and the paralysis of the London discount market, such drafts became for a time unsalable. Yet in the course of a few weeks this financial difficulty was largely overcome, at least as to shipments which could be satisfactorily insured, and cotton for England went forward in a volume that was substantial, though below normal.

The following table shows the exports to England up to June 1, 1915, compared with exports to England in the corresponding months of 1913-1914.

COMPARISON OF COTTON EXPORTS TO ENGLAND, BY MONTHS, 1913-1914 AND 1914-1915. IN BALES

	1913-14	1914-15	Changes 1914-15	
August........	77,488	6,370	Decrease	71,118
September.....	376,426	50,980	"	325,446
October.......	514,105	232,065	"	282,040
November.....	530,355	333,700	"	196,655
December.....	473,028	572,396	Increase	99,368
January.......	437,231	585,534	"	148,303
February......	328,794	633,574	"	304,780
March.........	264,999	440,490	"	175,491
April..........	147,298	378,828	"	231,530
May	140,618	359,675	"	219,057
Period Aug. 1 to May 31...	3,290,342	3,593,612	"	303,270

All this meant that in the early months of the shipping season, the months vital in fixing the price paid the farmer, the largest purchaser of American cotton was not buying. Therefore, there was double reason why the second largest purchaser, Germany, should without hindrance take its share.

For reasons to be explained, direct shipments to Germany were at first very difficult. Hence during the early months of the export season, beginning August 1, cotton had to move into Germany via adjacent neutral European countries. That is, instead of being shipped from the United States to Hamburg or Bremen, cotton was shipped to Genoa, Rotterdam or Copenhagen and forwarded to Germany overland. Or it was shipped to Norway or Sweden, particularly to Gothenburg, and thence forwarded to Germany by sea.

In the month of October these indirect shipments into Germany began to go forward and appeared in our export figures, which showed an increase in shipments to the neutral countries adjacent to Germany, compared with the corresponding shipments in the same month of the year before. But not until January did these increases, representing cotton for Germany, begin to compensate for the loss in direct shipments. This whole situation is illustrated by the following table:

BALES OF COTTON EXPORTED FROM THE UNITED STATES TO GERMANY, DIRECT AND INDIRECT

	Germany-Austria			Italy-Holland-Scandinavia		Excess of 1914-15 over 1913-14
	1913-14	1914-15	Decrease	1913-14	1914-15	
August.................	73,228	52	73,176	15,267	2,246	Decrease 13,021
September.............	294,055	—	294,055	53,666	33,548	Decrease 20,118
October...............	481,726		481,726	62,454	107,199	Increase 44,745
November..............	528,340	1,000	527,340	80,945	224,442	Increase 143,497
December..............	350,298	47,076	303,222	91,750	354,614	Increase 262,864
January...............	326,968	99,913	227,055	69,172	491,681	Increase 422,509
February..............	222,967	88,508	134,459	45,701	503,652	Increase 457,951
March.................	223,144	6,112	217,032	54,657	425,076	Increase 370,049
Period Aug. 1 to Apr. 1........	2,500,726	242,661	2,258,065	473,612	2,142,458	Increase 1,668,846

Figures later than March are not given; for after March 31, as we shall see, England let no cotton sail for Germany either direct or indirect. Much of such cotton as sailed even in March was held up and bought by England.

The remarkable thing about the table of exports to England is that they show that the total exports of American cotton into England have been larger in the present year than in the past year. The increase for the August 1-June 1 was over 300,000 bales. It was only in the early months of the war that cotton did not move in good volume to England.

Moreover, the decrease in the total cotton movement into Germany and Austria has not been so large as many think. The drop in direct exports to Germany and Austria was 2,258,000 bales. But the increase in shipments via adjacent neutral countries was about 1,668,000 bales. So the real decrease in exports to Germany was perhaps not over 500,000 bales, assuming—and we cannot quite assume—that Germany got all the excess exports moving to adjacent neutrals.

It is recalled that the New York and New Orleans Cotton Exchanges closed on July 31. For later quotations on the price of cotton we are mainly dependent on individual transactions reported from different parts of the South. All tell the same story of sinking prices.

Cotton had sold in New York for 11¾ cents in the last days of July. On August 10, southern shippers were willing to deliver it to New England factories for 11 cents. On August 21 it sold in Augusta for 10½ cents, on August 26 for 9½ cents. On September 2 cotton touched 8 cents; on October 6, 7½ cents; on October 12 it dropped to 6¾ cents; and on October 19 sales from southern points were reported at 6 to 6⅛ cents per pound. This was a price of desperation. As a matter of fact, cotton on the farm was selling for 6 cents all during September and October. These 6-cent sales are what finally forced the United States to act.

If there had been the customary monthly regularity of movement from the United States to England and Germany, the price of cotton in this country would not have dropped in any such manner as it did. The rapid fall was occasioned partly by the fact that in August and early September little cotton was bought or moved either to England or Germany. The fall was caused partially by the fear of Americans that England would not let cotton move to Germany at all.

Just as long as England could, she fostered this impression, and she allowed a free movement only when an irresistible force was applied to her; namely, the force of a direct demand from Washington. This demand, brought about by irate southern senators, was supplied with a promise of real consequences should it not be met. The story of the quiet English ban upon our cotton trade, and its removal in October, is worth reading.

It is recalled that, under the codification of international law represented by the Declaration of London, cotton was on the "free list"; that is, it was one of those articles which could not be declared contraband by any belligerent. The reason is obvious. It is a prime necessity for the life of civilians and the raw material for the greatest single peaceful industry of countries; namely, the textile trades. Upon the unhampered movement of cotton in international commerce depends the prosperity of the workers in great sections of the civilized world. Excepting after a complicated manufacturing process, cotton is not available for purposes of war.

England, we know, in her Order in Council of August 20, adopted the Declaration of London as her rule of international law, with certain exceptions. Cotton was not affected by the exceptions either in the August 20 Order or in any successive one. That is, England by announcement was pledged to consider cotton as a free good that could move unhindered to Germany in all but German ships or those of Germany's Allies.

During August there was the same initial difficulty in getting cotton started for Germany as in getting it started for England. This cotton normally moves in full shiploads in "tramp" steamers, chartered for the voyage. Most of these steamers are under the German or the British flag. Those under the German flag dared not venture on the seas, which England controlled. Those under the British flag were of course not available to carry cotton to England's enemy. That left for consideration ships of neutral countries: the United States and other neutrals.

Since the United States owned few ships built to cross the Atlantic, the most promising candidates seemed the ships of other nations. These were, however, out of the question with regard to direct exports to Germany, because of the peculiar conditions surrounding hull and cargo insurance, without which no shipowner or shipper can let his property sail. This difficulty is connected with British control of the vessel insurance business for the whole world, a control which was naturally exercised to injure the enemy of England.

As for marine insurance, neutral vessels could without difficulty obtain it from the German and neutral marine insurance companies, including the American. But they could obtain no war risk insurance to cover them in the German trade. The large field of British private companies was closed to them. Neutral insurers, in so far as they participated in the war risk business, confined themselves to lesser risks than on shipments into Germany, in the face of the attitude England was exhibiting toward all such commerce. The War Risk Insurance Bureaus of other neutral governments than our own were restricting their insurance to their own vessels engaged in the home trade. They had no intention of insuring shipments between America and Germany.

Our own Government War Risk Insurance Bureau, established in September, was unfortunately limited by law to insuring American cargoes in American vessels, under the pleasant delusion that there were enough American vessels to carry the cargoes across the sea.

Other neutral vessels being eliminated from the American-German trade through this war risk insurance difficulty, only American vessels remained. With few exceptions, we had no oversea merchant carriers. Most vessels flying the American flag were constructed for the coastwise, Gulf, Caribbean and Great Lakes trades. They were not fit for long transoceanic voyages. The Government Bureau offered to take war risk insurance on these vessels, but required first that they get their marine insurance elsewhere.

Since they were not built for crossing the ocean— which no one knew better than the insurance men— the small American steamers had a long fight to get this marine risk insured. It is not the custom for a single insurer to assume the whole risk of insuring a vessel. Such a risk is jointly carried by a number of insurance companies, or underwriters. So far as oversea insurance is concerned, the American companies have been mere participants with the big English companies in the business. The Americans were unable to secure English aid in furthering shipments to Germany; they long seemed incapable of carrying those risks themselves.

Finally, so Washington claims, the American underwriters were forced to do this insuring by the threat that, if they did not, a bill would be introduced in Congress empowering the Government War Risk Insurance Bureau to enter the marine insurance field. The prospect of perhaps permanent government competition was too much for the American marine companies. They shifted to British insurers some of the risks that they (the Americans) were carrying on English and neutral business, and set free part of their own resources to enable them to handle German trade. The rates charged on steamers not built to cross the ocean were naturally high.

When the cotton exporter had the marine risk on his American vessel covered, he turned to the Government War Risk Bureau and found it quite inadequate for his needs. The government limited the risk on any one bottom to $500,000, hull and cargo included. Even under normal conditions this amount would cover only a very modest hull and cargo. As the demand for American tonnage had brought about a great rise in its value, the shipper found, after he had covered the value of his vessel in the Government War Risk Bureau, that the margin left for the cargo was insufficient. There were occasions when the vessel alone was valued at more than the government's limit.

Eventually Washington instituted a more liberal policy and, in some cases, the insurance limit was increased to $1,000,000. But the time lost in getting this limit extended, after overcoming the other difficulties described, helped hold up direct shipments to Germany for many months. The first American ship in this trade was the Greenbriar, reaching Bremen on January 9, 1915. She was followed by others, mostly vessels withdrawn from the coastwise trade. The high marine risk charged on them was shown to be justified when one, the Denver of the

Mallory Line, foundered on her return trip from Germany.

All the cotton that has been shipped direct to Germany the past season has moved in these American steamers. But the capacity of even the considerable numbers of them withdrawn from the coastwise service was totally inadequate to the situation. This is illustrated by the smallness of our exports to Germany from August 1 to April 1: 250,000 bales compared with 2,250,000 bales last year ·in the same period, a shortage of 2,000,000 bales. If cotton to Germany had moved only in direct shipments in American steamers, the movement would never have afforded the relief which it eventually did afford. There were simply too few American ships and those who knew the situation promised themselves no results of value from the elimination of insurance difficulties that forbade even these few ships to sail.

The fundamental dearth of American vessels for this German cotton trade was early apparent to the government at Washington. The simple way to create such American tonnage was to buy it from foreigners and put it under the American flag. The obvious tonnage in the market was the German, tied up inactive in American ports. All other ships were on the seas earning such rates as never before; no one wanted to sell them.

American laws already allowed the transfer of foreign-built vessels to the American flag, within five years of their construction. In August, 1914, a new law was passed removing the age maximum and permitting ships so entering the American registry to retain their foreign officers. This last measure was designed to remove the last objection to such purchase, in the mind of the American buyer.

Yet no one came forward to buy the German ships, or any others. Nobody felt quite sure of support in exercising his right to purchase belligerent merchant ships in war time and operate them under the American flag. Everyone could count on the active opposition of the British Government to such purchase, an opposition only too plainly indicated in the despatches from London. Under such circumstances the American buyer of a German ship ran the risk of purchasing one which he could not use when purchased.

Precisely this situation was created for the buyer of the former Hamburg-American liner Georgia. In March an American bought this steamer after obtaining, from a representative of Great Britain, what appeared to be an assurance that His Majesty's Government would make no opposition to the purchase and operation of the vessel, provided she did not run in the German trade. She was bought to run to the West Indies and South America. However, with the vessel bought and the money paid, the British Government announced that it would seize the ship if she left port. The buyer had a ship he could not sail.

The case of the Dacia is better known. In December and January Senator Walsh, spokesman for the administration, proved to the satisfaction of the reading public that there was nothing in international law that prevented Americans from acquiring any belligerent merchant vessel they chose, provided the purchase were bona fide and the transfer absolute and unconditional. It was shown that Great Britain's own precedents would not permit her to oppose such transfer. There was considerable miscellaneous criticism of American citizens for neglecting to seize the golden opportunity to upbuild our merchant marine. An American, Edward N. Breitung, tried to seize it.

Breitung purchased outright the Hamburg-American steamer Dacia, which lay in Port Arthur, Texas. He hoisted on her the American flag, signed an American crew and American officers, and loaded her with Texas cotton at Galveston. She was to clear for Bremen. Evidence was submitted of the validity of the transfer, satisfactory to the State Department at Washington.

Great Britain announced that it would capture the Dacia if she sailed. The State Department tried to induce the British Government to let the vessel make just this one trip to Rotterdam, Holland, the Dacia's original destination having been altered in order to improve her chances of getting across. His Majesty's Government, being by this time apparently immune against our communications, could not see its way clear for such a concession.

Yet for England to have seized the Dacia, in the face of English precedents that justified just such

transfers, and while complications of other kinds
were accumulating in the diplomatic relations of
that country and America, would have been clearly
impolitic. It happened that the allied French Government was embarrassed by no such conditions,
either as to precedents or diplomatic complications.
In fact the French precedents did not recognize the
validity of transfer of a belligerent's merchant vessel during war time.* So England allowed a French
cruiser to capture the Dacia and tow her into Brest.
There she was thrown into a French prize court.

In view of the reluctance of private citizens to
create American tonnage, the administration during
the early months of the war determined to acquire
the necessary ships with government funds and to
arrange for their operation. Two reasons were behind this measure. One of these was a desire to relieve
the distress of the cotton states and to start the movement of grain, which for a time was halted by lack
of ships. One reason was the desire of the Democratic administration to call into life an American
merchant marine, about which the Republicans, without practical effect, had talked and agitated for so
many years.

But the main problem was to get cotton moving
into Germany. Since private citizens had failed in
their attempt to acquire ships and start this movement, the task seemed to many an appropriate one

*However, the Declaration of London, under which England
and France were both acting, recognized the validity of such
a transfer as the Dacia.

for the government itself.* There were men who supported the Ship Purchase Bill on this ground, believing that it would put the government in possession of a large number of ships, and that these vessels would be at the service of the South for the export cotton trade.

Had the administration been entirely frank with the public, the bill might, quite probably, have passed. In such case, government-owned ships without interruption would have carried cotton and food to Germany, bringing back dyes, potash, and other German imports. The British so-called "blockade" would never have been established against such a government line.

The bill was projected in August and September of 1914. It provided for a corporation in which the American Government was to be the main stockholder. The corporation was to have $40,000,000 at its disposal, available for purchasing ships. It was claimed that the ships were needed to carry American products to market. What ships, what products, what market, were not specified. Yet everyone knew that the market that called for our product was Germany, that the product that chiefly required American ships to carry it was cotton, and that the ships available for purchase were the interned German steamers.

For two main reasons England was opposed to the bill. In the first place, the purchase of German

*See Minority Report of the Merchant Marine Committee of the U. S. Chamber of Commerce, Appendix, p. 322.

steamers would have created in this country credits available for purchases by Germany. More important than that, the British Government could not have continued to exercise against a line backed by the United States the "economic pressure" which they had been exerting, and which they proposed to exert, on Germany.

The British opposition to government purchase of German interned vessels was manifested in the despatches from London and in unofficial warnings at Washington. Eloquent Republican senators denounced the Ship Purchase Bill as likely to involve us in a war with England, and in their speeches solemnly referred to the warnings from London. The administration itself was confused.

Very possibly the country would have stood behind the administration if it had said:

"The South is prostrate. Cotton is 20 cents in Bremen and 6 cents in Augusta. Germany is ready to take large quantities off the southern market and relieve the situation. It happens that we must have American ships to get that cotton through. We propose to buy them, and to buy them where we can get them cheapest and quickest, put them under the American flag and send them full of cotton to Germany."

Unfortunately nothing of this sort was done. Intentions were veiled until no one knew what was intended. The word Germany was taboo, either as a market to be sought or as a source for ships. People in Washington spoke of buying English and neutral ships. It was specifically said that no ships would be bought that would involve us in any difficulty with the belligerents. Officials spoke generally of running the ships "wherever needed," particularly to South America, to develop our trade there.

As to buying other than German vessels, however, England and many neutral countries put embargoes on the sale of their merchant ships away from the home flag; so that proposition was a futile one. And South America, as was easily pointed out, was in no shape to have its trade with us developed. That continent found itself unable to sell to a large part of Europe, and hence was unable to buy from us or anyone else. Vessels in the regular lines to South America were sailing out of New York only half loaded.

That is, the administration seemed to be asking for these ships from an impossible source, to institute South American services which were unnecessary and superfluous. If this was the real purpose of the Ship Purchase Bill, no money should have been voted for it. If it had some other purpose, that purpose ought to have been declared. Under our apparent concern for the displeasure of England, the bill had become a measure to buy ships nowhere in particular and run them everywhere in general. It was on this rock that the project foundered after a stormy contest in the Senate that carried through most of January and February.

It has been seen that American ocean-going ships were necessary to carry cotton to Germany. Private

individuals failed to acquire such ships and the
attempt to acquire them by public action failed.
Long before this result had been worked out in the
sensational Republican filibuster in the Senate, the
real cotton shippers gave up hope of ever getting
much cotton into Germany direct, and bent their
efforts towards starting the movement to Germany
via neutral ports, in neutral ships.

England met this contingency by two means.
One of these was to urge the neutral countries adjacent to Germany to place re-export embargoes on
cotton, such as they had placed on many other articles, under virtual compulsion from England.   The
second means was the fear created in the minds of
the shippers that cotton might be declared contraband; and this fear interfered with its shipment to
Germany via all neutral countries.

Pressure designed to compel re-export embargoes
was first exerted on neutral Holland.   In the first
days of the war the Netherlands Government placed
a re-exportation embargo on cotton, and the ban
was never removed until January 9, 1915.   This
meant that the natural way into Germany was
barred: the route through Holland and up the Rhine.
In times of peace much of West Germany is so
supplied from the oversea world, since Rotterdam,
at the mouth of the Rhine, is in Dutch hands.

Another neutral country which maintained an
embargo for a considerable period was Italy.   The
other "adjacent neutrals" at first refused.   They
contended for the right of their merchants to for-

ward cotton to Germany, since cotton was on the "free list" of the Declaration of London, according to which England—barring certain modifications—professed to be acting.

That England sought deliberately to prevent cotton from moving to Germany via the neutral countries by fostering rumors that cotton was likely at any moment to be declared contraband, cannot be denied. The fear of such an event was such a potent influence in banking and insurance circles that it made cotton exports very difficult. No one knew that cotton might not be peremptorily declared contraband, as copper had been, while cargoes were in mid-ocean. What the situation called for was clear. A definite declaration from England was needed, to the effect that cotton was not and would not be considered contraband of war.

In the latter half of September and early October, attempts were made to have our government get such a declaration from England. If the State Department made an effort in this direction, the effort was not successful. Shippers who pressed for the declaration received at Washington the answer that it would be an affront to ask England to make such a statement. Was not cotton on the "free list" of the Declaration of London, and was not His Majesty's Government guiding itself by the principles of that Declaration, with certain exceptions that did not affect cotton? Therefore, ship cotton freely.

To remove the last vestige of apprehension, Solici-

tor Cone Johnson, of the State Department, issued
on October 10 the following statement of his personal opinion as to the ease with which cotton could
move to Germany:

"There is no impedient to the shipment of cotton
to any country, not excepting the belligerents. Cotton is non-contraband, for the manifest reason that
in its raw state it cannot be used for the purposes
of war. In order to be available for use by armies
and navies, or forces of the belligerents, it has first
to undergo a long process of manufacture. It is
ranked as a non-contraband in the London Convention.

"Of course shipments of cotton to foreign countries, if they are to escape detention, must be shipped
in American or other vessels flying neutral flags.
There is no legal impediment to a shipload of cotton
going direct to Hamburg consigned to German
spinners, and, personally, I hope to see the exportation of cotton to the countries at war increase.
The English give preference, I understand, to Egyptian cotton, but other countries at war, no doubt, are
in need of raw cotton. Apparently the American cotton interests should, if they have not already done
so, seek out these markets."

The solicitor's optimism did not infect the cotton
trade or start the cotton movement. He was right
in believing that England was preferring Egyptian
cotton, and that there was a market for American
cotton in belligerent countries other than England.
He seemed to underestimate the subtle difficulties
in reaching that market. The trade waited for
assurance from someone more closely in touch than

the solicitor with the practices and purposes of His Majesty's Government.

That the absence of a definite British declaration that cotton was to be considered non-contraband had prevented export shipments from moving even for neutral consumption, is made clear by a telegram of the president of the New York Chamber of Commerce to Mr. Bryan on October 24. It repeated the reports that the Allies had announced cotton for Germany and Austria as on their prohibited list and had warned vessels trading with Scandinavia, Holland and Italy against carrying cotton for Germany or Austria.

Therefore, the telegram read, even shipments to neutral countries were in danger. They might be brought before a British prize court and have to establish their innocency; yet no one had been told what proofs of innocency would be satisfactory. Therefore, it went on, neither shippers nor insurance companies dared handle trade for neutral countries, to say nothing of Germany. The whole cotton trade was represented to be in a serious predicament. The message then asked that Great Britain be requested to give some authoritative statement of its attitude, both with regard to shipments destined to neutrals and shipments destined to Germany and Austria.

Indeed there was need for relief. Through September and October, cotton had been passing out of the producer's hands at a price of six cents per pound. Speaking broadly, the small southern

farmer has been for years in a state of near economic slavery. He lives on credit. When the cotton-
planting season comes, the general store gives the
farmer on credit the seeds, fertilizer and implements
he needs. During the growing season it advances
him clothing and food for his family. The understanding is that the debt will be paid when the cotton
is harvested. It is frequently paid by direct delivery
of cotton to the store, where the farmer is credited
at the current cotton price.

So in September and October of 1914, when the
current price was six cents, the farmer could not
hold his product until better times came. He was
in debt; he was living on credit; and unless he turned
his cotton in, his credit would be cut off and he would
be in positive want. The storekeeper had his bills
and notes to meet also; and he, too, generally had to
sell the cotton at once for what it would bring.

It cannot be denied that there are large farmers
in the South who are financially independent and
capable of holding back their product. Some did
hold it back. But even of those who could carry
the cotton, there was many a cautious spirit who did
not care to take the risk of cotton going still lower
than the six-cent level which it reached. These men
sold at eight and seven or six and one-half cents
when they saw cotton falling, and later congratu-
lated themselves on having gotten off so well.

Shippers were pressing the State Department to
give them the true remedy for the evil times in the
South,—the remedy that worked when applied. In

the meantime, the country was full of nostrums for the malady. There was talk of the government buying the entire cotton crop and holding it. There was formed a cotton pool loan fund, which bound northern banks to help out their southern confrères, but little of the fund was ever used. The President headed the "buy-a-bale" movement. The daughter of the Speaker of the House of Representatives planned a "national cotton goods bargain day."

The final sacrifice of patriotic devotion was made by the august judges of the Mississippi Supreme Court, who, according to news despatches from Jackson, of October 26, held court clad in overalls and cotton shirts, while the lawyers argued in the same garb. The function was reported to be part of a local "cotton day," in furtherance of the "wear cotton clothes movement" in the South. War, as General Sherman said, is indeed hell.

While the learned judges were doing their best, those who had studied the export situation were applying other, and more effective, remedies. Discouraged at the failure of their efforts through the State Department, the southern senators finally turned to the British Government direct. On October 22, Senator Hoke Smith, of Georgia, introduced in the Senate a resolution providing for the appointment of a committee of five senators to look into the matter of facilitating shipments abroad. The resolution was passed and the President of the Senate appointed Senators Smith, of Georgia; Vardaman, of Mississippi; Smith, of South Carolina; Jones, of

Washington; and Smith, of Michigan.   The next
day this committee was in touch with the State
Department and the British Ambassador.   The
committee seemed to galvanize the British Government into action.

To have refused the southern senators would have
meant legislation to enforce their demands (possibly
an embargo on the exportation of something England wanted); for the South at that time still held
the whip hand in Congress.   No one knew this better
than the British Government.   And there were mur-
murings also from the great textile centers in New
England and the Atlantic states, for the manufacturers had been told by Germany that if they desired
the German dyestuffs vital to their industries it
would be necessary to send cotton cargoes to pay
for them.

Under the pressure thus exerted the British authorities gave way.   On October 26, the following
letter was addressed by the British Embassy to Mr.
Lansing, Acting Secretary of State:

"The British Embassy, Washington, October 26,
1914.

"Dear Mr. Counsellor: In compliance with your
request, I telegraphed on the twenty-third instant
to my government to inquire what was their view
with regard to cotton and whether or not they considered it to be contraband.   You addressed this
question to me, as you said there seemed to be doubts
in certain quarters in this country as to the attitude
of my government.

"Last night I received a reply from Sir Edward Grey, in which he authorizes me to give the assurance that cotton will not be seized. He points out that cotton has not been put in any of our lists of contraband, and, as your Department must be aware from the draft proclamation now in your possession, it is not proposed to include it in our new list of contraband. It is, therefore, as far as Great Britain is concerned, in the free list, and will remain there. I am, dear Mr. Counsellor,

"Yours sincerely,

"CECIL SPRING-RICE."

By this same declaration, the heavy restrictions on the export of cotton to neutral countries of Europe, as well as to Germany, were also removed. No one had felt safe shipping to these countries so long as there was danger that England would declare cotton contraband. England had been detaining conditional contraband like meat and copper destined for neutral countries and neutral consumption on the pretext that the goods might be en route to Germany. No compensation was in sight for the cargoes detained and still unloaded.

When the British declaration was once made, certain officials in Washington were quick to see its political value. Not one, but five or ten of them will each admit that he was the one responsible for getting the export cotton movement started. In the Senate, on December 21, Senator Walsh delivered the most complete commentary on the glory for which they were competing. He said:

"I have not dwelt on the just causes of complaint given to our shippers of foodstuffs and cotton to neutral ports. I know nothing of them in detail, but I do know that there never was a day when shipments of cotton from our shores to any port should have been interrupted, save for the want of vessels in which to carry it, and there is no achievement in any arrangement by which they have been finally permitted to move. No blockade has ever been declared, and yet it is notorious that such cotton as goes to Germany, goes with the permission of England."

CHAPTER VIII

STOPPING THE COTTON MOVEMENT

After the British Embassy's letter of October 26 to Mr. Lansing, England seemed under definite obligations not to interfere with our cotton exports to the Continent. But we were to learn that the hindrances were by no means at an end. On October 30, four days after the note of Sir Cecil Spring-Rice to Mr. Lansing, Denmark for some reason declared an embargo on the exportation of cotton. This closed the route to Germany via Copenhagen which, after Rotterdam—a route already closed—was the most natural entrance into Germany through an adjacent neutral.

Moreover, while England's position as to cotton was now on record, it was also important that assurance should be had from France. In general, that country joins England in such communications. In this case, however, by some unexplained circumstance, Secretary Bryan was not able until December 17 to announce that France also would not consider cotton contraband.

When cotton for Germany direct finally started moving, not the least of the grievances of our cotton trade was the extraordinary rigidity of the British Government with respect to precautions against suspected concealment of contraband in cotton cargoes. It was a sufficient tax upon the patience and resources of cotton exporters that German-bound cargoes should be submitted to the examination of English consuls, the process in some cases including even the sealing of the vessel's hatches by these officials. Even this gave no assurance that the ships would not be detained and searched by British cruisers. The consular certificate and the British seal on the hatches of ships were considered as merely partial proof that cargoes contained only cotton.

The further suggestion was made by England that it would be a valuable precaution against the possibility of detention and search if shippers would have the cotton bales photographed by X-ray process and the photographs sent along with the British consul's certificate as additional evidence that the cotton contained no contraband. The first of these photographic seances took place December 25 at a pier in New York in behalf of the cargo of the City of Macon, an American coastwise steamer bound for Bremen. All this was of course at the cost of the shippers.

But the most serious difficulty with a free cotton movement is to be found in still another episode of the period. On October 27, one day after the State Department had published the note of the British Ambassador, the British Admiralty alleged that the Germans had laid mines in the waters north of Ireland. On October 29 the further news came from England that this measure on the part of Germany might cause England to close the North Sea to shipping.

On November 2 the British Government declared the whole North Sea a military area, mined and dangerous for navigation. It was stated that merchant craft of all kinds would there be exposed to the gravest dangers excepting as they followed the specific sailing directions of the Admiralty. Though this announcement was not issued until November 2, the Admiralty disclaimed responsibility for accidents after November 5. All vessels trading to and from Scandinavian countries and Holland were instructed to come, if inward bound, via the English Channel and the Straits of Dover, whence they would be directed up the east coast of England and thence to destination.*

It will be noted that no directions are given for getting through to Germany. This mining of the North Sea had the effect of terrorizing the owners of American ships who were approached with regard to chartering of their vessels for cotton exports to Germany. It had a similar effect on the insurance men approached to insure such boats. As a result, the first American ship sailed for Bremen about the middle of December, though the British passport for cotton had been issued October 26. The requirement

* Amsterdam despatches reported that, up to March 10, floating contact mines had been taken up and rendered harmless along the Dutch coast to the number of 378. Of these, 214 were of British origin, 22 German, 33 French, and 109 unknown.

that all vessels for Holland and Scandinavia should pass through the English Channel, simplified the British practice of seizing, examining and detaining this traffic.

All this while, the British Cabinet was congratulating Great Britain on the success of the "economic pressure" applied to Germany.   At a London banquet for the Lord Mayor on November 9, the Right Honorable Winston Churchill, First Lord of the Admiralty, declared that the economic pressure— Churchill invented the phrase—brought about by the naval blockade, would ultimately spell the doom of Germany as certainly as winter struck the leaves from the trees.   On November 27 in parliament he announced: "The economic pressure on Germany continues to develop in a healthy and satisfactory manner."

It is interesting to see his Lordship even as early as November 9 speaking of the "naval blockade" of Germany.   Then, as now, the British authorities were exercising by indirection the rights of blockade without undertaking its responsibilities.

Yet Great Britain has successively denied accountability for any distress of the American cotton trade. In the British communication dated February 10, the second answer to our December 26 protest, is found the following:

"Any decrease in American exports which is attributable to the war is essentially due to cotton. Cotton is an article which cannot possibly have been affected by the exercise of our belligerent rights, for, as your Excellency is aware, it has not been declared by His Majesty's Government to be contraband of war, and the rules under which we are at present conducting our belligerent operations give us no power in the absence of a blockade to seize or interfere with it when on its way to a belligerent country in neutral ships. Consequently no cotton has been stopped."

The point, of course, was that England's pressure upon cotton had been exercised so early in the course of its movement that for months it never got far enough to have a chance to be stopped by British cruisers.

While the economic pressure upon Germany was the purpose of England's measures, British merchants were by no means averse to taking advantage of the depressed cotton prices brought about by the stagnant market in the South, and buying their 1915 supply at famine rates. Of the heavy stock of cotton carried in the South during the cotton year 1914-1915, a considerable proportion was in the hands of persons who carried it for British importers and spinners. Some German buyers, as well, profited by the opportunity offered them, buying cotton to hold pending favorable conditions for shipment.

Such circumstances as these elicited a fiery outburst from Governor Colquitt of Texas. Great Britain had bought her cotton low after depressing the price, he said. The business of the South, he declared, was prostrated, its credit was impaired, and thousands of its people were starving. He proposed sending "American ironclads to England's door" to enforce our rights.

Significant of the southern feeling was the adoption of the following resolution by the State Farmers' Union of Louisiana:*

"Whereas the cotton farmers of the nation are suffering from the worst depression that has overtaken this country since 1860, and the business interests are correspondingly affected in common with the farmer; and

"Whereas, taking the European War as an excuse, England placed such restrictions on the exporting of cotton from the United States that it caused a ruinous decline in the price of cotton, owing to our inability to ship it to our customers in foreign countries, and England did not relax her interference with the shipment of cotton until her subjects had practically bought a year's supply of cotton at about six cents per pound from our farmers, who were forced to sell in order to exist; and

"Whereas the waters of the seas are the only means of carrying the commodities interchanged between the various nations of this earth; and

"Whereas great injustice resulted from the efforts of some nations to interfere with the untrammeled and free use of the interchange of commodities of all kinds and interchange of intelligence; so be it

"Resolved by the Louisiana State Farmers' Educational and Co-operative Union of America, that we hereby pledge ourselves to do all in our power to obtain for ourselves and our fellow citizens and mankind generally, the freedom and unhindered use of

* Reprinted in Congressional Record, February 3, 1915, pp. 3232-3233.

the seas and of the air, and we hereby respectfully petition our Federal Government to give due notice to all nations, in view of the losses sustained by the people of these United States, that in future we henceforth shall ship all of our products at all times and to our customers in any nation just as in the past; that this nation, being neutral, will not favor one over the other, but will treat all alike, as it ought to do, but that our government proposes to send its own ships, under its own flag, with the products of its own citizens, to its customers in any nation on earth, and will brook interference from no one in protecting the rights and the property and trade relations of its own people."

We have seen that, in the face of all difficulties, cotton in good volume did get moving to Germany, via neutral countries, during November.* In a previous analysis of the movement it was assumed that most of the exports to Italy, Holland and Scandinavia in excess of their takings in 1913 may fairly be credited with German destination. In November 1,000 bales cleared for Germany direct; the indirect exports via neutral countries were approximately 143,000 bales. In December 47,000 bales cleared for Germany by the direct route, and 263,000 bales by the indirect. In January 100,000 bales moved directly, no less than 423,000 indirectly, to Germany. In February 89,000 bales were exported by the direct and some 458,000 by the indirect route. In March 6,000 bales cleared for Germany, while the excess movement to neutral countries was 370,000 bales.

* See table on p. 117.

The effect of this movement was seen in advancing cotton prices.   On November 16 the New York Cotton Exchange reopened, fifteen weeks from the date of closing.   In the initial trading, spot cotton was quoted at 7.75 cents per pound.   From then until Christmas the price varied between 7.35 and 7.75 cents.   On the day after Christmas the price was 7.60 and on January 4 passed 8 cents.   During the second half of January it reached 8.50 cents.   At that point it held until March 5, when a gradual rise began which carried the price up to 9 cents on March 20.

The great British and German takings had braced the market.   The relief was cumulative, and in spite of the British blockade action on March 1, the price advanced to 10 cents on April 9 and to a maximum of 10.60 on April 24.

Yet from the day when Britain made an exception in favor of cotton and allowed us to ship it to Germany, there were English voices that protested against the exception.   For some time no real excuse for interfering with the movement could be found. The first one offered came from Sir William Ramsay who, at the end of January, 1915, wrote the London *Times* advocating the placing of cotton on the absolute contraband list and pointing out that nitro-cotton is an ingredient of all modern powder.

"If copper lies under an embargo, cotton *a fortiori* should be prohibited.   To place it on the list of contraband of war is a necessity, unless the whole theory of contraband is given up."*

If Sir William was following the successive British contraband lists he must have known that his government was by no means sacrificing the whole theory of contraband. But the inclusion of cotton in the list was not so simple as it looked.

In the first place, great American interests were at stake. In view of these, the London *Daily Mail* advised against the Ramsay proposal, and declared that Germany already had enough cotton for military purposes. The *Mail* suggested that America might retaliate by putting an embargo on ammunition exports to England.

Moreover, the main uses of cotton are so far removed from the purposes of war that to declare it absolute contraband would be an affront to international intelligence. It would be a particularly drastic violation of the Declaration of London, where the common sense of mankind had been expressed in putting cotton on the free list. And it was British

* British scientists seem not to agree as to the importance of cotton in the making of explosives. On July 16 W. F. Reid, formerly president of the Society of Chemical Industry, addressed that society in London. Apparently referring to Ramsay, he said:

"There is practically no cotton used in the manufacture of high explosives. The whole thing is a great fraud. There may be some trace of cotton in the explosive but the bulk of it is coal products. *Eminent scientists* have made erroneous statements on this subject. If people associated with science would speak only on the branches with which they are connected, the advantages would be very great."

representatives who at the London Conference insisted upon including cotton in this list.

Above all, the British Government as a neutral is on record as declaring that no belligerent can make cotton absolute contraband. Such action was attempted by Russia in the Russo-Japanese War. Upon instructions from Lord Lansdowne, the British Ambassador at St. Petersburg protested against this procedure. His letter to the Russian Minister of Foreign Affairs, resulting in forcing Russia to take cotton from the absolute contraband list, read:

"British India is by far the largest exporter of raw cotton into Japan. The quantity of raw cotton that might be used for explosives would be infinitesimal in comparison with the bulk of the cotton exported from India to Japan for peaceful purposes, and to treat harmless cargoes of this latter description as unconditionally contraband would be to subject a branch of innocent commerce to a most unwarrantable interference."

If cotton was to be banned it was imperative that some other way be found of dealing with this commodity, and before long the desired opportunity arose. On February 4 the German Admiralty, in retaliation against England's alleged violations of the Declaration of London and all international law in general, declared the waters around Great Britain a War Zone where enemy merchant ships would be torpedoed and where neutral vessels and citizens would not be safe. The War Zone Decree was to be effective from February 18.

Retaliation by England in the form of a complete stoppage of our exports to Germany was foreshadowed in a cable from the British Government to the British Embassy in Washington, given out for publication on February 5, the day after the War Zone announcement. The cable read in part:

"The apparent intention, however, of the German Government to sink merchant ships by submarines, without bringing them into port or providing accommodation for their crews, and regardless of loss of civilian lives, and the attempt to effect this even against a hospital ship, has raised very seriously the question whether Great Britain should adopt in retaliation more stringent measures against German trade.

"It is recognized that when any such decision to this effect is reached, due care must be taken not to inflict loss upon neutral ships which have sailed before any warning has been given or the decision announced."

This purpose was further indicated in the last paragraph of the note of February 10, addressed by Sir Edward Grey to the American Ambassador at London.* On the following day, February 11, Premier Asquith in the House of Commons made a statement thus reported in American press despatches:

Premier Asquith, in an announcement made to the House of Commons this afternoon, said that the

* The paragraph ends: "It is impossible for one belligerent to depart from the rules and precedents and for the other to be bound by them."

British Government was about to take more stringent measures against the trade of Germany.

Replying to a question put by Admiral Lord Charles Beresford "whether the government will place all food and raw material used in German industries on the list of absolute contraband," the Premier said:

"The government is considering the question of taking measures against German trade in view of the violation by the enemy of the rules of war. I hope shortly to make an announcement of what those measures are to be."

It is instructive to note the tentative form in which the blockade proposal still remained. To Lord Beresford's question whether Great Britain would place on the contraband list raw materials for German industries, the Premier would only state that the government was considering what measures should be taken. The measure it was considering could as well have been announced in parliament on February 11 as on March 1, when the blockade was finally proclaimed. But one thing had to be assured: that American public opinion, which in October had revolted against the interference with cotton, would not again revolt. The intimation of Mr. Asquith on February 11, cabled to this country, served to test whether that opinion was still active.

On February 17 a test was again made. Despatches from London stated that a proclamation was momentarily expected declaring "a blockade of the German coast, *or, at any rate*, the prohibition of foodstuffs destined for Germany." England still left the way clear for a strategic retirement should Washington speak. Washington was silent.

The preliminaries having been completed, on March 1 the now famous March 11 Order in Council was announced by Mr. Asquith in parliament, though it was not formally published until March 15. The announcement produced the desired effect on insurance companies, carriers and shippers. The Order in Council was in practical operation on March 2. When finally promulgated it declared subject to capture all movement of goods to or from Germany whether direct or via neutral countries. Such an Order could have but one meaning: that Great Britain proposed a blockade.

Steamers at once refused to take any more cotton or other shipments of German destination or origin. Insurance was withdrawn on all such shipments, no matter over what route they moved. A large volume of cotton had been contracted for German delivery, but had not yet moved from this country. Its owners faced a severe situation.

It is interesting to learn how for one month this hardship was modified. An American government official called to ask the Washington Ambassador of Great Britain to do him a personal favor. America, he said, not recognizing the Order in Council or the validity of the British blockade, obviously could not officially ask for a modification of that which we considered non-existent. It is a palpable absurdity to modify what is not. However, could not His Majesty's Ambassador as a personal favor consent to some measure that would permit the cotton shippers, who before March 1 had sold cotton to Germany, to forward their cotton?

The British Ambassador yielded and wrote a telegram. It was sent to London, resulting in the following special cotton dispensation being granted by the British Embassy in Washington, in a communication issued by it on March 8:

"Many inquiries have been received as to the treatment to be accorded to cotton shipped to Europe in view of the restrictive measures proposed to be taken by the Allied Governments.

"As already announced, there is no question of confiscating cotton cargoes that may come within the scope of the Order in Council to be issued. The following arrangement has been come to in London as to cotton consigned to neutral ports only.

"One—All cotton for which contracts of sale and freight engagements had already been made before March 2 to be allowed free (or bought at contract price if stopped), provided ships sail not later than March 31.

"Two—Similar treatment to be accorded to all cotton insured before March 2, provided it is put on board not later than March 16.

"Three—All shipments of cotton claiming above protection to be declared before sailing, and documents produced to and certificates obtained from consular officers or other authority fixed by (Allied) Governments. Ships or cargoes consigned to enemy ports will not be allowed to proceed."

That is, cotton contracted for Germany before March 1 might be shipped to neutral countries up to

March 31, though not to Germany direct. The modification of the original Order was a slight one; it merely prevented that Order from being retroactive. Moreover, the provision that vessels should be allowed to proceed *or be bought at the contract price* meant that England reserved the right to stop and requisition cargoes from America to neutrals in the future.

One vessel with a cargo destined for Germany was allowed to go forward after March 31. The conditions under which the vessel sailed are an instance of what England described as sympathetic consideration of the cotton interests. Due to a lateness in arrival of the S. S. Kina at her berth in Savannah, it became impossible to load her before the end of March. Permission for time extension on this one ship was sought by the State Department from His Majesty's Government. His Majesty's Government, through the medium of the American Ambassador at London, accorded this favor to the State Department in a cable from Mr. Page, dated March 29, 1915. It was firm, as well as kind, and read as follows:

"I am informed by the Foreign Office on the 24th that the S. S. Keit (Kina), in view of the special circumstances of the case, will be permitted to go forward on her prearranged trip from Savannah to Rotterdam, Göteborg, and Copenhagen, provided, however, that her cargo of cotton is covered, with the exception of the date of sailing, by the terms of the agreement recently concluded concerning such shipments, and further provided that there shall be

allowed no undue delay to occur in reloading this
steamer on arrival at Savannah and in the departure
of the steamer from Savannah.

*"Sir Edward Grey most earnestly requests that it
be distinctly understood that this indulgence must
not be used as a precedent for further exceptions
from the provisions of the agreement above referred
to."*

The request was distinctly understood, and no further indulgence was asked. The British allowed the
Kina to go forward. They did not allow her to reach
her destination. She was stopped and thrown into a
British prize court.

Indeed, it became evident not only that His
Majesty's Government, as announced in the Order
of March 11, would allow no cargoes to go directly
to German ports, but also that even the German
cotton for which indirect shipment was nominally
permitted was by no means to be allowed to reach
its destination. To be sure there was nothing in
international law or the English law to justify
the stoppage of these neutral cargoes—they were
mainly cargoes consigned to forwarders in neutral
countries. Yet the contingency was met by the
British diplomats. On March 31, as we have seen,
during trial of the Wilhelmina case, the British
crown lawyers, to the astonishment of this country,
produced a new Order in Council empowering His
Majesty's Government to requisition the cargo of
any neutral vessel in a British port.

The rest was easy. Since a British cruiser could
bring into a British port any neutral merchant

vessel on the high seas, this Order meant that no
vessel carrying goods to neutral European countries,
whether cotton or anything else, was exempt from
the unloading and impressment of its cargo by
England.   In order to make sure that no cotton
would reach Germany many cargoes destined for
neutral consumption were bought by England.   For
cargoes thus unlawfully seized the compensation
promised by His Majesty's Government was by no
means sufficient.   The interference with established
trade, the breaking up of commercial relationships,
were matters of more serious import than the values
of the shipments directly involved.   If you in Scandinavia buy a cargo of cotton and never receive it,
I may be relieved by Great Britain from loss on this
particular shipment.   But I get no more orders from
you.   You will not order what cannot be delivered.
One of the country's large cotton exporters wrote on
May 17:

"The exporter of cotton today can sell at a good
price cotton to Sweden, Norway, Holland and
Switzerland for immediate delivery or for next fall's
shipment, but he is prevented from so doing by the
fact that under the British Orders in Council every
bale is subject to detention and seizure though
shipped in neutral, even American ships.   It is obvious that the spinner in Sweden or the dealer in Norway cannot afford to buy and pay cash for cotton
when the chances are that there will be delivered to
him not the cotton itself, but a claim against some
government for detention and seizure of his goods."

It is, of course, far from a handicap to the British manufacturer of cotton goods, when competitors in Scandinavia find their supplies of raw cotton scarce and high in price. The British market is kept flooded with diversions of neutral-bound cargoes. On August 5, 1915, despatches from Washington quoted the Department of Commerce as stating that British exports of cotton goods and cotton yarns to Scandinavia and Holland in the first six months of 1915 showed a great increase over 1914. At the same time that our exporters are hindered in their exports to European neutrals, British raw cotton dealers expand their re-exportation of cotton imported from us. In June, 1915, Holland and Sweden each took from England five times as much raw cotton as in June, 1914.

In March and April, 26 cargoes of cotton destined for neutral European ports were held up in England. The "unofficial" Foreign Trade Advisers of the State Department were conferring with the British Embassy in Washington in an attempt to get these shipments released or paid for. On May 20 the pressure was so great that the British Foreign Office included a reference to cotton in the press statement which it gave out, primarily regarding the detained meat cargoes.* It was stated that the cotton would be purchased in accordance with the "agreement" reached with American cotton interests regarding cotton shipped in March. It was averred that this arrangement was highly satisfactory to the cotton

* The statement is abstracted in Chapter VI.

interests and that "His Majesty's Government were given to understand that the provisions of the arrangement were acceptable to the United States Government."

The cotton interests had no means of bringing to Britain knowledge of how little satisfactory to them was an arrangement which limited to one month the continuance of their trade with neutral countries and Germany. Our government, to indicate that England was under a misapprehension in supposing that it approved of any arrangement supporting the Order in Council, ordered its Foreign Trade Advisers to withdraw from conferences with the British Embassy until England clearly understood the matter. Three days later the British Ambassador issued an official statement saying that the unofficial arrangements in question of course did not in any way involve a departure by either government from its expressed views regarding the blockade.

Not until June had Britain begun making payments on the cotton. On July 19 Sir Robert Cecil announced in parliament that $3,500,000 had been paid on the seized cargoes, which by this time were sixty in number.

The procedure through which our shippers had to go, in order to get any return for their detained shipments, was one of unexampled complexity. When the ship sailed from this country duplicate copies of papers, such as shipping documents and contracts, were to be given to British consular officials in our ports. The papers were forwarded to London and arrived in England at about the same time as the cargo which was detained for examination. The papers were referred to the British Admiralty, thence to the Foreign Office and finally to the Board of Trade. The Board of Trade took two weeks to examine the contracts. The papers were then sent to the Admiralty and by it to the Foreign Office, which had to deal with the shipper.

In the meantime six weeks were consumed. The shipper felt by this time that he ought to have his cargo freed or paid for. The "arrangement" by which the Admiralty detained cargoes provided that they should be purchased "at contract price" or released. If the shipments were contracted for when they left this country, the price appeared in the contract. If they were sent to a broker—for example, in Gothenburg—to be sold, the fair price was obviously the market price at Gothenburg on the date when the cotton would have arrived, had it not been detained by England. But when the American owner attempted to get payment on either of these bases, the British Foreign Office was willing to do no more than make a payment "on account" (maximum ten cents per pound), insisting that the eventual price should be arbitrated.

On July 20 the Board of Trade announced a ruling that detained cotton cargoes whose ownership had passed to Germans would be confiscated without payment.

One of the most novel forms of "pressure" which Great Britain has exercised has been applied to cotton dealers in this country. Many of the most prominent are associate members of the Liverpool Cotton Exchange. The Liverpool Exchange has sent these American dealers, to be signed, an agreement not to deal directly or indirectly with enemies of His Britannic Majesty. Those who so sign will have their names posted in the Liverpool Exchange and receive preference by the Liverpool members. By implication, those who do not sign will be blacklisted by those who handle the great cotton trade of England.*

These then were the measures which England took to stop the movement of American cotton to Germany. The "blockade" made contraband of everything. In the spring of 1915 this was explained by His Majesty's Attorney General to a group of British scientists, who, better versed in natural science than international law, followed the lead of Sir William Ramsay and, even after March 1, demanded that cotton should be made contraband. The Attorney General explained that the blockade prevented everything from going to Germany by sea and hence it would be superfluous to name cotton as an especial object of embargo. The Order in Council, he said, was very effective in preventing cotton from reaching England's enemies. Moreover, he continued, to declare cotton contraband would be to set a precedent which might return to plague Great Britain in the future.

* For the text of the agreement, see Appendix, p. 322.

The effectiveness of the British policy in preventing the Germans from buying and getting our cotton is measured by the fall in cotton prices in the American market.

We have seen that the cotton market reached its high level at the end of April. Though shipments toward Germany had been cut off on March 31, the effect of the great British and German imports carried through. But early in May the trend of prices began to reflect the apprehension of the market as to the future, an apprehension that was justified as the months went by.

The German takings were over. What might have been exported to that country lay a dead weight on the market. Spot cotton in New York, which was 10.60 cents per pound on April 24, dropped to 10.05 cents on May 6. Through May and June it averaged 9.50 to 9.75 cents. By the middle of July the July option had sunk to 8.25 cents. The prospects for a successful marketing of the 1915 crop had indeed become bad.

What is the military value to England of all this economic pressure that she is exercising in the South? Will the German ammunition makers in the fall of 1915 be embarrassed for cotton? It is used mainly in the form of gun cotton to make charges for the artillery and torpedoes. Certainly no reports from the front indicate that the German heavy artillery is sinking into a state of inactivity and there seems to be no excessive economy of torpedoes. That any such result will occur can be asserted or expected only by those who shut their eyes to the plain facts of the case.

At the opening of the cotton shipping season, August 1, 1914, the stock of cotton in Bremen (to say nothing of the stock in German spinners' hands) was 309,000 bales, a quantity in excess of other recent years. The direct imports of American cotton into Germany from August 1, 1914, to April 1, 1915, were 242,661 bales. Adjacent neutral countries in the same period imported 1,668,846 bales more than in the same months last year. Assuming that all these excess imports of adjacent neutrals were destined for Germany, the total stock which that country had up to April 1, 1915, amounted to 2,220,507 bales.

It is likely that part of the excess exports to adjacent neutrals were for the consumption of these countries themselves. In particular, it is possible that Italy needed considerably more cotton than last year to supply her own textile mills, which appropriated some of the foreign trade in cotton goods with countries that Germany had difficulty in reaching, such as Mediterranean lands and South America.

Assume, therefore, that Germany to April 1 had 2,000,000 bales of American cotton to meet her requirements. This is only 800,000 bales short of our exports to both Austria and Germany in the year ending August 1, 1914. Moreover, what of the 150,000 bales annually raised in Turkey? What of the 100,000 bales of Persia; and the 1,000,000 of Russian Turkestan? Is there any doubt that the

Jewish dealers who handle this Russian trade smuggled a part of it into Germany, to get the high prices which Germany, alone of all buyers, was offering during the winter? Why in May did England forbid the export of Egyptian cotton to Italy, if it was not moving through to Germany?*

No one can imagine that the military will not be able to meet its needs from the vast store at hand, not only its needs for this year but also for a long time to come.   Besides, so Hudson Maxim says, there are substitutes for raw cotton in making the explosive gun cotton.   One, he informs us, is cellulose.

Great Britain is aware of all this.   She knows that in the case of cotton, as in the case of grain, the military is fully supplied.   The pressure will fall upon the civil users of these products, if it falls at all. The hope is that the pressure on these civil users will become unbearable and that they will force the military to sue for peace.

What is the prospect of a cotton famine in the German textile industries?   For certain reasons, Germany needs less cotton than formerly.   She has a large export trade in cotton goods.   In 1912 this trade amounted to $31,055,000.   Since the Orders

* In a letter written to the London *Times* in April, James G. Peel of Manchester, a large cotton dealer, shows that the exports of Egyptian cotton to Germany and Austria dropped from 99,000 bales in the months October-March of 1913-1914, to nothing in those months of 1914-1915.   But the exports of Egyptian cotton to Italy and Switzerland, neighbors of Austria and Germany, increased exactly 99,000 bales to the period under question.

in Council of March 11 placed a ban on all German
exports, even if shipped from neutral ports, the only
countries Germany can reach are those accessible by
land or via the Baltic, which England does not control. Other oversea shipments have ceased. The
only foreign markets still available are Turkey, Roumania, Bulgaria, Austro-Hungary, Switzerland,
Holland and Scandinavia. In 1913 the shipments
to these countries from Germany were about $4,000,-
000,* or only 13 per cent of her exports of cottons.
Therefore less raw material than normal is needed
to work up for the export trade.

Yet there is reason to believe that more cotton
could have been used by German textile industries
than was sent them from the 1914 crop. It is recalled that up to April 1 we sent to Germany about
250,000 bales; and to adjacent neutrals 1,650,000
bales more than last year. Assuming that 250,000
bales of our excess exports to adjacent neutrals were
actually destined for these neutrals, it appears that
up to April 1 we sent Germany, directly and indirectly, about 1,650,000 bales. With regard to
German consumption, other estimates agree pretty
nearly with those of Ambassador Gerard, who in
December wired the State Department that in the
year 1914-1915 Germany could take about 2,000,000
bales, Austria about 800,000, together 2,800,000.
If that is the case, 1,150,000 bales more of the 1914
crop could have been sold to the Teutonic Allies.

* This does not include exports to Bulgaria, Austro-Hungary
and Denmark, for which figures were not available.

If this cotton had been allowed to move, it would have probably kept the price since May 1 at or near 11 cents. At 11 cents per pound, 1,150,000 bales would have meant sales of $63,000,000 of cotton to Germany, to say nothing of the better prices that holders of cotton would have received for sales to American mills. Above all, the large quantity of the 1914 output which we are carrying into the 1915 crop year (beginning August 1) would have been considerably reduced. All this indicates the sacrifice which the South is demanded to make to a blockade which, the American Government says, England does not lawfully maintain.

With the great German-Austrian market closed by a blockade, the prospects for this 1915 season are not bright. The yield will be a good one. Early reports of a larger acreage reduction have not proved true. There has been some reduction in the use of fertilizer, especially of the potash elements, but this reduction will not greatly affect the crop, the first year it occurs.

It is simple to illustrate why no large acreage reduction is not made. As a southern planter I may know it to be in the general interests of the South, and of high prices in general, that the cotton acreage should be reduced. But I want the higher prices to apply to as much cotton as I can raise. Therefore I will let the other fellow carry out the reduction in acreage. No considerable voluntary curtailment of independent agricultural producers has ever yet come to pass. We look for a good crop; namely, at least 12,000,000 bales.

Much of the 1914 crop will be carried over. In April Mr. Harding, a member of the Federal Reserve Board, speaking before the Baltimore Chapter of the American Institute of Banking, estimated this carry-over at 5,000,000 bales, due to the fact that by April foreign and domestic spinners had already laid in supplies with an eye to the future, in excess of their current requirements. More recent estimates place the surplus at 4,000,000 bales. In any case it will be very large. The visible supply of cotton in the world at the end of July, 1915, was 2,500,000 bales higher than last year. The quantity of the 1914 American crop still in the hands of producers was 1,000,000 bales more than usual.

There is a simple solution to the crisis that confronts the South. Another autumn like the last will ruin it. The present and prospective elimination of the German-Austrian market through an unlawful blockade is the largest single element depressing prices and threatening the future. Nothing would clear the situation like the lifting of that blockade. If it is not lifted, and if cotton prices are not to sink to low levels, either the cotton raisers must have advanced to them money with which to hold millions of bales of cotton until something happens—perhaps peace—to restore the normal purchasing power of the world, or someone else will have to carry enough cotton to relieve the weight on the market.

The problems here involved go far beyond the

limits of this book.   The financial aid necessary will
be in the nature of a valorization of the cotton crop.
Banks which are asked to participate in the proceeding point out that the South is not built to hold the
export cotton crop.   It has not the warehouses.   The
export quota moves abroad and is held there.   Besides this physical difficulty, the financial risk of
carrying cotton for the indefinite period that this
war may last is very great.

In the middle of July, 1915, a renewed agitation
arose in England for making cotton contraband.
The British Government announced its definite intention of confining European neutrals to the quotas of
cotton which they had imported in normal years.   The
London *Times* suggested that Britain spend $175,-
000,000 to buy up the amount of American cotton
usually sold to the Central Empires and European
neutrals and then declare it contraband.   The cotton
so bought was to be held off the market until the
close of the war.   It was the most magnificent bribe
ever proposed.   His Majesty's Government has not
adopted the suggestion.

From the British Embassy at Washington, near
the end of July, seemed to emanate a suggestion that
a cotton pool be formed, under the auspices of England and America, to distribute among the cotton
interests such shipments as England would allow to
go forward to neutral countries.   It was said that
England would abolish her policy of detaining cotton
moving to neutrals if America would agree to ship
neutrals no more than their normal takings.

All these false remedies for the disease remind us of those proposed in the fall of 1914. Now, as then, the true remedy is the recovery of the closed German-Austrian market. Now, as then, we need to think straight, to ask with the power at our command and to break a blockade which we declare is illegal and which threatens with ruin an entire section of the country.

CHAPTER IX

Copper as Lawful Commerce

Cotton, as has been seen, is our most important article of export. It is also the one which has suffered chiefly through belligerent activities on the sea. By a coincidence our second largest item of export, copper, is the one to which the second largest measure of interference was allotted.

While the actual monetary loss which befell copper interests (and they suffered heavy losses in the first six months of the war) was not so great as in the case of cotton, such losses as did occur were traceable to violations of international law and the rights of neutral trade, of a character especially flagrant.

Copper, like cotton and petroleum, is a resource conferred upon this country more richly than on any other. In its raw state it is found principally in Michigan, Montana, Arizona and Utah. Of the normal production of 140,000,000 pounds per month at the refineries, mainly at the Atlantic seaboard, about 110,000,000 pounds come from domestic and 30,000,000 pounds from imported ores.

America turns out over half of all the copper produced in the world but consumes only a third of the world's output. Over half our product has been exported in recent years. This means that of the growing number of our citizens employed in copper mining and smelting, about 70,000 in all, over half are normally working to supply foreign markets.

The principal foreign taker of our copper is Germany. This is due to the development of the German industry in manufactured copper, ranking second only to our own. Normally, exports to Germany move both directly and via Rotterdam. The copper consumption of the Netherlands itself is not large. Practically all of the heavy Dutch takings, usually nearly equal to the direct shipments to Germany, may be considered as destined for Germany.

Our shipments to Germany and Holland—that is, our exports to Germany—have amounted in recent years to one-half our entire exports of copper, or one-quarter of our entire production. There were indeed great interests affected by the British measures which for three months hindered the movement of copper to Germany while it was a free good of commerce or as conditional contraband, and eventually made it absolute contraband, subject to the same summary treatment as guns or shrapnel.

Immediately after the outbreak of war the copper producers, excepting in the Lake Superior region, reduced their output to 50 per cent of normal. No one knew what was to be the effect of the war upon our exports. Of the current output, just before the war began, two-thirds had been going abroad and only one-third absorbed by the slack home consumption.

On August 1, 1914, the refineries had on hand a stock of 100,000,000 pounds. Copper before the outbreak of the war was selling for thirteen cents per pound, which for the majority of mines allows a very small margin of profit. The price started to decline immediately, in August. With copper below thirteen cents, the cheapest place to store what cannot be sold is in the ground.

The reduction to 50 per cent of normal output, designed as an emergency measure, was destined, through the force of events, to carry beyond the New Year.

Copper exports to Germany being so important to the copper industries, we had from the beginning a vital interest in the manner in which copper shipments were treated by England, the belligerent power which controlled the seas. Upon that treatment depended the possibility of continuing the German trade. As in the case of cotton, copper during the first week of August could be shipped nowhere, for financial reasons and lack of marine tonnage. Because of the unsettlement of the foreign exchanges as a means of making international payments, shippers would export their copper only on the terms of "cash against shipper's documents in New York." This method of payment was such an innovation that it was some time before foreign buyers could make the necessary arrangements with the New York banks.

With this difficulty overcome, as it was in a short time, shipments of copper should have gone forward to all nations of Europe with the same freedom as to England. Nothing in the international law code by which England was acting, namely, her modified Declaration of London, permitted the preventing of copper shipments to Germany.

In August, 1914, England took twice as much of copper as in August of the previous year—24,600,-000 pounds, against 12,100,000 pounds. In August, 1913, the shipments to Austria, Germany and Holland—the total German takings—were 44,300,-000 pounds. In August, 1914, not a pound of copper moved to Germany or Austria; and only 5,350,000 pounds to Holland, compared with 14,-200,000 pounds in August of the year before.

To appreciate the situation fully, it is necessary to consider the status of copper as defined by the Declaration of London. We recall that in an Order in Council of August 20, England announced the Declaration of London as her code of naval warfare, making certain important modifications. Therefore, it is to this Declaration that we must look to find the treatment that copper might reasonably have expected from the British authorities. Since copper was not named as either contraband or conditional contraband in the British contraband list of August 4, accompanying the August 20 Order, it technically remained a free article of commerce, transportable direct to Germany undisturbed, in all but German ships. Still less could there be interference with shipments to Germany via adjacent neutrals.

At the outbreak of war direct shipments of copper

to Germany were impossible, since, as is recalled from Chapter VII, no vessels reached Germany from the United States until 1915.   However, copper should have moved to Germany indirectly through Italy, Holland and Scandinavia.

In August the British agents in this country could report that no copper was going to Germany directly and apparently none by the indirect route. There were no exports declared for Germany, while the copper shipped to the adjacent neutrals was only 7,200,000 pounds compared with 29,200,000 pounds in August, 1913.   The neutrals were getting only one-quarter of their normal takings; they were obviously not receiving a surplus which could be sent forward into Germany.

In September, however, the situation changed. Our copper exports to Holland and Italy reached normal, while those to Scandinavia jumped to six times their volume in September, 1913.*   That the

*COPPER EXPORTS TO EUROPEAN COUNTRIES ADJACENT TO GERMANY
COMPARISON OF SEPTEMBER 1913 AND 1914

Country	Sept. 1913 Lbs.	Sept. 1914 Lbs.	Increase, 1914 Lbs.
Holland	12,175,048	12,211,509	36,461
Italy	3,127,053	3,352,606	225,553
"Other Europe"	1,209,132	7,443,688	6,234,556
	16,511,233	23,007,803	6,496,570

It is fair to assume that the *increase* of shipments to "Other Europe" was for the Scandinavian countries.   "Other Europe" means Europe exclusive of England, France, Germany, Austria, Belgium, Holland, Italy and Russia.

excess was all destined for Germany was by no means a necessary inference, as will be shown. But German destination was a possible construction to be put upon those excess shipments.

American copper interests regarded this development with satisfaction. They seemed likely to regain their market on the Continent, just as they had already more than regained the English market, closed in the first few days of the war.

But the British Government looked at the situation with anything but pleasure. England, of course, did not wait until the tardy American government statistics were published, to get news of the destination of our copper exports. These facts were ascertained by British agents from the ships' manifests, filed at the American Custom House, and were promptly cabled home.

Though in the September statistics given, the increase in copper exports was greatest in the case of "Other Europe" (Scandinavia), yet the largest amount actually moving into Germany was probably via Holland. Therefore the British Government set out to make Holland an example which should be heeded by other adjacent neutrals.

The September measures of England were confined to Holland alone. These measures were four in number.

(1) Dutch dealers were induced to sell to the British Government the stocks of copper in Dutch warehouses, about 2,400 tons.

(2) Holland was induced to enact an embargo

forbidding the re-exportation of copper that entered her borders.

(3) The Holland-American Line, which has the only important regular line steamers that operate between America and Holland, was induced to refuse copper shipments consigned to individuals in Holland. It was required that such shipments be consigned to the Dutch Government.

(4) As an extra precaution, England made sure that the Holland-American Line knew what was meant.

On September 21, while 1,500 tons of copper were afloat for Holland on the steamship Rotterdam and 389 tons on the steamship Sloterdyk, the British Government made copper conditional contraband. At the time, this looked like a comparatively harmless proceeding. Neutrals had not yet learned what it meant for a commodity to be on the British conditional contraband list. On the same September 21 the Westerdyk sailed for Holland with 605 tons of copper in her cargo, and on the day following the Potsdam went out with 1,805 tons. These were all Holland-American steamers.

When these vessels reached the English Channel, Great Britain halted every one of them, took them into British ports, and detained them each several days while their copper was being discharged. This was no trifling matter to the vessels' owners. Great steamships make money only when in operation. One day's detention for a vessel like the Potsdam or the Rotterdam means a loss of $2,000. These September and October seizures of the Holland-American boats were sufficient. The company learned its lesson, and never needed to be taught again.

From these four ships England took a total of 9,500,000 pounds of copper.

These seizures could be justified by no known rule of international law. So long as copper was a free article of commerce, of course there was no excuse for interfering with it on its course to Germany, even directly. Even after copper had been declared conditional contraband, there was as little excuse for seizing it when destined to Germany via Rotterdam. The Declaration of London, Article 35, provided that

"Conditional contraband is not liable to capture, except when found on board a vessel bound for territory belonging to or occupied by the enemy, or for the armed forces of the enemy, *and when it is not to be discharged in an intervening port.*"

That is, when conditional contraband for the enemy is to be discharged in an intervening port, such as Rotterdam, it is not subject to interference. Nor is there any precedent in international law—for example, in cases where treatment of conditional contraband has come before the courts—to justify the stoppage of such traffic to a belligerent via neutral ports.

In defense of the stringent British policy of interfering with supplies for Germany via adjacent neutrals Great Britain's second note (of February 10) in answer to our protest of December 26, dwelt

CONSERVATION *of* WATER *by* STORAGE

By GEORGE FILLMORE SWAIN, LL.D.

Gordon McKay Professor of Civil Engineering,
Harvard University

"It is the most masterly, comprehensive and authoritative deliverance on the general subject of the Conservation of Water by Storage that has ever appeared, and the chapters particularly devoted to the water power question, in which the author is a recognized leading expert, are most timely in view of the large amount of irrelevant talk and political bias that has characterized much of the public discussion of this important economic question, not only in the National Congress but also in the National Conservation Congress."—HENRY STURGIS DRINKER in *American Forestry*.

"Interesting as the book must be to the engineer and the student, it is of special value to the general reader because it gives complete and precise information, expressed in the clearest language, about a matter that is of great and growing public importance; one that every man should be prepared to understand and judge for himself."—*New York Sun*.

Price $3.00 net, postpaid

YALE UNIVERSITY PRESS

209 Elm Street,
New Haven, Conn.

225 Fifth Avenue,
New York City.

ORDER FORM

Date .... *191* .....

Yale University Press,
209 Elm Street, New Haven, Conn.

Enclosed please find .... *for $* .... *for which you will kindly send me:*

.... *cop* .... *of CONSERVATION OF WATER BY STORAGE* (*Swain*).

Name ....

Address ....

upon the principle of "continuous voyage" as applied to shipments into the Confederacy during the Civil War, in our so-called Bermuda cases.

During that war it was found that the Confederacy was drawing large quantities of supplies from the island of Nassau, in Bermuda. It appeared that British vessels were carrying these supplies to Bermuda, where the cargoes were transhipped. From Bermuda small blockade runners waited their chance to slip through the cordon of Federal warships before the southern ports. Warships of the United States then intercepted British vessels bound to Nassau and brought them before our prize courts, where all their Confederate supplies were condemned, on the ground that the ultimate and not the immediate destination was the controlling factor. That is, to those Confederate goods was applied the doctrine of "continuous voyage," previously developed in British courts.

But it is to be noted that these cases referred not primarily to the application of contraband law with the seas open, but to a condition of blockade and attempted violations thereof. And in September and October of 1914 there was no British blockade of Germany, even on paper.* Nor were the captured

* Even today when a so-called "blockade" is maintained, the Bermuda cases are no justification for Britain's stoppage of our exports to Scandinavia, for forwarding to Germany by sea. These goods are to be forwarded to German ports which Britain admittedly does not blockade; namely, the German ports on the Baltic. British exports to Nassau were to be forwarded to Confederate ports which we *were* blockading.

goods destined to be forwarded to Germany by sea. They were going forward by land.

This fact—that the traffic was to continue to Germany by land—turned our Civil War precedents against Britain. In the same British note of February 10 mention was made of the Matamoros cases, also of Civil War time. The Federal war vessels held up British goods destined for Texas via Matamoros, Mexico, on the Mexican bank of the Rio Grande. Brownsville, opposite Matamoros, was blockaded by the Federal fleet; Matamoros obviously was not. Our Supreme Court decided that we might seize only the contraband on board such ships, and then only if it had a clear destination for belligerent use. That is, absolute contraband destined overland to the Confederacy was condemned, but all other goods with the same destination were ordered released.

None of the copper seized from Dutch boats, while traveling to Germany via Rotterdam, was seizable under these precedents. Copper was not declared absolute contraband until October 29.

For America to have interfered to greater extent than described with the lawful traffic between England and Matamoros would have been intolerable, and would never have been suffered by Great Britain. To be sure, the limitation imposed seriously impaired the tightness of our blockade of the Confederacy. But we had something other than our own wishes to consider. As the Supreme Court said:

"Neutral trade (*) to and from a blockaded country by inland navigation or transportation is lawful and therefore that trade, between London and Matamoros, with intent to supply goods for Texas from Matamoros, violated no blockade, and cannot be declared unlawful. Such trade . . . with unrestricted inland commerce between such ports and the enemy's territory, impairs undoubtedly, and very seriously impairs, the value of a blockade of the enemy's coast. *But in cases such as that now in judgment, we administer the public law of nations and are not at liberty to inquire what is for the particular advantage of our own or another country.*"

England in September and October was not maintaining a blockade of Germany. Even had she maintained one, the American "continuous voyage" cases, which she calls to her aid, would, if they had any application at all, declare illegal the seizure of 4,290 tons of copper from the Dutch boats. And this was true quite apart from the further question as to a retroactive decree causing the condemnation of a free article of commerce by declaring it conditional contraband after it has set out upon its voyage on the high seas. The Sloterdyk and the Rotterdam were over halfway across the Atlantic when anathema fell upon their copper cargoes.

It must not be supposed that the injury to this country was in any way measured by the 4,290 tons of copper illegally seized. That copper was eventually paid for by the British Government. But Dutch consignees, and those whom they represented, sent

* All but absolute contraband trade.

in no more orders. No one continues to order what he cannot get. The purchase by Great Britain of 9,500,000 pounds of copper, for which payment was made after a long delay, was a poor substitute for the cancelled normal trade of 12,000,000 pounds monthly with Dutch ports. The magnanimous action of His Majesty's Government in finally paying for the copper it seized did not support the men and families in Butte and Ray whose markets and whose ultimate employers were by that seizure obliterated.

Great Britain in the September seizures did not act without law. However, what she acted under was not international law, but her own substitute for it; namely, the August 20 Order in Council.

In that Order, we recall, His Majesty's Government repudiated the principle which its own precedents had done the most to create; namely, that conditional contraband moving to the enemy territory is immune unless the captor can prove that it is destined for the enemy's hostile forces. The August Order made conditional contraband seizable when moving to anyone under control of the authorities of the enemy state; which obviously banned all such traffic going to Germany.

Yet this would not have affected the copper seized. It was moving to Germany through Holland, and was to be discharged in "an intervening port," which, according to the Declaration of London, freed it from suspicion as to its possible destination for German forces. The Order in Council made conditional contraband for Germany by indirect routes capturable under the same condition as if it moved direct. In plain words, it was capturable if it moved at all. Under this "law" the Dutch shipments described were seized.

We have seen that in September measures were taken by England to put an end to the movement of copper through Holland to Germany. In October and November came the turn of Italy and the Scandinavian countries to learn that they too must not play the middlemen for German buyers. British representatives in this country could report that in October a quantity of copper far in excess of October, 1913, was exported from the United States towards the neutral countries in question.

EXPORTS OF COPPER TO NEUTRAL COUNTRIES ADJACENT TO GERMANY

COMPARISON FOR OCTOBER 1913 AND 1914

Country	Oct. 1913 Lbs.	Oct. 1914 Lbs.	Increase in Oct. 1914 Lbs.
Holland........	11,119,819	———	11,119,819 (decrease)
Italy,..........	3,698,042	22,166,413	18,468,371
"Other Europe"	1,939,327	13,670,445	11,731,118
Total	16,757,188	35,836,858	19,079,670

It is noted that in October Holland did not receive a pound of copper. That country had been disposed of as a possible purveyor to Germany. The Dutch had learned their lesson. The Holland-American Line would accept no more copper for carriage.

Still more drastic measures were adopted toward Italy and Scandinavia in October, November and

December. In October and November, fourteen steamers for Italy were detained and their 21,403,-200 pounds of copper piled high at Gibraltar.* In November and December, thirteen ships for Sweden were stopped by England and 12,555,200 pounds of copper taken off.* The Swedish copper lay in British east coast ports.

Every pound of copper with neutral destination seized before October 29, the date of declaring copper absolute contraband, was seized illegally. The legality of such action as to shipments that were already on the seas on October 29 is doubtful, even assuming that copper may properly be declared absolute contraband.

England herself had appeared to feel technically justified in her September and early October seizures of Dutch-bound copper while it was still conditional contraband. But the seizures of Swedish and Italian consignments promised to assume so vast a scale that the flimsy structure of the August 20 Order in Council and the September 21 contraband list did not look able to bear them. Moreover, the United States on October 22 addressed to England a protest, never published, on its interference with our commerce. So on October 29 copper was made absolute contraband.

The justice of considering raw copper as contraband is a subject worth considering. The British Government by its Order in Council of August 20

* For the vessels detained, dates, cargoes and destination, see Appendix, p. 323.

had accepted the Declaration of London as binding, precisely as though it had been ratified by His Majesty, except for certain modifications. That Declaration gives no authority for considering raw copper contraband. The items mentioned by Article 22 in the first class (as always subject to treatment as contraband) are all manufactured goods. They do not include materials for ammunition.

According to Article 23, this list could be increased by proclamation of a belligerent so as to include "such articles *exclusively* used for war as are not enumerated among the eleven groups of the first class." The protocol of the drafting committee indicates that this addition was to care for possible future inventions or discoveries. The committee admitted that it had specifically included in the contraband list all known items that properly belonged there. Raw copper was of course known, and it was not included.

When not a belligerent, His Majesty's Government has demanded more emphatically than any other that the contraband list should be restricted in war time to the narrowest possible limits. Great Britain has even appeared before the international public favoring the total abolition of contraband lists. Witness the charge of Sir Edward Grey to the British Delegation to the Second Peace Conference at The Hague:

"His Majesty's Government recognize to the full the desirability of freeing neutral commerce to the utmost extent possible from interference by belligerent powers, and they are ready and willing for their part, in lieu of endeavoring to frame new and more satisfactory rules for the prevention of contraband trade in the future, to abandon the principle of contraband of war altogether, thus allowing the oversea trade in neutral vessels between belligerents on the one hand and neutrals on the other to continue during war without any restriction, subject only to its exclusion by blockade from an enemy's port. They are convinced that not only the interest of Great Britain, but the common interest of all nations will be found, on an unbiased examination of the subject, to be served by the adoption of the course suggested.

"In the event of the proposal not being favorably received, an endeavor should be made to frame a list of the articles that are to be regarded as contraband. Your efforts should then be directed to restricting that definition within the narrowest possible limits and upon lines which have the point of practical extinction as their ultimate aim.

"If a definite list of contraband cannot be secured, you should support, and, if necessary, propose regulations intended to insure that *nations shall publish, during peace, the list of articles they will regard as contraband during war, and that no change shall be made in the list on the outbreak of or during hostilities.**

"A list might be prepared and submitted for adoption by the Conference, specifying the articles which in no event shall fall within the enumeration of contraband, e.g., mails, *foodstuffs destined for places other than beleaguered fortresses, and any raw materials required for the purposes of peaceful industry.* It is essential to the interest of Great Britain

---

* It is instructive to compare this statement of principle with the continued British action in this war of expanding the fixed contraband list of the Declaration of London.

that every effective measure necessary to protect the importation of food supplies and raw materials for peaceful industries should be accompanied by all the sanctions which the law of nations can supply.

"His Majesty's Government would further be glad to see the right of search limited in every practicable way, e.g., by the adoption of a system of consular certificates declaring the absence of contraband from the cargo, and by the exemption of passenger and mail steamers upon defined routes, etc."

Obviously the British Government, when it prepares for the eventuality of being a neutral in war time, is no believer in an extended contraband list.

If, as Sir William Ramsay tells us, copper is less properly considered as contraband than cotton is, there is indeed little excuse for declaring it contraband of war.

On December 26 we sent England a note protesting primarily against her seizures of copper on the high seas. It contained only the following reference to the inclusion of copper in the absolute contraband list:

"The government of the United States does not intend at this time to discuss the propriety of including certain articles in the list of absolute and conditional contraband, which have been proclaimed by His Majesty. Open to objection as some of these seem to this government, the chief ground of the present complaint is the treatment of cargoes of both classes of articles when bound to neutral ports."

But it was hardly to be expected that our authorities, while accepting the listing of rubber and hides as conditional and absolute contraband, respectively, would protest strongly against the inclusion of copper in the absolute list. Copper has a secondary connection with the operations of war. But both rubber and hides are so distantly removed from war's uses that they are on the free list of the Declaration of London.

Had copper been kept off the absolute contraband list (it was off the first three months of the war), and if conditional contraband had been treated by Britain as in previous wars, the nearly 35,000 workmen in American copper industries laid off on August 1 would have soon returned. As it was, these men were out of work until after the first of the year. Not until April, 1915, were the mines and refineries working to 75 per cent of their capacity. Not until June were they fully employed, ten months after the lay-off on August 1. Senator Walsh of Montana declared in the Senate at the end of December:

"Multitudes of the latter (the miners) in enforced idleness must make such provision as they can against the rigors of an inhospitable winter climate. No little destitution must follow, and great industrial loss."

Nor did the loss fall entirely on the workmen. The Order in Council of August 20 cost the copper export trade $6,000,000 per month, the average exports to Germany.

Yet in the early part of the war our main complaint is not with Britain's declaring copper absolute contraband. Up to October 29, 1914, the period with which this chapter has dealt, we protest against the illegal treatment of copper while Great Britain still carried it on her free or conditional contraband lists.

CHAPTER X

COPPER AS CONTRABAND OF WAR

In the preceding chapter the propriety of Britain's
declaring copper absolute contraband of war was
discussed. Once that declaration was made, on
October 29, and once it was accepted, the British
Government had the right to prevent copper from
moving to Germany direct or via the adjacent European neutrals.

After October 29 America's chief trials and losses
sprang from the extraordinary severity with which
England proceeded against trade with neutrals. In
its eagerness to intercept all such trade which might
by any chance get through to Germany, Great
Britain went far towards making impossible even
bona fide shipments to neutrals. The severe measures which England took included the imposition on
neutrals of re-export embargoes, the subjection of
detained neutral shipments to unprecedented delays
in the prize court, and finally the stoppage of our
neutral copper trade until we submitted it to the
complete direction of the British Admiralty.

The other neutrals early followed the example of
Holland in prohibiting the export of copper from
their boundaries. The State Department at Washington, as soon as the September copper seizures

began, co-operated in the attempt to induce European neutrals to lay these embargoes. On October 5 the following Associated Press despatch was sent from Washington:

"Secretary Bryan at once set to work to obtain from Holland, Italy, Spain, Norway, Sweden and Switzerland guarantees that copper imported from the United States would not be re-exported. These guarantees will be accepted by Great Britain. It is believed the neutral countries will not hesitate to approve the plan, which is similar to that already arranged with Holland with regard to foodstuffs."

Yet even with these embargoes in existence, neutral trade was difficult to carry on. It is recalled that, according to the August Order in Council, ultimate German destination of a consignment to a European neutral would be presumed "from any sufficient evidence" and that it then devolved upon the neutral consignee to *prove* that the shipment was *not* going to Germany. The difficulty lay in knowing what proof of innocence would be satisfactory.

For example, it was insisted by the copper trade that all of the copper seized at Gibraltar in October and November was destined for Italian consumption. The shipments were from the largest and most responsible firms in this country, such as the American Smelting and Refining Company, the United Metals Selling Company, and the American Metal Company. The consignees were the largest and most responsible consumers in Italy, such as Corradini, Naples; Schiapparelli, Turin; Unione, Genoa; Trafilire and the

Metallurgica, Leghorn. Moreover, for any of these dealers to have re-forwarded copper to Germany would have been in violation of an Italian law, especially enacted to prevent such occurrences.

Yet cargoes unloaded and detained on suspicion—like the 9,500 tons at Gibraltar—lay for indefinite periods without action of a British prize court and without any indication of what was to become of them. The first of this Italian copper was taken off at Gibraltar on October 26, the last on November 18. Through December, January and February and into March these cargoes waited, unapproached by any prize court proceedings. Long before, the drafts which our exporters drew against these exports had been returned to them and had caused them financial embarrassment.

Fortunately, we have the opinion of the great English jurist, Sir William Scott, with regard to the propriety of these leisurely proceedings. In giving judgment on the Madonna del Burso, seized in the last months of 1797, he severely condemns a three months' delay in disposing·of the case.

"It would be highly injurious to the commerce of other countries and disgraceful to the jurisprudence of our own if any persons, commissioned or noncommissioned, could lay their hands upon valuable foreign ships and cargoes in our harbors, and keep their hands upon them, without bringing such an act to judicial notice in any manner for the space of three or four months. The complaints which such a conduct tolerated by this country would provoke against it from foreign countries are not to be described; and it is not very easy to suggest how the real honor of the country, connected as it is with its justice, could be defended against such complaints."

Further, the eminent jurist lays down the principle that a belligerent nation which is in the exercise of the rights of war is bound to find tribunals for the exercise of such rights, where neutrals should enjoy speedy and unobstructed justice. He dismisses the plea that the "court's full calendar precludes rapid trial," with the words:

"It is no secret that this court has never thought it a breach of that equal justice which it owes to all suitors to suffer a cause to be interposed that from its magnitude of interests or other circumstance of just weight had a peculiar claim to pre-audience."

In point of fact the copper at Gibraltar never came before His Majesty's prize courts. It was eventually bought by the British Government on March 18, 1915, four months to a day after the last consignment of it had been seized, and nearly five months after the first consignment had been captured. Before that, the British Admiralty had offered to buy it, but—a rather important detail— at less than the cost of producing copper. The offer was thus described by an American copper official in an interview in the Boston News Bureau of November 30:

"The British Government not only blocks our mining companies from the Italian market, but, after

having seized their copper, they open negotiations
to buy it and intimate that they are prepared to
pay for it a price that will net the shipper about
10½ cents a pound, less than the average cost of
producing copper at the present time."

However, on March 17, the copper men in this
country were informed that their representative had
made an arrangement with the British Admiralty.
The Admiralty agreed to have 1,000 tons of the
copper that was held at Gibraltar sold on the London market. The rest the Admiralty was to take
at an agreed price, excepting for forty tons carried on the Ascot, which was still regarded as suspicious. The Americans were to pay the expense
of transporting the copper to London on a British
government collier.

During the first half of November, the copper
exporters were desperate. Domestic consumption
of copper was at a low ebb. Steamship lines to
European neutrals were refusing to accept it for
export upon any condition. The British Government was finding one excuse after the other for
detention of such shipments; there seemed no possibility of fathoming the British mind and discovering what would satisfy it. At last England itself
solved the mystery and cut the Gordian knot that
had baffled the copper producers and even the
official minds at Washington.

Great Britain decided what its own intention was
and what would satisfy itself. As a result of this
decision, Mr. Gardner, chairman of the board of

Henry R. Merton and Company, Limited, of London, the world's leading copper merchants, arrived in America in early November, with peace and concord in his hand. He brought with him a glowing prospect for the copper interests, a prospect of the early trade revival for which they had longed.

The story of Mr. Gardner's mission, of its wide and deep bearings, finally—to the credit of Americans—of its rejection by American copper people, is an honorable chapter in our history, even if in the spring of 1915 we were forced into practically the same surrender we had refused in the fall of 1914.

Under the conditions brought about by the war, practically the only copper supply available for countries that did not produce the metal was the American supply. The Merton plan was a very simple one. Mr. Gardner appeared with powers from his government that have never been questioned. England would agree to take a large fixed monthly output of copper, upon the condition that American producers should ship to Europe through no other channels than British merchants.

The offer was indignantly rejected, and on November 16 Mr. Gardner returned to London, his prepared documents unsigned.

Had the proposal met with acceptance, it would have meant the desertion by American producers of hundreds of old customers who consumed copper in neutral countries, and the transferring of copper manufacturing in large measure from these coun-

tries to England, which alone could get the raw
material freely. It would have meant, further, that
England, controlling the world's supply of a material necessary for the manufacture of ammunition for
small arms, would have an influence of very special
potency over all countries not then at war.

While these events were transpiring, there was
developing a copper famine in neutral Europe. To
be sure, England was theoretically willing to let the
European neutrals, except Holland, receive the same
monthly amounts of copper which they had received
in 1913. The British Embassy at Washington said
in a note handed to our State Department on
November 11:

"A supply of copper sufficient for normal consumption in neutral countries will not be interfered
with, provided adequate guarantees are given that
the copper will not be transhipped to enemy countries."

Even if the British detention policy had allowed
the neutrals to receive their normal quotas, these
would have been insufficient for their needs. Italy
is a good example.

First, Italy was arming. This meant increased
imports of copper for the Italian ammunition factories and largely explained our abnormal shipments
intended for Italy in October. Moreover, Italy, like
most other European countries, has in normal times
heavy imports of copper manufactures from Germany. In 1912, Italy imported $4,235,000 of

copper manufactures and electrical apparatus from Germany. With Germany's importation of raw copper checked, that country naturally ceased exporting copper manufactures, retaining all the raw product available to her industries for domestic, especially military, uses. Italian manufacturers were therefore called on to supply what formerly had been imported, in products of copper, bronze and brass. In America we have seen the sudden growth of certain industries after imports from Germany were cut off. In Italy it could not have been different.

The normal annual Italian consumption of copper, apart from that contained in sulphate, is over 40,000 tons. In sulphate, 20,000 tons more are used. Copper sulphate, or what we call blue vitriol, is used throughout Europe to spray vines, for the purpose of destroying the phylloxera pest. Italy needed more copper from us to make the copper sulphate which she had hitherto purchased from Germany. She also needed copper to make sulphate and other products for France, for in the early months of the war the French copper industry was paralyzed. The high price of copper in Germany had induced German manufacturers to turn over to neutrals (Italy) the filling of many orders which they—the Germans—had booked. Finally the 11-cent price of copper during the fall months tempted Italians, like other good merchants, to buy stock for the future.

England itself took in the first three months of the war a vast excess of copper over the volume for the same months of 1913. Italy, in process of arming, was under the same compulsion to have more copper; perhaps under a greater one, because Italy was more dependent than England upon the barred German copper industry. England's imports of copper from us in August, September and October were over 64,000,000 pounds. Including these imports, and including the copper diverted from Dutch warehouses and the quantities taken off steamers bound for Dutch, Scandinavian and Italian ports, England in those three months received 103,000,000 pounds of copper, an increase of 69,000,000 pounds over the same period in 1913. In August, September and October, 1914, there left our shores for Italy 25,000,000 pounds of copper, 16,000,000 more than in those months of 1913. England, in suspecting and stopping those shipments, was refusing to allow Italy an increase less than one-fourth as great as England itself took.

What has been said of Italy's need for extra copper, and the famine resulting from British detentions, applies with equal force to the Scandinavian countries.

We have instructive evidence, in England's own experience, as to the importance of a stoppage of supplies from Germany in stimulating imports by neutrals from other countries. In parliament, on November 17, 1914, a member called attention to the large increase in exports of British coal to Holland and the Scandinavian monarchies. The member implied that some of this coal might be getting through to Germany, and adverted to the fact that Mr. Asquith's constituents were largely interested in the mining of it. Mr. Asquith explained that the increased exports were "not due at all to their being ultimately destined for Germany, but to the fact that these countries (the neutrals) were deprived for the time being of the supplies they have been accustomed to receive from the enemy country."

The interests of the British exporters of copper manufactures were by no means hindered by a policy that kept every other country from getting copper at any price, while the British market was abundantly supplied. Neutral manufacturers found their supplies uncertain as well as high in price, and could not give the guarantee of delivery which the protected English manufacturer could give. The British exports of copper manufactures and copper sulphate mounted steadily in the fall months of 1914.

It is recalled that the October 29 Order in Council prohibited American shipments to neutral countries "to order." This prohibition discouraged the copper trade in particular, for most copper exports are so consigned. Even if destined for a known buyer, a copper shipment is consigned to the order of the foreign agent or banker of the American shipper. The purpose of this is plain. The ultimate consignee might be unable, for some reason, to take delivery of the shipment upon arrival. The title then remains in the American shipper. Shipments "to order" allow our foreign representative, if he thinks best, to retain possession of the copper until the Italian or Swedish consignee has satisfied him with regard to payment. Once this assurance is given, the representative of the American copper firm orders the shipment delivered to the foreign buyer.

Moreover, large American dealers regularly carry heavy stocks abroad. The United Metals Selling Company had 16,000,000 pounds of copper in Europe at the outbreak of the war. These stocks are replenished, normally, by constant shipments "to order." Shipments so coming forward may go into stock or be diverted to buyers as buyers are found. Great Britain was perfectly familiar with this method of doing business. The prohibition of "to order" shipments compelled a complete readjustment of the method of marketing and financing copper.

As an excuse for Britain's detention policy, there came from London continued absurd tales of attempts to smuggle copper into Germany through the neutral countries of Europe. Some of the tales were gross plays upon popular ignorance of steamship practice.

For example, the grave suspicions of the Allies were declared justified when copper was found concealed under a shipment of oats, in a ship unloaded at Marseilles. On November 21, London despatched to American papers the following report:

"The Norwegian steamer Tyr has been detained at Glasgow, according to a despatch to the *Central*

News. It says that 4,000 tons of copper ore, which is contraband of war, was found in the bottom of the Norwegian steamer's hold, hidden under a cargo of general merchandise."

There is no claim made in either case that the copper in question was not upon the ship's manifest, or cargo list, open to inspection. Copper, being the heaviest of all cargo, is always placed in the very bottom of the hold to insure the stability of the ship. The lighter merchandise, such as oats, naturally is placed over it and "conceals" it. Were copper carried on deck where the boarding officers could see it at once, the ship would founder before she sailed.

When in December the Italian and Swedish steamship lines resumed the carriage of copper, they imposed the condition that none should be "in transit" and none should be consigned "to order." Moreover, a Swedish shipment would be accepted only if a cable had been received from the home government specifically reciting that it was for domestic consumption.

But even the sovereign voice of the state expressed in its re-export prohibition laws, and the certification of cargo by Washington Ambassadors of neutrals, did not suffice to prevent seizure of copper by England. On December 28, the New Sweden and Soerland, bound for Sweden, were diverted to English ports by English cruisers. One was relieved of 730 tons of copper, one of 600 tons. In each case the shipment was accompanied by a statement from the Swedish minister at Washington that the copper was for Swedish use.

At last the State Department was driven to protest. On October 22, they had sent an informal note, never made public, to England. The events of November indicated that the October protest had not severely touched the conscience of His Majesty's Government, that sensitive attribute of belligerent powers to which appeal is so generally made in the state documents of the war. As little was accomplished at the almost daily conferences in Washington between officials of our Statement Department and the British and French Embassies, devising ways and means for facilitating the trade in copper between this country and neutrals.

Our December 26 note of protest to England was primarily on behalf of copper. It was stated that great interests in this country were being deprived of their lawful markets. The note pointed out that England was going beyond the limits of international law. It stated that Britain did not seem willing to let shipments go to European neutrals even when they had imposed re-export embargoes on American products. British interference, our note stated, was so severe that a legitimate trade in copper was suffering greatly. Therefore, we said, we felt justified in asking for information as to the manner in which England proposed to carry out her policy, in order that we might determine the steps necessary to protect our citizens.

On January 7, we received an answer from England. It recited the fact that our exports of copper towards Italy and "Other Europe" from August 1 to December 21 exceeded those of 1913. It then asserted that there was strong presumption that this surplus traffic was destined for one of England's enemies, and against this contingency England must protect itself. In view of the circumstances—the note continued—surely neither the government nor the people of the United States could expect England to strain the international code in favor of private American interests.

This January 7 note was a preliminary answer to ours of December 26. On February 10, a final answer was despatched to us. It was a long note with plenty of general discussion. Mention was made of copper only once and then only incidentally. The note opened with a discussion of the reasonableness of the American complaint.

"Towards the close of your note of the 28th December your Excellency described the situation produced by the action of Great Britain as a pitiful one to the commercial interests of the United States, and said that many of the great industries of the country were suffering because their products were denied long-established markets in neutral European countries contiguous to the nations at war."

The British note then proceeded to indicate that American claims of distress due to the war had been exaggerated. It demonstrated that apart from cotton, American exports were getting to be larger than in 1913. (This was due chiefly to foodstuffs and war materials sent to the Allies.) The note stated that the difficulty of shipping to neutrals was probably closely connected with the shortage of shipping on the seas, due to the tying up of the German merchant fleet and the detention of certain British vessels in German harbors. It explained that steamships nowadays are larger than they were, and harder to search. It said that plans were alleged to have been made to move copper in cotton bales. It explained that since the German population had become identical with the army, all food for Germany was properly stopped.—All of which was interesting but in no way contributory to a solution of the copper situation.

Meantime, events were working to the end which Great Britain desired: the submission of our copper trade to her control. In December the Italian Ambassador in Washington received a proposal that he should certify that copper to Italy was for domestic consumption. He indignantly rejected the suggestion. He indicated that to require this was an affront to his government, which had already prohibited the export of any copper from Italy. The Ambassador said, "Italy has given its word that no copper will be exported from its boundaries, and we shall do nothing from here to appease the apparent doubt of our integrity in the mind of England."

But in January the Ambassador had melted. On January 7 the following was announced from Washington:

"Although the Italian Government considers that its embargo against the exportation of copper is sufficient guarantee, it has decided to help American shippers in getting their cargoes across the Atlantic without delay, by certifying the consignments before they leave the United States.

"Under this arrangement the Italian Foreign Office makes an investigation of the business of the consignee and the purpose for which he seeks to use the import of copper. On learning that copper is strictly for home consumption, it authorizes a certificate to that effect to be issued by the Italian Embassy at Washington, which is submitted to the British consul at the port where the shipment is being loaded."

The reason for the Ambassador's change of heart was not far to seek. Copies reached this country of the Italian newspaper *La Perseveranza*, dated about the first of the year. They explained that the Italian Metallurgical Corporation, which supplies the state railways and the army and navy, had closed five works, throwing 3,000 men out of employment. It closed them because of a lack of raw material to make copper tubes, plates and ammunition.

On February 22, a London despatch reported the procedure in the case of some copper bought by a Swedish contractor to fill a contract with his government. The copper was thrown into the prize court and counsel for the contractor asked for an assurance from the British Government that it would not take and use the copper before the case was legally settled. The Attorney General said that the

British Government, while it was prepared to act reasonably in the matter, could give no such assurance. If the Swedish minister desired to make any representations, he added, he must do so through the Foreign Office. The case was adjourned on the application of the Attorney General.

To be sure, British copper dealers, known to the Admiralty and naturally favored by it, had less difficulty in getting into neutral countries the copper that they ordered forwarded from the United States. For example, when the steamship Italia was seized by the British at Gibraltar on November 8, there were aboard two consignments of copper sold to Schiapparelli, Turin. One had been shipped by the American Smelting and Refining Company, one by the United Metals Selling Company. The United Metals had sold through the mediation of an English house. The American Smelting and Refining Company had sold direct. Only the United Metals shipment ever got past Gibraltar.

Such incidents as this indicated clearly the only safe course to pursue. Despite the original repudiation of the British monopoly plan, some of the exporters had made concessions such as selling through British agents. After such plain demonstrations of the good results of such a policy, others who had held out longer began similarly to see the point.

The sentiments of the exporters are well expressed in a letter from one of them early in April, after he had submitted to the English monopoly.

"We are simply forced to take the action because of the fact that some $800,000 worth of our copper was held at Gibraltar, and also because some of the representatives of our leading competitors, resident in England, signed the Agreement some two months in advance of our signing. We held out as long as we could, chiefly because we did not wish to give up our position of independence in the matter of trading where and when it suited us best, without having to consult with the British Government."

Getting no relief from the official action of the State Department the copper men had finally asked the State Department to authorize them to deal with the British Ambassador directly. Authorization was given.

Soon after the middle of March an Agreement between the Americans and His Majesty's Government was made.* It recited that England would do her best to keep copper from Germany but did not desire to hinder exports to neutral countries whose re-export embargoes were found effective. While England could not forego her right of search, she was willing to let copper proceed to destination if the terms of this Agreement were fulfilled. Shipments were to be made only to named consumers (not to merchants) in the neutral countries and copies of bills of sale were to be forwarded to the Admiralty. Bills of sale were to recite that the shipment was for neutral consumption. Under these conditions copper could be exported to Italy or

* For text of Agreement, see Appendix, p. 324.

Scandinavia. Exports to other neutral countries were not to be made except subject to permit of the British Admiralty. "Shipments of copper to Great Britain or her Allies may be made without restriction."

This was the contract signed by American copper exporters. This was the consummation of the British detention campaign.

What was the result on German military operations of all this organized system of annoyance, detention and loss, designed to keep copper from reaching Germany?

Economic pressure was no more effective in the case of copper than in the case of cotton. From London and from Copenhagen, Geneva and Amsterdam, via London and Paris, pathetic tales were forwarded of schoolboys in Germany begging door knobs for the military, housewives being stripped of copper kettles and pans, and roofs being de-coppered. But those who had been in Germany told no such tales.

German copper consumption in 1913 was 256,000 long tons. In order to keep the works operating, the German factories carry a stock of three months' supplies, about 64,000 tons. Because of large imports in the months just preceding the war, it is likely that on August 1 a supply much larger than 64,000 tons was on hand at the factories. In addition to this, on August 1 there were on hand in German warehouses 10,000 tons. German raw copper production in 1913 was 50,000 tons, and no doubt it was largely expanded after the war began by intensive working of the mines. Probably there were readily available not less than 50,000 tons of old metal. This made a total of at least 174,000 tons available for the first year. Further, the needs were reduced by the halting of Germany's large exports of copper products, amounting in 1913 to 125,850 tons, and the interruption of internal electro-technical developments.

There is a very large supply of old copper in Germany. The average annual consumption in recent years has been 225,000 tons of raw copper and average exports have not exceeded 100,000 tons, leaving 125,000 tons every year in the country. In case of need, this supply would care for military uses for an indefinite period.

A vast amount of scrap metal is brought forth by a rise in prices. At the end of 1914 the German price quoted was 200 marks per kilo, or at the then rate of exchange, 20¾ cents per 100 pounds. Scrap was pouring on the market just as it did in the eighties when Secretan's copper corner failed. Secretan got control of the world's supply of raw copper, but those who backed him could not finance the purchase of the huge amounts of scrap copper brought forth by the higher prices which the corner was causing.

A large quantity of copper has been recovered from used ammunition, and taken from positions captured from the enemy. No one has yet thought of requisitioning the hundreds of thousand tons of copper wire on the street railways of Germany. Before they are touched, the wiring and roofs of Belgium and Northern France will be stripped.

Invention of substitutes provide still another resource. It has been reported that Krupp has invented a soft steel which serves very well in place of copper.

One is tempted to subscribe to the opinion of one of the leading copper dealers of America, expressed at the end of December:

"Without denying the fact that the cutting off of the supplies of copper is annoying to the highly developed German industry, I believe it is of minor importance for the German army and navy, but I am sure the principal sufferers are the mine owners, miners and smelters in this country who are deprived of their best market.

"When 1914 statistics are going to be available you will find that while American copper production has been materially reduced owing to the war conditions, England and her colonies have continued to produce without any serious interruption; in other words, America though neutral and disinterested has to foot the bill for England's efforts to starve Germany, while the real profit goes into the pockets of the German copper mining companies and scrap dealers.

"England has gained little, America has lost much, while Germany is annoyed without being hurt."

CHAPTER XI

THE EXPORT SITUATION

A discussion of the effect of the Great War upon American interests would be lacking if it were not to include a consideration of our war exports. They demand attention for several reasons. There is general misinformation regarding their nature and extent and regarding the prosperity which they promise the country. The large extent of our exports during the war period has been frequently cited in the notes of Great Britain, both openly and by implication, as a factor which should influence the minds of the American public in their opinion regarding the stoppage of our normal trade with other belligerents in the war. Finally, the dependence of the Allies upon the United States for great quantities of war supplies, especially of munitions, gives us a vast economic power which might be used by this country, under clearly demonstrated necessity, for the protection of its proper rights and interests upon the seas.

During the greater part of the fiscal year 1915 (the year ended June 30), our exports were very large. The great extent of exports, together with a sharp falling off in imports—more marked than ever since the "blockade" of Germany—resulted in a large monthly balance of trade in our favor; that is, a large excess of exports over imports. In the five months ending August, 1914, we had an adverse balance of trade each month, meaning greater imports than exports. From September on, exports exceeded imports. By September, 1914, those factors were working which were to expand our foreign sales to very large totals, and which operated with increasing effect for many months. This development since September may be illustrated as follows:

EXPORTS AND IMPORTS BY MONTHS, SEPTEMBER 1, 1914
TO JUNE 30, 1915

	Exports	Imports	Excess of Exports
September...	156,052,333	139,710,611	16,341,722
October.....	194,711,170	138,080,520	56,630,650
November ...	205,878,333	126,467,062	79,411,271
December ...	245,632,558	114,656,645	130,976,013
January.....	267,879,313	122,372,317	145,506,996
February....	299,805,869	125,123,391	174,682,478
March	299,009,563	158,040,716	140,969,347
April	294,470,109	160,576,106	133,894,093
May	273,768,093	142,284,851	131,483,242
June........	268,601,599	157,746,140	110,855,459

This increase in our exports was entirely to Europe (including England) for Europe alone had the money to buy. Other continents buy from us, normally, with money loaned by Europe, or with the proceeds of their sales to Europe. Since the war, the monied European powers have been so drawn upon by war expenses that they have had no surplus to lend away from home, and no money to spend for anything but the necessities of life. Germany was prevented by British sea power from getting anything that was on the British absolute or conditional contraband list, and this included nearly every article in trade. The blockade affected other large sellers to Germany exactly as it affected us. And when the purchasing power of South America, for example, is crippled, we too are touched. All this meant that South America, Africa and Asia could not sell their chief customers nor borrow from their customary bankers. Hence they had no money with which to buy from us.

It is this condition that has disappointed the optimists who at the beginning of the war prophesied that America was going to sell to the oversea world what England and Germany used to sell. But the world in question could not buy from anyone. So, though we may sell them a larger proportion of their whole purchases than formerly, it turns out that our actual sales to this extra-European world are smaller than before the war. International trade is a great co-operative venture. No such disturbance as the present can occur among certain of the partners without adversely affecting all the others.

Our increased sales, then, have been to Europe. But the increase has not meant for us that prosperity which it would bring in normal times. Normally such a growth in exports would be extended to our whole field of industries and agriculture. In the present case, the large increase in some articles is met by a large decrease in others, a decrease in articles whose producers are absolutely dependent for their prosperity upon the state of the export trade. Such an article is cotton.

Our exports are "spotty." It is a condition that can no more mean prosperity to the country than an industrial community can be called prosperous when a part of its men are working overtime earning high wages and the other part are unemployed and growing poorer each day.

Contrary to the general impression, our main exports to Europe have not been the weapons of war. It is not possible to find the exports of big guns; they are not listed in the government statistics. But our ordnance shipments have not been large. For the nine months from September 1, 1914, to May 31, 1915, we shipped $34,000,000 of *munitions*, compared with $6,000,000 in the same nine months of the previous year. In munitions are included: firearms, cartridges, gunpowder and other explosives except dynamite. The increase in munitions exports is seen to be only $28,000,000. To be sure, shrapnel is not included in the munitions list; it also cannot be found in the official export figures. Even if we could add the statistics for ordnance and shrapnel, the larger figure would not go far towards explaining the vast growth of our export balance since November, 1914.

The explanation for our great increase in exports is found rather in the group we call *food*, especially in breadstuffs. By breadstuffs are meant flour and grain, except oats, the latter cereal being more correctly classed as forage. Some of the reasons why the European demand for our food was especially heavy have already been noted. Excepting for North America, the grain crops of extra-European countries in 1914 were below normal. The closing of the Dardanelles and German control of the Baltic held the great Russian and Balkan supplies of grain away from belligerent Western Europe. Neutrals like Scandinavia, Holland, Italy and Greece, which had always bought largely from the Black Sea, now turned to America. The great rise in the exports and the price of breadstuffs, especially wheat and wheat flour, were reviewed in Chapter II. In the nine months ended with May we shipped $431,000,000 of breadstuffs, compared with $107,000,000 in the previous year. The growth of $324,000,000 showed that the disappearance of Germany as an export market for our wheat was far more than counterbalanced by the great demand of the rest of Europe. In this one item the growing balance of trade is chiefly explained.

In the case of meat products, a similar development occurred. For some time the communication of the Allies with the Argentine was unsafe, owing to German cruisers in the South Atlantic. Even when those seas were cleared, our shipments continued large, the vast supplies required to provision the armies of the Allies causing a recovery of our export meat trade, which for a decade had been on the decline. The demands for a fighting army are far above those for the same number of men in peaceful occupations.* The European population in the field has advanced to a scale of living which it never knew before. Further contributing causes to the large meat orders from this country included the German occupation of part of the producing area of France; and the large purchases made by American relief bodies on behalf of the Belgians. We exported in the nine months $160,000,000 of meat products, $54,000,000 more than in the same months of the previous year. We sent $11,000,000 of dairy products, an increase of $9,000,000.

A similar advance was in our shipments of sugar. The stoppage of German exports to England resulted in keeping nearly half a million tons of German sugar at home, where it was made into cattle fodder. England therefore had to turn to us for her supply. To prevent a too great increase in price, she tried the experiment, which was not altogether happy, of a government monopoly of the purchase and distribution of sugar. Our sugar exports in the nine months to the end of May amounted to $21,000,-000, which was $20,000,000 more than in the same months of the year before. Finally, there was a growth of $4,600,000 in our shipments of vegetables.

In *forage* there has been another remarkable increase. In the nine months' period we exported $71,-000,000 of forage: oats, hay, cottonseed cake and meal. This was $60,000,000 more than in the same

* Exports of canned beef have increased from $350,000 to $9,900,000.

months of the year before. Five-sixths of the
increase was in the item of oats alone. As will
appear later, our exports of forage were paralleled
by our shipments of horses and mules to eat the
forage; that is, to eat it for the brief period during
which an army horse or mule continues to enjoy the
gustatory pleasures of this world.

Another great group of exports was *hides, leather*
and *footwear,* not including harness and saddlery,
which belong better in the category of war supplies.
The largest increase was in unworked leather and
miscellaneous leather products, though there has been
a notable movement of men's shoes and of hides. In
the whole group we exported $68,000,000 or $48,-
000,000 more than in the same months a year ago.

Somewhat closer to the business of war were our
exports of *textile manufactures,* mostly the result
of great equipment orders from the Allies. Probably
the largest single item was blankets, then woolen uniforms, then cotton knit goods. Of these items and
of wool and woolen rags we sent abroad $35,000,000,
which is $30,000,000 more than last year.

Nearer yet to the direct equipment of war we may
make a group called *war supplies.* It includes
horses, mules, harness and saddles, aeroplanes, commercial automobiles, automobile tires, wagons, gas
oil and fuel oil, barbed wire, horseshoes and surgical
appliances. The largest increase in this group was
in the means of transport: horses, mules, commercial
automobiles. In nine months ending May 31, 1915,
we sent to the war 250,000 horses, compared with

18,000 in the same period of the year before. We sent 53,000 mules, compared with 4,000 in 1913-1914. We exported $30,000,000 of commercial automobiles, which is $29,000,000 more than in the previous year. In the whole group of *war supplies* we sent abroad $148,000,000, an increase of $119,-000,000 over the year before.

It is apparent that up to the present time our great contributions to the carrying on of the war have been indirect contributions rather than munitions. Greater than the increase in munitions exports has been the increase in *material for making munitions.* Under this head should be included lead, zinc, brass and brass manufactures, wire rods, steel billets and metal working machinery. The last item means lathes for turning out shrapnel. American lathe makers have been totally unable to meet the demand for their product on the part of those in this country and abroad who have shell orders to fill. In this whole group the exports of zinc—generally called spelter—overshadow all others. This is because the German and Belgian stocks of spelter, which normally supply the world outside the United States, are cut off from the Allies. Spelter accounts for over one-third of the increase in the group, the foreign sales of which amounted to $62,000,000 in the nine months ending May 31, $46,000,000 more than in the same months of the year before.

Combining these groups and comparing them with the whole exports of the United States, we have a picture of the present situation.

EXPORTS OF UNITED STATES, CLASSIFIED COMPARISON OF NINE
MONTHS' PERIODS ENDING MAY 31, 1914 AND 1915

	Nine Months Ending May 31, 1914	Nine Months Ending May 31, 1915	Increase in 1915
Group I. Munitions	$6,283,953	$34,421,595	$28,137,642
Group II. Material for making munitions	16,291,624	62,360,423	46,068,799
Group III. War Supplies	25,856,921	147,702,807	121,845,886
Group IV. Textile manufactures.	5,293,155	35,239,110	29,945,955
Group V. Hides, leather and footwear	20,599,959	60,150,388	47,550,429
Group VI. Foodstuffs.	218,390,743	627,417,302	409,026,359
Group VII. Forage	10,419,041	70,640,989	60,221,948
Total, Groups I-VII	303,035,596	1,045,932,614	742,897,018
All other Exports . . .	1,529,255,043	1,146,942,879	*382,312,164**
Total Exports, U.S.A.	1,832,290,639	2,192,875,493	360,584,854

What is evident is that our total exports for the
nine months' period did not grow to any amazing
degree. There was a shifting of our output. We
were making and selling what we never made and
sold before. We were not selling much that we have
always sold. A huge decrease is seen in the exports
of articles not included in Groups I-VII. For example, there was a great falling off in cotton exports,
a decrease of $216,000,000 for the nine months'
period. Naval stores decreased. Iron and steel
manufactures fell off $17,000,000. Agricultural
implements decreased $20,000,000. Lumber and

*Decrease

manufactures of wood dropped $41,000,00. There were similar decreases in many other articles such as phosphate rock, mineral oils, electrical machinery and copper (copper fell off $36,000,000) ; though the lower exports of copper were, as we know, finally compensated by higher sales at home, to the ammunition makers. These things went to make up the decrease of $382,000,000 in our exports outside of the seven groups.

It may be doubted whether such a situation is a healthy one. It is a poor consolation to the pinched cotton farmers to know that the ammunition makers in Bridgeport are working day and night, that the machine tool works in Hartford cannot fill their lathe orders, that the railroads haul trainloads of war auto trucks from Detroit, that the harness makers of Cincinnati are full of business, or even that the wheat farmers of the West and the packers of Chicago are rich. Lumbermen cannot be shifted to a shoe factory and the tobacco raisers of Kentucky and Tennessee are not trained to make shrapnel shells.*

* On August 5 a New York importer of German goods said in the *New York Times:* "England says that the money that is being earned by manufacturers of arms and war supplies should be a compensation for the losses sustained by the importers. But let me say that if I were to go to any manufacturer who has earned money on war contracts and say to him, 'Brother, through obeying the British Order in Council I have lost my business, money, home and everything I possess in the world. Will you kindly let me have $100,000 of the fortune you have made on war supplies, to put me on my feet?'—you can pretty near guess his answer."

Until those who sell lumber, tobacco, phosphate rock, cotton, mineral oil, agricultural implements, and naval stores reach their accustomed foreign markets, we shall not again be a prosperous country. It is noted that most of our distress products come from the South. To a large degree the distress of these products is due to the ban which England laid upon the important German market. The removal of that ban will be the largest single step towards a return to prosperity.

Nor is it a matter for the South 'alone. Our inland business dwarfs our foreign trade. No one knows the exact figures of our interior exchanges but it is estimated that the volume of our inland trade is sixty times the volume of our foreign trade. The figures of export trade are published by the government and flashed in the papers. But most manufacturers know that on their books the foreign orders are a small quota of the whole. Most of our producers, especially of our industries, are perhaps sixty times more interested in market conditions at home than those abroad. The fact that some makers of clothing can sell to Europe does not compensate the clothing industry for not being able to sell to the South. So with the wagon and leather industries. We are all interested in the state of the South, and in its relief, not merely in some abstract way or even from humanitarian motives. We are also interested because we want the South to be able again to buy from the rest of the country.

Our main problem will not be in any way solved by the entrance into the export trade of the vast supplies of ammunition contracted for and now in the course of manufacture. They will go simply to make the rich richer.

CHAPTER XII

The Import Situation

One of the outstanding features of this war is its amazing demonstration of the economic power of England. Once Sir Walter Raleigh said that the nation which controlled the shipping of the world controlled the trade of the world and so the world itself. Sir Walter Raleigh stated the principle; the proof was in the great European War.

England at the outset of the war owned over half the merchant shipping in the world. This she withdrew from all service that might aid her enemies. She controlled the marine insurance business. The withdrawal of English companies from participation in the underwriting of risks on German-American trade was one of the obstacles to the recovery of that trade. The London discount market, through which most of international trade had been financed, was withdrawn from the service of England's enemies.

All this was a legitimate use of British economic power. For a belligerent to forbid trading with the enemy is as old as war itself. But England went further than this. We see uses of her power that strike us as more novel. The British naval power was used so to threaten with starvation the neutral nations of Europe that they agreed not only not to allow goods to pass through their territories in transit to Germany, but they even agreed not to supply Germany with their own products. Neutral merchants submit their books to English accountants who satisfy themselves that none of the neutral imports are resold into Germany.

Early in the war the British cut the German cable, leaving us largely dependent on British and French cables for communication with northern Europe. When Italy entered the war, our dependence was complete. No message to European neutrals is allowed to reach its destination if the British censor imagines that it refers to a transaction that may be benefiting Germany. Sweden has complained that this exercise of the censor's imagination has seriously impaired her legitimate trade with us. In August, 1915, the packers were in Washington complaining of the cable censorship. They complained that, after creating the Netherlands Oversea Trust and designating it as the sole consignee for our exports to Holland, Britain was refusing to let our cables reach even the Trust.

These cases represent unprecedented interference with the course of neutral trade. And yet Americans do not excite themselves unduly because of what Britain is doing to Denmark or Holland, even though it is our exports which are there being subjected to British supervision.

Another set of cases comes nearer. Some of them are detailed in this chapter. Rubber from the British empire was withheld from the American trade until

Americans signed an agreement not to manufacture rubber goods—from any rubber whatever—for the enemies of England. So with wool. So with tin.

Because of a blockade which we do not recognize, we are cut off from imports from Germany, and we face serious industrial disturbance through the failure of the potash and dyestuffs supply.

We already have seen that the Admiralty forced our copper exporters to place in its hands the direction of our copper trade. The Liverpool Cotton Exchange now apparently blacklists all Americans who do not sign an agreement not to deal with the enemies of Britain.

It is indicated by Great Britain to the steamship lines carrying our exports that American shipments to neutral countries, if approved by British consuls, are less likely to be detained. Steamship lines refuse to take shipments until they are so approved. British consuls in American ports are engaged in accepting affidavits from American shippers that none of our exports for neutral countries will get through to Germany; though in our official protest to England we assert that for us to accede to the purpose of the ineffective British blockade would be to violate our neutral obligation to trade with both belligerents.

It is impossible to reach this point without feeling that our American sovereignty is involved.

In 1793 E. C. Genet, an agent of the French Government, was operating in this country, France then being at war with Great Britain. Thomas Jefferson wrote to him in June, 1793:

"It is the right of every nation to prohibit acts of sovereignty from being exercised by others within its limits, and the duty of a neutral nation to prohibit such as would injure one of the warring powers."

It is not far from an act of sovereignty when a British consul decides whether we may ship anything—contraband, conditional contraband or "free list"—to neutral countries in Europe. When this sort of sovereignty is permitted and is exercised for the purpose of injuring the Germanic Allies, those Germanic Allies might perhaps justly feel they have cause for complaint against us as a neutral nation.

The present chapter and the following are the story of the strange documents we had to sign to get certain necessary imports from the British empire or even from the neutral world, of the stoppage of our imports from Germany and Austria, especially dyestuffs and potash, and of the pending loss to our Federal treasury from the disappearance of custom revenues from German goods.

First with regard to imports that do not come from Germany. The most important of these are rubber, wool and tin. At least part of our supplies of each of these comes from British colonies. Great Britain allows us to get supplies from British colonies only on condition that our manufacturers refuse to ship to Germany either these materials or the products of them. In practice we may not ship raw materials or their products even if the materials do not come from British colonies; even if they come from the United States itself. This policy of Great Britain has been aided by her manipulation of the contraband list, particularly by her making absolute contraband of wool and rubber, both on the free list of the Declaration of London.

The United States normally consumes about one-half the world's output of rubber, whose production has increased rapidly with each succeeding year. Over half of our material is grown in British colonies.

Apart from the obstacles in finance and transportation, soon overcome, there was no difficulty in getting rubber in the early months of the war. In August, 1914, we received 6,500,000 pounds less rubber than in the previous August, but after that month our imports steadily reached higher figures than in the corresponding period of the previous year with the single exception of January, which will be explained.

The chief excitement in the rubber trade during the first four months of the war was provided by the exploits of the German cruiser Emden, which in the course of her destructive career sank two dozen merchant vessels, three of them carrying $1,000,000 worth of rubber. The indirect influence which the Emden exerted, in the way of discouraging shipments from Ceylon and Singapore, was considerable. When the cruiser was sunk November 10, rubber prices declined, because these Far East supplies were free to move. Values were soon to recover, however, because of England's embargo on the exportation of rubber from the British empire.

On September 21, London had declared rubber and rubber goods to be conditional contraband, making it impossible for our dealers to export rubber and its products to Germany, and difficult to ship it to adjacent neutrals because of the suspicion which England cast upon such cargoes. For example, the rubber and copper for Italy in the cargo of the American steamship Kroonland led England to unload this steamer partly and subject her to a long detention at Gibraltar near the end of October. On October 29 rubber tires were made absolute contraband.

Still England was not content. The British officials believed that rubber goods and raw rubber were going through to Germany from this country, via adjacent neutrals, under false declarations on the ship manifests. Therefore on November 12 the exportation of raw rubber was forbidden, from all parts of the British empire to all destinations except England. The rubber trade at once became worried and appealed to the State Department. The State Department did not seem able to help the situation, and though American dealers offered re-exportation guarantees as a condition of being allowed to receive raw rubber, Great Britain seemed unwilling to accept them.

Because of the large volume of rubber on the seas for America at the end of November, this prohibition did not at once affect our receipts. Not until January did the imports sink below the corresponding month of the year before. Meantime, however, the rubber trade was getting alarmed. The Rubber Club

issued a statement saying that the employment of
250,000 men was imperiled, and that, if the embargo
continued, half of the 65,000 tons of rubber which
the trade needed for 1915 would be cut off.

By the end of December a peculiar problem had
arisen, due to the high prices ruling and the uncertainty as to how long the embargo would last. It
was apparent that if the embargo continued long
there would be a large accumulation of raw rubber in
the British market, and that the release of this
supply would so depress the price as to occasion
serious loss to prudent American manufacturers who
had bought supplies at the higher December prices,
compared with those who took a risk, waited until the
ban was lifted and later bought their rubber cheaper.

In December the large rubber interests arranged
that B. G. Work, president of B. F. Goodrich and
Company, should visit London and attempt to
arrange for rubber imports into this country. He
found the British Government none too eager to co-
operate with him, because of its conviction that rubber goods were reaching British enemies from the
United States, and because of what it evidently considered as the suspicious action of the American
Government in withholding the publication of ships'
manifests for thirty days after the ship sailed.
Nevertheless, the negotiations of Mr. Work were
successful, partly owing to a promise on the part of
the Rubber Club and the Rubber Association of
America jointly to seek the co-operation of the
Treasury Department in investigating and prevent-

ing illicit practices, such as false declarations of exports to neutrals adjacent to Germany.

In his January 7 note, Sir Edward Grey, in answer to our protest of December 26, speaks of an arrangement by which Americans were to be allowed to get rubber. Under proper guarantees, provisional licenses to ship to the United States were, he said, being granted to British rubber exporters.

On January 8 Washington despatches, inspired by the British Embassy, announced the conditions which Americans must fulfill. Large manufacturers were allowed to have rubber consigned to them direct, upon condition of their giving a bond in London which would be forfeited if they were caught exporting or allowing exportation to Europe. American dealers in rubber, as distinct from manufacturers, were to be allowed to get rubber only by having it consigned to a New York bank, to be delivered to the buyer when he filed with the British consul general in New York a guarantee against re-export which was satisfactory to that official.

The leading manufacturers in the country signed a guarantee, undertaking not to sell or export any raw, waste or reclaimed rubber, except to England and British possessions. Raw rubber then in the hands of American producers was to be used in their factories, and not sold to anyone. The manufacturer bound himself to execute no orders for manufacturered goods for any enemy of Great Britain. Orders for European neutrals were to be filled from stocks previously accumulated in Europe, or, if manufactured in America, were to be shipped first to London and re-exported thence under license. A distinctive mark was to be put upon all products exported or sold for export and notice was to be given to His Majesty's consul general of shipments destined for non-European countries. The manufacturer pledged himself not to sell rubber manufactures to any person in the United States without first ascertaining that the person would not export the goods to Europe except to Great Britain or her Allies.

This guarantee was published in May by the Rubber Club, with a request to customers to co-operate with the manufacturers in preventing rubber from getting to the Teutonic Allies, and so avoiding a second British embargo.

But more than good will on the part of dealers was required. The manufacturers, having obligated themselves, proceeded to bind their customers, the latter being required to sign an agreement of which the following is a copy:

"We hereby agree that any quotation asked for, and any purchases made by us from you or another of any of your products, shall be in each and every case only for domestic use or shipment to Great Britain, France or Russia. We pledge ourselves to this fact, and agree that the execution of this document shall be binding on us for such length of time as you shall consider it to be effective, and cancellable only by you.

"We further agree to submit to any and all investigations that may be necessary on your part, and to give free access to any and all of our books, if called on so to do, to establish the fact of our non-exporting, or selling to another to export, in violation of this agreement.

"And further, we agree that any order, even though accepted by you, may be cancelled without redress on our part at your option, for any cause whatsoever, during the period that a state of war exists abroad, between Great Britain and any other country.

"In case we tender any order that is for shipment out of this country, we will in each instance state thereon its destination."

It will be noted that the guarantee signed by the manufacturers with the British Government bound them not to manufacture any goods for the enemies of Great Britain, whether made of British-grown rubber or not. It is supposable that a manufacturer might have refused to sign the agreement on the ground that it was a combination in restraint of trade, and might have declared that he would work with Brazil rubber and sell his products where he chose. But Brazilian rubber is of a different quality from plantation rubber from Ceylon and the Straits; and manufacturers cannot do without the British material.

Moreover, without signing the agreement with the British Government, no American manufacturer could get Brazilian rubber. The product of Brazil could get to the United States at this time only via England; or, if it came direct, via the Booth Line. But the Booth Line was an English concern and

would accept no rubber for New York unless consigned to the order of the British consul general.
The latter would deliver, naturally, only to the
faithful.

It is true that rubber or its manufactures did get
into the hands of dealers who would have been willing
to sell to Germany. But they could not ship it.
There were no steamship lines to Germany, and from
September 21, when rubber was declared conditional
contraband, the lines to adjacent neutrals had refused rubber that by any chance might be destined
for Germany, out of fear that its presence on board
would subject their ships to long detention by the
British cruisers.

After American manufacturers were prohibited
from exporting to neutral countries except via England, lines to those countries refused to accept articles with any rubber in their composition, even
rejecting American exports of carpet sweepers and
of the harmless necessary clothes wringer.

The export of American automobiles and motor
cycles to European neutrals was greatly hindered,
because their tires were not allowed to go with them.
A motor cycle for a customer in Sweden had to be
shipped to him without tires. The American company found it necessary to deliver the tires from
stock in England, or to send the tires to its London
agent with instructions to request a license for their
shipment to the Swedish buyer. Whether the tires
were allowed to be exported depended upon the state
of mind of the duly authorized British official. If

the official thought that the name of the Swedish
buyer had a German sound—and most Scandinavian
names have to British ears—he would refuse the tire
license and the Swedish buyer would find himself with
an automobile or a motor cycle for which he had no
particular use. If he was wise, next time, he would
order his motor cycle from England, whence the
motor cycle would not be exported unless the tires
were licensed to follow. The acquaintance of the
British license officer with the British exporter gave
the exporter the opportunity to explain that it was
a racial and not necessarily a personal or business
relationship between a gentleman in Gothenburg and
a gentleman in Hamburg which made their names
sound alike.

Naturally, the market for rubber products which
our manufacturers had built up in European neutral
countries disappeared, excepting so far as the British
would still allow us to supply that market through
English agencies; and for this loss an increase in our
exports to the Allies could be hardly a legitimate
compensation.

On December 23 Great Britain declared rubber
and its products absolute contraband. To be sure,
this was practically no more effective than the ruling
of September 21 which made such goods conditional
contraband. But just as in the case of copper,
placing rubber in the absolute contraband list was
designed to "keep the record straight."

Rubber is one of the items on the free list of the
Declaration of London. That is, it is so necessary

for the arts of peace, and has so little direct connection with the uses of war, that nations are forbidden to hinder its movement to a belligerent. There is nothing in the use of rubber today that was not known in 1909; hence the reasons for listing it as a free article of commerce must still exist.

And when one examines the connection of rubber with the operations of war, the justification for declaring it contraband does not appear. One of the uses of rubber is for automobile tires. These tires may be used upon machines that are part of the military equipment of the enemy. Rubber, just as oils, hides and copper, should be free, listed according to the Declaration of London, an international code to which Great Britain was the leading contributor.

As to Great Britain's course in restricting our re-export of rubber goods made from British materials, this embargo must be accepted as a necessary incident of war, on the ground that for Britain to allow such trade would be to allow an indirect form of "trading with the enemy." But for a system that prevents us from furnishing without hindrance rubber and rubber goods to European neutrals, and from furnishing to Germany Brazilian rubber and such products as we can make from other than British materials, there is no logical defense.

As for the British measures exerting any pressure upon Germany which will influence the outcome or duration of the war, this is out of the question. Not even in England does anyone think of

that. As usual, the pressure is being exerted upon a
civil population, and upon the manufacturers in Germany and elsewhere by whom this population is supplied. At the outbreak of the war all tires in the empire are said to have been commandeered for the use
of the military. Does anyone think that there were
not enough tires in Germany to serve the military
for an indefinite period? In a country with such an
old and developed rubber industry there is a great
store of old rubber which can be reclaimed and used.
Finally, synthetic or artificial rubber is a fact, not
an experiment. It cannot yet be produced so as to be
a commercial competitor of natural rubber, but with
the element of cost disregarded, it can be produced
in large quantities. In the production of synthetic
rubber for military purposes cost is not considered.

So much for rubber. The history of wool is similar. Of the wool which our manufacturers make
into dress goods and manufactured clothing, we
import more than we produce. Our imports fall
into two divisions: Class I and Class II wool, which
are the finer sorts used for clothing and blankets;
and carpet wool. Carpet wool comes from China,
Russia and Turkey. Russia and Turkey placed
embargoes on the exportations of carpet wool but
this resulted in no material embarrassment to our
mills because by far our largest supply of this wool
is from China and our trade with that country was
not disturbed. Our difficulties were concerned chiefly
with the better classes of wool, of which we obtain

normally about 60 per cent from the British empire, and the rest mostly from South America.

The war came at an opportune time for the woolen manufacturers. The Underwood-Simmons tariff law had placed raw wool on the free list on December 1, 1913, and there were large importations of foreign wool up to the time that the war began. From December 1, 1913, to August 1, 1914, we received 35,000,000 pounds more of raw wool than in the same period of the preceding year. At the opening of the war there was a considerable supply of wool afloat for this country or contracted to be delivered here, so until the end of October the wool receipts continued in large volume.

But with the opening of the wool auction sales in London, early in October, Great Britain announced an embargo on wool exports from the United Kingdom. The wool trade was not alarmed, assuming that the imports from Australia and New Zealand would not be affected. Anxiety began to be felt, however, when despatches from Washington early in November announced that Australia and New Zealand had imposed embargoes on wool exports; and it was asserted that England had forbidden British vessels to carry South American wool to the United States. As a result of these factors, our receipts of wool declined in November and fell to a very low level in December. They did not reach their normal volume again until March, after the February agreement of our importers with the British Government. That we were allowed to get as much wool as we did in those winter months was due partly to the clamor of the Australians at being deprived of their customary American market. Some shipments of Australian merino wool moved forward under temporary licenses granted American firms; but nobody knew how long the system would last, or what there might be in the future.

The difficulty in the negotiations between the American woolen manufacturers and the British Government arose from the nature of the required guaranty, namely, that the wool would not reach Germany in any way or form. Americans considered it impracticable and unfair to be asked to put up a bond supporting such a guarantee, because of the numerous stages and the many hands through which the wool must pass in its progress to the ultimate user. Meantime, the woolen manufacturers complained that the Allies were overwhelming them with war orders and were not letting enough wool supplies come forward to make the filling of those orders possible.

The Textile Alliance comprises the four leading textile associations in America and was originally formed to correct certain abuses connected with the purchase of mill supplies. It was through this organization that the plan was eventually worked out which allowed wool to come forward.

Under this plan a license to receive wool in America could be had by an American only after approval of the purchaser by the Textile Alliance, acting through its president, A. M. Patterson. Theoretically, it was possible to apply to London direct for a license, but the British Government let it be understood with quite sufficient distinctness that it would grant no license not approved by the Alliance.

The plan required that a separate application must be made for each shipment. The application was to be forwarded by Mr. Patterson to the British authorities. If the wool was to be shipped to an American, he must sign a non-export guarantee before delivery could be had. All imported wool, it was provided, must be consigned to Mr. Patterson or to one of a group of banks approved by the British Government. The banks, however, could release the wool only upon written word from Mr. Patterson.

The Textile Alliance, in explaining the plan to the wool trade, stated that it had assumed strong moral obligations towards the British Board of Trade, to discourage by every lawful means the export of wool, tops or yarns from the United States. If such exportation occurred it would be considered by England as prima facie evidence that the United States was supplied with more than enough wool for its own use, and the imports would be restricted by the British Government. Therefore all wool users and dealers were urged to refrain from such action. That is, even wool raised in Montana might not be exported without bringing upon this country a British embargo on wool from Australasia, and possibly other measures that would shut us off from supplies from South America in British ships.

In addition to the measures already reviewed, the

export of wool products to Germany was prevented, and export to adjacent neutrals hindered by Great Britain's August 4 contraband lists, and the treatment which the August 20 Order in Council prescribed for conditional contraband. Blankets were listed as absolute contraband in the August 4 lists; woolen clothing was absolute when of obviously military nature, and otherwise conditional. This policy reached its full effectiveness on March 11, when raw wool, wool tops and noils and woolen and worsted yarns were suddenly made absolute contraband. Again, in the making of raw wool contraband, the situation arose of Britain forbidding us to trade with Germany in innocent American products, necessary for the German civilian population. Wool was on the free list of the Declaration of London.

The measures taken regarding wool and rubber were paralleled by those regarding tin. Tin comes from England and the Straits Settlements. All of it now comes through London. After a period of complete embargo, we were allowed to import the metal under license, with a guarantee that tin and its products would be sold only to our own country and the Allies.

CHAPTER XIII

The Import Situation (Continued)

Passing from commodities imported largely from British possessions, it is of interest to consider the effect of the war as to articles for which our great source of supply is Germany, notably potash and dyestuffs.

One of the most important and necessary of our imports is potash, in which Germany has a monopoly of the world's supply. Potash is an essential ingredient of commercial fertilizer, which becomes increasingly necessary for soils that have been worked long and have had extracted from them, by the growing crops, important chemical properties. Our use of fertilizer is naturally most extended in the older parts of the country, especially in the southeastern cotton states where the land has been tilled without interruption for a century.

Commercial fertilizer is compounded of phosphoric acid, lime, nitrogen and potash. All the necessary elements are present and readily available in this country, except potash. We import from Germany 1,000,000 tons annually of salts with various percentages of potash, containing about 240,000 tons of the pure chemical. In normal times this material is used principally in making fertilizer, though it is also employed in making various chemical products, among them gunpowder.

The war came at a bad time for the fertilizer manufacturers in this country. The annual supply of potash from the German Syndicate comes in eight installments, running from May to December. The manufacturers ask for small installments during the early months, as they do not begin to ship the fertilizer until the following February, and large takings in the early months mean a corresponding tying up of money during the summer and fall. Hence, on August 1, 1914, little had been shipped to us.

At the outbreak of the war Germany declared an embargo on the export of muriate of potash, the sort used in gunpowder. This restriction lasted only five or six weeks, but its relaxation was not followed by large imports, owing to difficulties in arranging payments, lack of transportation, and shortage of labor at the German mines.

Potash comes from the Potash Syndicate. The contracts under which our manufacturers had been supplied contained a war clause, and so had become invalid.

The Syndicate offered, however, to continue shipping at contract prices if the Americans would carry part of the higher cost of delivering potash in America. The higher cost consisted of a larger inland freight rate—from the mines to Rotterdam, since the German ports were closed—a higher ocean rate and war risk insurance. The Syndicate offered to carry the higher ocean rate, if the Americans paid the higher inland rate and assumed the war risk insurance. The effect was to make potash cost us only $4 per ton more than before; which meant for muriate, for example, a price of $37.50, instead of $33.50 per ton delivered.

Under these conditions potash was brought to this country, subject only to the limitation imposed by scarcity of ocean tonnage, until at the end of January Germany forbade its further export. Yet it had never moved freely. Only in January and February did our receipts equal as much as one-quarter of the corresponding receipts in the previous year. In October, because the German railroads had been largely used for military purposes in August and September, we received only 1,800 tons of potash compared with 92,000 tons in October, 1913.

The German Government ostensibly looked with increasing concern upon the amount of muriate of potash being used in this country for exportation to England as pure gunpowder, or as gunpowder in ammunition; and therefore, on January 29, declared an absolute embargo on the export of all potash salts.

The British blockade action on March 1 showed that England was prepared to stop potash or anything else from Germany. Against our receiving further shipments there was apparently a double bar.

It so happened, however, that at the beginning of the war there were three cargoes of potash in Ham-

burg: two in ships of British registry, one in a
German ship. With the outbreak of the war these
vessels were tied up in port. The German boat could
not venture out for fear of capture; the English
boats were detained by the Hamburg authorities.
These cargoes had been bought before the beginning
of the war. In March, after the British Order in
Council, potash in this country was very scarce; so
the users urged the State Department to obtain from
Britain permission for these cargoes to be barged
from Hamburg to Rotterdam and there put on ships
for America. It was explained to London that these
goods, like other imports allowed to pass in March,
had been bought before the Order in Council went
into effect.

In April, after long negotiations, Great Britain's
permission was obtained. It was agreed that potash
on its way to Rotterdam and America should not be
molested. In America, provision was made for super-
vising the distribution of this potash by a government official, to assure the German authorities that it
would reach only fertilizer factories and chemical
manufacturers, who would put it to other use than
the making of explosives.

Though apparently suspicious as to the possibility of keeping muriate away from American
powder manufacturers, who were willing to pay high
prices for it, Germany agreed to let the potash go
to Rotterdam and be exported thence, on condition
that we would send three American ships, loaded
with cotton, to take it away. This our government

declared itself unable to do, in view of conflict with the British blockade Order.

The result was that the potash was still withheld. Because we would not send Germany the things she wanted, that country in effect set out to deny us the things we wanted. She apparently was looking for a pressure which would make us feel the inconvenience as keenly as we felt the illegality of the British blockade. The withholding of potash as a measure of pressure against us was no doubt the real reason for the January 29 embargo, rather than any hope of crippling our exports of explosives by that action. Potash is not used for smokeless powder.

As a result of these conditions the use of fertilizer in this country for the agricultural season of 1915 was greatly curtailed. This was especially true of the cotton states, where a reduction of 40 to 50 per cent was reported. Such fertilizer as was used contained less potash than usual. The effect on the cotton crop may not be noticeably great for the year 1915; but if the war continues and in 1916 no more potash is available than this year, the results, according to agricultural experts, will be very marked.

Apparently the resumption of our potash imports is dependent upon the successful assertion of our right to ship our products to Germany. It may be an additional incentive for us to start the movement of cotton to Germany, if that movement is the price we must pay for potash to raise more cotton.

We Americans are fond of saying that we are a

self-sufficient nation, independent of the world. We raise everything we need. No one can hurt us, we say, for we are a complete world in ourselves. The war will serve to awaken us from this self-hypnotism. Of some products, such as cotton, we raise a great deal more than we need, and a war that cuts off our exports brings us distress. Of some vital products like potash we produce less than we need, or none at all; and war cuts us off from the necessary raw material. We suffer as to potash because German mines have a monopoly of the supply. We suffer as to dyestuffs because German industry has created a practical monopoly of their production.

In olden days our textile manufacturers did their coloring with vegetable or animal products from such sources as logwood or the cochineal bug. These natural dyes have been displaced by synthetic dyes which are derived from coal-tar. We have no longer the apparatus and trained men for making and applying the old natural dyes. And the development of the synthetic dyes, their manufacture on a vast scale and the supplying of them to the rest of the world, have been an achievement of industrial Germany.

The manufacture of coal-tar dyes is complex. By distilling coal-tar ten products called *crudes* are produced. By treating these crudes with non-coal-tar products, like acid and gases, 300 *intermediates* are produced. These intermediates are assembled or combined to form, all told, some 900 *finished dyes*, of which a considerable proportion are in use in the

United States. It is as if ten fibers were used to make 300 yarns, these in turn being woven into 900 patterns.

There are several reasons why no dyestuff industry has developed in America. One difficulty is in the production of intermediates. The making of some of these is a process kept secret or patented by the Germans. In the case of others, by-products are developed for which the Germans alone have found a use and a market. The German industry is largely in the hands of four great concerns which produce all of the intermediates and finished dyes, and use all of the by-products. To compete with such industries, it would be necessary to operate upon the same scale. Some of the intermediates and finished dyes could not be made in this country until secret processes were discovered or until the expiration of German patents. We could not operate with efficiency until we had trained the thousands of chemists who watch over every division and subdivision of the dye-making process in Germany.

While the shortage of dyestuffs has given some stimulus to the industry in this country, it is a perilous business to embark upon the manufacture of dyes for the war period alone, only to encounter disastrous competition with the lower-cost German product upon the return of peace. The development of a real dyestuff industry in America would be a slow matter at best, but even much of a beginning is dependent largely upon a heavy protective duty and perhaps a change in our laws to prevent foreigners from dumping their products here at famine prices after the war. An increased protective duty would be opposed by many of the manufacturers who use dyestuffs. It would be unfavorably received, at present, by the American public and be out of line with the policy of a Democratic administration.

There are a few dyestuff plants in America, but these have been employed largely on intermediates imported from Germany. To solve the problem of war shortage they can help but little. It is vain to say that we have the largest supplies of raw material for dyes in the world. It is true that by collecting the great quantities of coal-tar which we could collect from our enormous coking industry, we could produce more of this material than anyone else. But the problem is to make the intermediates. It is a problem of processes, patents, trained men, organization and markets. To meet the war situation there is no prospect of American substitutes taking the place of German dyes; the difficulty that confronts dye users must be solved by regaining the German supply.

At the outbreak of the war Germany put an embargo on the export of dyestuffs, but in the latter part of August shipments were allowed to come forward to the United States via Rotterdam. Before the end of September, however, German consular agents here reported to their home office that we were shipping dyes to England. This seems indeed to have been the case, though the extent of such *direct re-exports* was small. For the nine months ending March 31, 1915, we re-exported to England $54,000 of dyes or dyestuffs, compared with $23,000 in the same months of the year before. More important than this, the export of *American* dyes increased from $244,000 in 1913-1914 to $538,000 in 1914-1915. These American dyes are largely made from imported German intermediates, and hence may be looked upon mostly as re-exports of German dyes to England. The figures given show only the declared movement of dyes from here to England, and do not indicate a movement which is said to have occurred under false declaration of the contents of shipments. Whatever the actual extent of the re-exports, they occurred in spite of obligation assumed by those who imported dyes, not to reship them to England.

Since England is as dependent as we are upon the importation of German dyes, Germany was bending every effort to keep her products from England, and so to bring pressure to bear upon the dyeing industry in England and upon the people employed. It was the same game that England was playing with rubber. After the discovery of the movement of dyes from here to Great Britain, already apparent in September, the German relaxation of the dye export embargo, when it did come, was so arranged that American manufacturers said it was designed to keep our industries in a chronic state of "dyestuff hunger," in order to prevent us from re-exporting. Our embarrassment was, in fact, probably due to another cause. From July, 1914, to the end of March, 1915, we received $1,700,000 more of dyes and dyestuffs than in the same months of the previous year. To be sure, prices were higher, and this accounted for part of the increase in the value of imports. Yet the quantity imported was heavy and apparently sufficient. There was no marked increase in the home demand for dyes. So, if, in spite of large imports, our industries were in a "chronic state of dyestuff hunger," it was either because the supplies were held off the market by speculators or sent across to England.

When negotiations took place with the German Government, in early October, 1914, to induce Berlin to allow dyes to be shipped to us, the German authorities insisted in return that the dyes should be called for by American ships and that these ships should bring cotton, or something equally desired, to Germany. This demand had much to do with the starting of direct shipments of cotton to Germany, and the use of American boats therefor. American vessels were insisted upon, because it was assumed that England would be less likely to stop our returning ships, and requisition their desirable dyestuffs cargo, than it would be in the case of ships carrying a less imposing neutral flag.

By a mistake which was probably due to excessive timidity, the Matanzas, the first American steamer that went over for dyes (in October), left America in ballast. The German Government nevertheless allowed the boat to bring back a cargo of dyes. The Matanzas arrived with her first cargo on November 15, brought another in January and a third in March. In the meantime, other American boats sailed with cotton, some of them direct to the German ports. Dyestuffs were sent to us theoretically in an amount equal to our average monthly receipts in recent years; practically we received more than this average. Shipments came to this country in good volume until the British Order in Council, announced March 1, shut off all movement to and from Germany. The Order in Council, above all else, stopped the movement of our cotton; and it was in return for our cotton shipments that the dyes had been sent to us.

On March 23, the steamer George E. Warren arrived in New York with a large cargo of dyestuffs and at about the same time the Matanzas came with her last load. The skipper of the Warren said that his were the last German dyestuffs that would reach us until after the war, and until the present writing (August) his prediction has proved practically true. American vessels which were in Bremen on March 1 loading dyes and other German exports, received the announcement of the British Order in Council and at once discharged what they had loaded and came back to America empty. The American steamers were afraid to sail with goods in the face of the Order in Council, and the shippers were afraid to ship, in view of the danger of detention or confiscation of their shipments. Moreover, the Germans, who were doing everything possible to keep dyestuffs out of the hands of Britain, were unwilling to let dyestuffs be exported while a British Order was in effect which allowed one of His Majesty's cruisers to take into a British port any cargo from Germany, unload it there and sell it in the British market.

When the shipment of dyestuffs ceased, Americans who were interested began to appeal to Washington. Congressman Herman Metz of New York sent out letters of inquiry to about 1,000 users of imported dyes: manufacturers of textiles, leather, paper, wall paper, colors and printing inks. Replies from 270, he said, indicated that about 250,000 employees would be affected by an interruption of dye imports. He estimated that the total number of workers affected directly and indirectly would be not under 2,000,000. Whether or not such figures were too large, it was certain that the threatened effects were serious. To some extent it was possible to substitute white goods for colored, but even that meant deprivation of employment for those ordinarily engaged in the coloring process.

In April it was estimated that the supplies of dyestuffs in the country would take care of our demands until July 31. The pressure brought to bear at Washington was strong. The British Government perhaps shunned the odium of bringing disaster upon dyestuff users; moreover it was not in a good position to resist the pressure. England had declared herself willing to allow the export of cotton which had been contracted for before March 1. She was now asked to allow the importation from Germany of dyestuffs under similar terms. Such a concession was suggested not only by her own policy with regard to exports, but also by her own interests as a dye-stuff user, for experience had taught her that she could buy German dyes that reached America.

So in the middle of April a London representative of the Textile Alliance obtained from England a free passage from Rotterdam for two cargoes of dyes, consisting of goods said to have been purchased before March 1. The dyes were to be consigned to Secretary Redfield of the Department of Commerce, and by him distributed to the members of the Textile Alliance. Many in this country were dissatisfied with the arrangement, because the membership of the Textile Alliance by no means comprises all those entitled to receive dyes. The German Government was dissatisfied, and refused to let the dyes come forward under such an arrangement. Berlin is said to have claimed that the dyes must move not by the grace of England, as an extraordinary shipment, but by right of the United States as a part of the free commerce with Germany which was being illegally obstructed by England. The dyes in question did not come forward.

All this meant, in plain English, that Germany was determined to hold up our supplies of dyestuffs until we re-established regular communication with her; to keep from us something that we wanted until, in accordance with what we claimed as our clear rights, we should begin to send our goods to her. It was believed that dyes were a more powerful inducement to us than potash, for we could see in the immediate future the result of a dye shortage, whereas the result of a potash famine probably would not be fully felt until the gathering of the 1916 crops.

As in the case of potash, so with dyes, we cannot say that Britain was directly responsible for the threatened shortage. Britain was willing to allow us to bring a small quantity of both potash and dyes through the blockade. But Britain must be held responsible for the sudden stoppage, on March 1, of all commerce between us and Germany, a commerce of which potash and dyestuffs form an inseparable part.

With regard to the stoppage of imports from Germany other than dyes and potash, the British Government bears the full responsibility. These imports are normally very large and serve a wide range of manufacturers, dealers and consumers. They include hides, skins and furs, toys, crockery, linens, hosiery, laces, woolen and silk goods and gloves.

It has been noted above that when the March 11 Order was promulgated, all American boats loading German goods discharged what they had loaded and came home. Moreover, the lines of steamers from European neutral ports gave notice that henceforth no goods of German or Austrian ownership or origin would be accepted for transportation, and discharged whatever goods of this nature they had aboard. Such lines included the Holland-American, Scandinavian-American, Swedish-American and Norwegian-American. Their refusal to bring any more goods was natural, since their doing so would expose them to detention and to whatever penalty His

Majesty's Government might choose to impose for disobeying the British Order.

This Order decreed that no vessels sailing from a German port after March 1 should be allowed to proceed. All goods aboard must be discharged in a British or Allied port. If discharged in a British port, the goods were to be turned over to the marshal of the prize court, and, if not requisitioned for the use of His Majesty, they should be detained or sold under the court's direction, the proceeds of such sale to be dealt with as the court deemed just. However, no money should be paid over by the court before the conclusion of peace, unless it were shown that the goods became neutral property before the issue of the Order. "The proper officer of the crown" was authorized to modify this last provision, and also to authorize the release of neutral property laden at a German port.

The provisions of the Order thus far cited affected shipments direct from Germany. Further provisions concerned shipments of German goods via neutrals. Any vessel sailing after March 1 from a neutral European port with goods of German ownership or origin, was similarly to be stopped and required to discharge its cargo. If the goods were not requisitioned by the British Government, they might be sold and the proceeds paid to the court. The court, however, was not to pay over any of these proceeds until after the conclusion of the peace, unless it were shown that the goods became neutral property before March 1. The "proper officer of the crown" was empowered also in this case to release neutral property of enemy origin.

It is recalled that we protested with vigor against this tie-up of exports from Germany to this country, in our note of March 30 directed against the Order in Council. We asserted the

"rule sanctioned by general practice, that even though a blockade should exist and the doctrine of contraband as to unblockaded territory be rigidly enforced, innocent shipments may be freely sent to and from the United States through neutral countries to belligerent territory without being subject to the penalties of contraband traffic or breach of blockade, much less to detention, requisition, or confiscation."

That is, we denied the right of Britain, even if she were maintaining a blockade of Germany, to stop the movement of German traffic to us through neutral countries adjacent to Germany.

This communication, as shown elsewhere, was not answered until the end of July. By a series of events, however, the original decree was somewhat modified.

It is recalled that the English Government first modified its Order by allowing us to export through neutral countries, until March 31, cotton which we had sold to Germany before the first of that month. The cargoes were to be allowed to proceed, or else bought at contract prices. It was natural for Britain to grant American importers a similar modification of the Order so far as it affected westbound

traffic; namely, to allow us to receive goods which had
been paid for before March 1. The object of the
westbound blockade being to deprive Germany of
the opportunity to make profits by exporting, there
was no insuperable objection to letting those exports
come forward for which Germany had already been
paid, and whose detention would injure only the
American buyers.

This was the nature of the British modification.
The period during which such goods might be
brought out of Germany was twice extended, but the
principle was adhered to that nothing should go
forward which had not been paid for before March 1.

The efforts of Washington to help importers without compromising the government on legal questions
resulted in a curious official complication. Although
our State Department never recognized the legality
of the blockade, two of its officials, its Foreign Trade
Advisers, were deputized to act as representatives of
American shippers in presenting to the British
Embassy at Washington proofs that their desired
imports from Germany were paid for before March
1. It was specifically stated that these Advisers did
not officially represent the government, and that
nothing they might do could legally bind their supe-
riors. Yet they were government officials, and they
were acting with the British Embassy in its method
of enforcing what their Department said was an
illegal stoppage of our commerce.*

* The situation could have been paralleled with regard to
our attitude towards Germany. We protested the sinking of

Early in April the Foreign Trade Advisers received a note from the British Embassy at Washington, containing the following:

"The British Embassy are authorized to state that in cases where a merchant vessel sails from a port other than a German port, carrying goods of enemy origin for which American importers claim to have made payment prior to March 1, 1915, proof that such goods were paid for before March 1 may be submitted for examination to the Embassy. If such proofs are presented at a sufficiently early stage to enable the report thereon to be communicated in time to the British authorities, the result of the investigations will be taken into account and due weight attached to them in deciding whether the goods concerned should be discharged under the provisions of Article 4 of the Order in Council of March 11."

The Foreign Trade Advisers sent to importers a statement containing this note and a list of the documents or affidavits which would be considered as evidence by the British Embassy.* Proofs were afterward submitted as fast as received.

However, perhaps greater relief was afforded elsewhere. The British Government saw that it must not cut off short all commerce from Germany to the United States. So it appointed the Holland-Ameri-

passenger vessels with Americans aboard. After doing that, we might have appointed two Foreign Travel Advisers, attached to the State Department, whose function would have been to inform prospective travelers what ships the German Ambassador, on behalf of his government, would agree not to torpedo.

* For this circular of the Foreign Trade Advisers, see Appendix, p. 327.

can Line as the route for such traffic as might be
allowed to move. The Holland-American Line is the
one most amenable to England, because of necessity
it runs through the Channel and is at the mercy of
British cruisers. This line was allowed to issue a
notice that upon certain conditions it would accept
German and Austrian goods after March 1. The conditions were that the goods should be of American
ownership, and should have been paid for before the
first of March. Moreover, this fact had to be sworn
to before an American consul in Germany, and certified by him. It was not simply a question of attest-
ing an oath; the consul must certify the fact.

Under this arrangement there was no doubt that
American consuls gave their certification in some
cases where nothing but ownership had changed
hands before March 1; that is, where an order had
been given but no payment had been made. If the
British requirement had been strictly met, few goods
would have come out of Germany after the first of
March. The very important reason for this was the
fact that imports are not generally paid for before
they are shipped. In the case of 90 per cent of them
a bill is drawn by the seller on the buyer, or his
banker, at the time the goods are shipped. This
draft does not become payable—i.e., the goods are
not *paid for*—until at least 30 days later. One of
the largest import firms in New York had placed
heavy orders in Germany, but on March 1 had only
ten cases of goods in that country for which it had
actually paid.

Probably because of this freedom with which the American consuls interpreted the circular of the Holland-American Line, the British Government caused the company to require the certification of the Netherlands Oversea Trust in addition to that of the American consul. During May the United States Government notified its consuls that they had no authority to certify, but merely to attest the oaths of others.

The time limit within which German goods could be taken from Rotterdam was extended to June 1, and then to June 15. It was definitely announced that after June 15, nothing more would be certified by the Netherlands Oversea Trust, and hence nothing more would be accepted by the Holland-American Line. On July 1 the Foreign Trade Advisers notified our importers that on June 15 the British Government had ceased issuing permits for the importation of German goods into America.

This final announcement, which had cast its shadow before it, stirred the New York importers of general merchandise to action. They met in New York on June 10 and thence some of them proceeded to Washington. They claimed that before March 1 they had ordered over $50,000,000 of merchandise for the fall trade. German manufacturers had proceeded with these orders, and the American buyers would have to pay for them.* In opposition to this view it was

* Moreover, these goods have been sold to American retailers who may take measures against the importers for failure to deliver.

asserted by the British that ample time had been given to get all legitimate and bona fide purchases out of Germany. In the case of orders placed after August 1, 1914, when war began, ordinary business prudence—the British said—must have caused the buyers to have in their contracts war clauses absolving them from liability in cases such as this.—That may be doubted. Nobody foresaw, until shortly before March 1, an attempt to blockade even German ports. A policy that forbade German shipments through neutral ports was undreamed of.

However this may be, our importers seem entitled to protection, whether they should have foreseen the British action or not. Their business is an established trade in German goods, upon which our manu-facturers and our people have become dependent. The livelihood of the dealers, the prosperity of manufacturers and the comfort of many people are conditioned upon a continuance of this trade.

Further, in this as in many other matters arising from the European War, it is a question of more than our right. If we continue to trade with England and allow our trade with Germany to be stifled, we violate an obligation of neutrality. We can no more rightly refuse to buy from one belligerent and not from another than we can rightly refuse to sell to one belligerent while continuing to sell to another. Failing to enforce our neutral right to trade with Germany is not in strict terms a refusal to trade; yet the principle is as true today as when clearly stated by Jefferson, that between restraining commerce our-

selves and allowing belligerent countries to restrain
it there is no difference.

On July 23, as we saw in Chapter VI, the British
answered with a complete refusal our protest of
March 30 against the blockade. The essence of its
contention was necessity, and the application of the
inapplicable Civil War cases.

In addition to this general denial of our contentions, we received a specific denial. On July 15 we
protested against the seizure and continued detention of the Belgian cargo of the American steamer
Neches.

In our July 15 note, the issue was first stated.
The American steamer Neches with a general cargo
sailed from Rotterdam for the United States. She
was held up at the Downs, taken to London and
compelled to discharge goods which belonged to
American citizens. The British had justified the
seizure on the ground of the March 11 Order in
Council, prohibiting German commerce from moving
via neutral ports. (The Neches cargo was of Belgian origin and as Belgium was in German hands
this was considered as German commerce.)

Our note stated that we considered the Neches
case an illustration of the international invalidity of
the March 11 Order in Council. We declared illegal
the seizure of goods from a neutral port merely because they originated with an enemy of Great Britain. Our Ambassador was requested to communicate
to England our desire that goods on the Neches, the

property of American citizens, be expeditiously released and forwarded to destination.

The unsatisfactory British answer was sent on July 31. With regard to what Britain considered its legal rights, this note referred us back to the British communication of July 23. Our attention was called to the inhumanity of Germany's submarine warfare on merchant vessels and it was asserted that this contrasted with the humane British procedure with regard to vessels seized. It was stated that Britain was unaware, except for the published correspondence of America and Germany, to what extent neutrals had demanded damages for the unlawful acts of submarines. So long as this German warfare continued, the note went on, Britain could hardly be expected to abandon her rights and allow goods of German origin to pass freely through waters patrolled by British cruisers.

However, it was stated that in particular cases of hardship in neutral countries England was willing to examine the facts with a spirit of consideration for the interests of neutrals. England declared herself willing so to proceed, if the Neches were held to be such a special case.

In preventing a stoppage of imports our government has an especial interest, because customs duties furnish the largest single item of our national revenue. In recent years we have collected each year approximately $700,000,000 in the form of taxes, nearly one-half of this sum, about $300,000,000, being duties levied on imported goods. German goods are, as a rule, manufactures; they are thus subject to duty and are sources of revenue to the Federal Government. In the last four years Germany has furnished 10½ per cent of all of our imports. She has furnished 14½ per cent of our imports subject to duty.

Precisely how much revenue is collected upon imports from Germany it is impossible to say. The statistics of the customs service are not kept in such a manner as to show import revenues by countries, nor can the figures be so combined as to produce this result. However, it is possible to get a fairly close estimate of the amount so collected.

We know our total imports from Germany, and we know the value of our imports of a certain number of the leading articles in this trade, thirteen in all, some of them dutiable and some of them free. In the calendar years 1912, 1913 and 1914 these specified articles represented one-half of all imports from Germany. The average rate of duty applicable to these goods was 25 per cent in 1912, and 26 per cent in 1913 and 1914. It is a fair assumption that the average duty we collect on all German imports is 25 per cent. Before the war we were importing from Germany at the rate of $120,000,000 per year. A 25 per cent duty on this amount would yield us an annual revenue of $30,000,000. In reality we probably collect more than this. Germany sends us 14½ per cent of all the dutiable goods that we import. If these goods pay the average rate of duty they would yield 14½ per cent of the total we collect. That total is over $300,000,000 per year. So the German imports would contribute over $45,000,000. The true amount lies somewhere between the estimates of $30,000,000 and $45,000,000.

It may be objected that imports from Germany would in any case have fallen off during the war, and that our revenues from these imports would inevitably have decreased even if Britain did not interfere with our trade. In a degree, that is true. In the eight months ending March 1, when the Order in Council went into effect, we imported $76,000,000 of goods from Germany, compared with $127,000,000 in the same period of the previous year. That is, our imports were 60 per cent of normal. Presumably we were collecting that proportion of the normal amount of duties or at the rate of $20,000,000 per year on German goods.

But with an absolute stoppage of German imports, our revenues will decline from $20,000,000 to nothing. And this $20,000,000 is a sum whose prospective disappearance has concerned those in the Federal Government who must take care of our revenue. No one will be popular who suggests taxes to meet a $20,000,000 deficit, which is the contribution England demands that our government should pay towards the enforcement of a non-intercourse policy, though that policy, we officially contend, violates our rights and our neutrality.

CHAPTER XIV

The Practicability of Starving Germany

A sentiment has existed among many people, not excessively partisan in their views as to the general merits of the war, in favor of allowing England a free hand in the treatment of commerce for Germany. They feel that a policy on the part of Great Britain which would tend to end the struggle quickly by bringing to bear upon Germany not only the force of heavy military odds but also the force of severe economic pressure ought, perhaps, to meet the approval of neutral countries, even though these countries might suffer in their own material interests.

This point of view is expressed in an editorial of the New York *Journal of Commerce* of March 2, the day after the British announced their ban on our trade with Germany.

"If it is in the power of the Allies to keep from Germany the supplies which would enable it to maintain its hostile operations against them indefinitely, whether these supplies are intended for the direct support of armies or to replace those taken for their support from such as would otherwise sustain the civil population, that may be the most effective and humane means of shortening the ruthless process of slaughter, desolation and misery, the destruction of all manner of values and the huge losses which neutral nations cannot escape sharing.

"All can afford to share in the cost and the sacrifice to secure this consummation as speedily and effectively as possible."

In the discussion of Great Britain's action with respect to cotton, and also as to copper, some attention was given to the practical effect of the British policy in bringing to bear upon Germany pressure which might shorten the war. It was seen that in neither case was there any considerable probability of such a result.

It is now proposed to consider further the efficiency of England's "attrition" measures, especially with regard to foodstuffs. It will be instructive to note the resourcefulness with which Germany has negatived the English policy. Not only is it probable that Germany will "get through"; but it is also possible that, under the English economic pressure, she will develop permanent substitutes for some of the products we formerly sent her.

The common opinion is about as follows. Everyone knows that at the time of the Franco-Prussian War Germany had a population of 40,000,000. In 1870 Germany had about as many people as its farms would feed. Everyone knows that this population has in the meantime grown to nearly 70,000,000. Germany's land area has not increased. Therefore, there must be about 30,000,000 people supported by imported food, mostly from Russia and from oversea. If Germany were deprived of Russia's exports, and if

England shut off the supplies from oversea, then, it is reasoned, a population of 70,000,000 would be left with food materials sufficient for less than 60 per cent of that number.

It is generally assumed that the 30,000,000 people added to the German population since 1870 have been supplied with food brought into Germany by the great expansion of that country's trade, which has advanced along with the growth of population. This is the more easily believable, because it is the explanation of the feeding of the increasing British population. Britain, like Germany, is an industrial country and is the only foreign land that we know much about.

There are, however, important differences in the economic situation in the two countries as regards foreign trade and the food supply.

Britain was the first "industrial nation," for the great industrial inventions were made there. In Britain the steam engine was invented and first applied to the manufacture of goods. The old order of production by hand was here replaced by the new order of production by machinery. This great advance so cheapened goods that, aided by the low transportation charges brought about by the steamship and the steam railroad, England began to supply with manufactures that part of the world which could be reached by modern means of communication and which did not erect a tariff wall high enough to keep England's products out.

In return for these manufactures, England took

food to supply her rapidly growing population, and raw materials—such as our cotton—to work up into more manufactures. But the undeveloped countries could not pay England with their own products for the enormous supplies she delivered to them. So they went into debt to her and sent to her stocks and bonds and mortgages for the railroad equipment, the harbor cranes and the mining machinery delivered to them. For instance, it is estimated that we owe England three and one-half billion dollars or more; that is the sum of English "investments" in this country.

The British population, which grew from eleven to forty-four million in the nineteenth century, was being fed from abroad. British agriculture positively declined, especially after a policy of free trade in the fifties left it defenseless against the cheap grain of the American prairies, the cattle of Texas (later the Argentine), the mutton of Australia, the dairy products of the thrifty Dutch and the Danes. Cheap transportation worked against the British agriculturists just as it worked in favor of the British manufacturers. Britain became a vast industrial town, with the rest of the world as the surrounding country.

If Germany had followed the course Britain pursued she would be as vulnerable as Britain is today in her dependence on food from across the sea.

The German states, like other European nations, had not been able to meet the competition of the established British industries. Germany was an agricultural land when it came into existence in 1871. It was supporting about as large a population as its land would maintain, in the agricultural stage. Every year a larger number of natives had to emigrate. German emigration to the United States reached 110,000 in 1870; 149,000 in 1873. It rose to 210,000 in 1881, and 250,000, the high-water mark, in 1882. By 1882 the influences were already at work by which the exodus of Germans was to be checked.

The annual loss during the seventies of emigrating soldiers, taxpayers and laborers was regarded by Bismarck with grave misgivings. He decided that further growth of Germany and the retention of its increasing population depended upon a development of its industries. These industries would employ the increasing numbers of Germans. The products of these industries, just as in the case of England, would pay for the food of those employed in them. In 1879, therefore, Bismarck consented to the establishment of a protective tariff, to shield infant German industries from being overwhelmed by British manufactures.

It took time for the effect of this tariff to be seen. The industries had to grow up before they could compete with England on international markets. Emigration was still high during the eighties and early nineties. Prices were low and trade depressed everywhere during the period of 1880-1894. But in 1895 a recovery set in. The German industries were established and ready to take advantage of the recovery. In 1895 emigration to America dropped to 32,000, and it has never since passed 50,000 in any one year. Since 1906 the total German emigration to all lands has not exceeded 32,000 in any year.

Every year this outward movement has been more than balanced by an immigration into Germany of Poles, Galicians and Italians, to work in the industries. That is, Germany has been able to take care of her normal increase in population, and more. It has been the popular impression that Germany has needed land to care for her teeming millions, and that a huge military establishment has stood ready to seize more territory when the least opportunity offered. The truth is that she did not need more land for her people but more people for her land.

The growth of German export trade, a growth larger than that of the other great nations, is indicated by the following table:

EXPORTS OF LEADING COUNTRIES 1880 AND 1912

	1880	1912
Germany......	$ 718,375,000	$2,421,050,000
England.......	1,393,833,000	2,994,805,000
U. S. A.......	853,638,000	2,204,322,000
France........	890,200,000	1,764,780,000

Germany, then, has proceeded along the same paths as England in developing herself into a nation that manufactures for foreign countries. Germany differs from England, however, in not having become dependent on oversea lands for food supplies.

This would have been the result had Bismarck followed the British policy of free trade in food. Unprotected, the old high-priced German farms could no more have competed against American grain than could the English farms.

When in 1879 a protective tariff was levied to protect industries, the German manufacturers clamored to have foodstuffs on the free list. They said that they could not compete with the English manufacturer, if the English workmen were allowed to buy their food in the cheapest markets, while the German workmen could not. The argument was sound, if the sole object was to become a great industrial country like England, importing food from abroad. Germany's purely industrial development would no doubt have proceeded more rapidly if no duty had been levied on grain and meat. But German agriculture would have declined, as did that of England.

Bismarck considered that dependence on foreign food supply was perhaps a tolerable situation for a country like England, commanding the seas, but an intolerable one for Germany. Such a dependence would put Germany at the mercy of any nation with a stronger navy, and Germany did not have a navy of any size, nor did she then propose to have one.

Therefore the Chancellor determined upon a high protective duty on meat and grain (particularly wheat). The duty kept German agriculture in the field. The duty was later increased with the purpose of stimulating intensive production and keeping this production adequate to the needs of the growing industrial population. The attempt has been largely successful.

Protective tariffs generally bring burdens in the shape of higher prices paid by the people who live under the tariffs. So in Germany. The German laborer has paid more for his meat and bread than the Englishman. Through the payment of higher prices for food, the German laborer has been taxed to supply the nation with the economic equivalent of England's navy; namely, assurance of food supply in the time of war. But England's people, meantime, have been taxed in other ways to support their navy.

To be sure, England uses her navy for other purposes than the protection of food supply. But, on the other hand, Germany's policy has attained a desirable result that England misses; namely, the retention of a large population on the land. This has a great and definite social value. The country is the tired city's recruiting ground. The possession of very large agricultural contingents in Germany's armies is of not inconsiderable importance to her in the terrible strain of modern warfare.

Germany's production of food, stimulated by the protective tariff, increased more rapidly than the population it was designed to support. In the admiration expressed for Germany's industrial development, this agricultural success has passed unnoticed. In the years 1883-1887 the population of Germany averaged 46,700,000. This grew to 67,-000,000 in 1913, an increase of a little less than 50

per cent. An increase has occurred of more than 50
per cent in the production of every important article
of food and fodder; namely, wheat, rye, barley, potatoes, oats and hay. This result was due less to an
increase of the acreage cultivated than to a more
intensive cultivation and hence a greater yield per
acre.

In the early eighties Germany was self-supporting
in the matter of foods; that is, everyone was fed with
the products of German soil. Since then, products of
the soil have increased faster than the population.
It follows that if the people were satisfied with the
same scale of living as they enjoyed in the eighties,
they could still be fed from German products. But
in Germany, as elsewhere, in these twenty-five years,
the standard of living has advanced. People have
learned to live better. They eat more. The per
capita consumption of wheat and rye was 40 per
cent higher in the years 1902-1906 than in the years
1886-1890. Hence the growing food imports in
recent years.

The rye, wheat and flour imports for industrial
West Germany have been partly balanced by exportation to Scandinavia of rye, wheat, rye flour and
wheat flour from agricultural East Germany. These
exports were of course stopped when the war broke
out, with a view to conserving Germany's home
supply. But there was still a clear balance of imports into Germany, a supply which was sure to be
missed, and for which no substitute could be found.

It must be recalled that the war broke out on

August 1, before Germany was able to import any of the 1914 agricultural products. When Britain cut the German oversea supplies, the problem that faced the Germans was not one of absolute starvation, as the British assumed. But it was the difficult problem of returning to a scale of living that had been outgrown, but which was nevertheless more than sufficient for actual physical needs.

To prevent extortionate prices for the limited supply of food on hand, the German Government early in the war set maximum prices that could be charged for many foodstuffs. The maximum prices served their purpose well. They kept nourishing food within reach of the poor and of the great masses of those dependent on men fighting at the front.

Next, an effort was made to restrict consumption by appealing to the patriotism of the people. The government exhorted the people at home to cut down their use of food and so supplement the work of the soldiers in the field.

Unfortunately this was not sufficient. If there had been no maximum prices set, rising prices would have automatically reduced the use of food as it became apparent that the supply would not last until the next harvest. The government could have controlled the use of food at any time by repealing its maximum price law. But this would not have reduced the consumption equally on the part of the whole population. The rich and the well-to-do would have bought as much as before. The reduction would have fallen entirely on the poor and dependent.

One way was left to combine the benefit of maximum prices with the necessity for making the food supply last until the next harvest,—namely, for the government to take over the supply and distribution of the foods of which a shortage was threatening. By the end of the year 1914 such a shortage seemed possible in grain and flour. One serious difficulty had arisen from the circumstance that the maximum prices that could be charged for grain were such that it paid the farmer to feed grain to live stock rather than sell it in the market.

Hence the now famous Decree of the German Federal Council, dated January 25, 1915. This document was 3,500 words long, and bore the title "Announcement concerning the Regulation of the Trade in Bread-Grain and Flour." The essence of the Decree was contained in the first paragraph, which read:

"On and after the first of February, 1915, all supplies within the empire of wheat, rye (oats and barley were later included), pure or mixed with other grain, thrashed and unthrashed, are seized on behalf of the War Grain Society, Limited, in Berlin. In the same way all supplies of flour made of wheat, rye, oats and barley will be seized in behalf of the communities in which they are found."

The terms of the Decree did not apply to supplies belonging to the empire, to a state, to the military or naval authorities or to the Central Bureau which provisioned the army. The Decree was designed to

guard, essentially, the food of the civil population.
Moreover, as noted elsewhere, all imported grain and
flour were excepted.

The exceptions included, further, farmers' seed
grain supplies, and supplies for their households.
Mills and flour dealers were put under regulation as
to the amount of their sales. Bakers were restricted
to the use of three-quarters of their former amount of
flour. Such were the provisions of the ordinance.

Later a special Kriegsbrot (War Bread) was prescribed for the bakers to make, consisting of wheat,
rye and potato flour. Pure wheat bread was not to
be baked. Above all, a reduced consumption was
assured by the bread card system. Each person was
given every week a commutation card calling for
bread to equal 225 (later 200) grammes of flour per
day. Bread could be obtained at bakeries or restau-
rants only upon the presentation of the card, which
was duly punched. When 7 x 225 grammes were
punched out of the card, the person could get no more
bread until the following week.

It was considered an act of patriotism to go
through the week with some of the bread allowance
on the card unused. The equivalent of 225 grammes
per day is 150 pounds of flour per year. This is
well over the amount that will support life, but far
below the amount that had been used by the German
population in recent years. For example, in 1902-
1906 the average annual German consumption of
wheat and rye was 495 pounds per person, over three
times as much as was allowed on the bread cards.

It is well to note this reduction. It is a common statement that Germany was never in danger of starvation and that she could not possibly justify her submarine campaign as a proper defense against Britain's plan to starve her. Today we can make light of any plan of starving Germany. But on February 4, when the submarine campaign was launched, starvation was by no means impossible. The danger which the German Government felt is measured by the drastic measures of self-denial which it imposed upon civilians.

Von Loebell, German Minister of the Interior at that time, wrote to Professor Sering of Berlin:

"We shall be able to subsist during the war only if our mode of life is radically different from that to which we have been accustomed during the long period of peace. The soil of Germany is fertile and can maintain the population of the country, but what it produces has not always in the past most appealed to us. We need not starve, but we must be saving and live simply, eating less wheat and white bread and more black bread and potatoes and utilizing what formerly was waste. We must begin our saving now, if it is not too late. Every household must be placed on a war footing. Economy and self-denial at home are like readiness to face death and courage at the front."

A problem quite as serious as that of food for the population was that which confronted Germany with regard to fodder for its live stock. Under normal conditions fodder constitutes a large portion of the cargoes that fill ships going to Germany. The great items are barley, oil-seed and oil cake, bran and corn. Altogether, imports of fodder exceed exports by more than 7,500,000 tons. Evidently, with imports of fodder cut off, there was necessary either a reduction of live stock or a diversion to the feeding of live stock of grain that ought to be reserved for human beings.

Two measures were adopted: one, to reduce the numbers of live stock, and the other, to increase the supply of home fodder.

At the opening of the war there were 25,000,000 swine in Germany. With imports of fodder cut off, farmers tried to keep their swine alive by feeding them grain and potatoes. At the ruling maximum prices of grain, potatoes and meat, it paid the farmer to turn grain and potatoes into pork before selling to the public. By the end of January the swine had eaten most of Germany's oats, and a large portion of the potato crop.

At the same time that the January 25 Decree confiscated supplies of grain and flour, there was passed a Decree of the Federal Council aiming at a reduction of the number of swine. Towns of 5,000 and over were ordered to purchase and preserve quantities of pork, and for this purpose were empowered to confiscate the swine supply. How many of the 25,000,000 swine were thus appropriated we do not know. In February Professor Schumacher estimated that it would have been possible to save alive 18,000,000 of the 25,000,000 swine, if the precautionary measures described had been taken earlier in the war. As it was, he expected that 9,000,-000 would be saved.

In any case, vast quantities of pork have been preserved by the German communities, and swine reduced to the numbers which can be conveniently supported without drawing upon the foods that support men—notably potatoes. All potatoes were needed for men, to help eke out the supply of bread-grain. Potatoes were withdrawn from fodder use, both by the drastic reduction of the number of swine and by a raising of the price maximum by 35 marks per ton, which occurred February 15. This price increase induced the farmer to sell his potatoes for human use.

So much for the means taken to reduce the supply of swine. The second problem of Germany was to find a way to replace out of her home supplies a large amount of fodder formerly imported, in order to support the remaining live stock. There were two possibilities. First, a large volume of potatoes are ordinarily distilled into alcohol, used in beverages and in the industries. Further, about 400,000 tons of beet sugar are annually exported, mostly to England. This exportation, of course, ceased with the opening of the war.

A determined and successful war has been carried on against alcoholic beverages in Germany; and the industrial demand for alcohol has diminished. This has set free such a mass of potatoes that there is now a quantity available for fodder even after all human wants are met.* Moreover, a method was found of making the unexportable raw sugar tonnage available for fodder. Nitrogen in the form of ammonium sulphate, a by-product of the coking industry, has been mixed with the sugar to make a fodder with over 50 per cent of albumen. This discovery was the work of the Institut fuer Gaerungsgewerbe (Institute for the Yeast Industries) in Berlin. It means a substitute for the fodder albumen formerly contained in imported barley. A new straw meal has made the food values in straw available for live stock.

So successful have been the German restrictive measures that at the end of May, 1915, the price of flour was reduced, and the communities were stopped from further slaughtering and pickling their swine. For the first war year the problem is solved. It is now known that several million tons of grain and fodder will be carried over to the next season, along with the crops now being harvested. Any shortage of grain in the future will be met by a reduction in the supplies for food animals. This means a reduction in the German meat consumption which is, however, now far above the physiological minimum.

The best measure of the success of the German policy of price maxima and government distribution is that at present food prices in blockaded Germany are lower than in unblockaded England.

Next year's harvest has already been planned to meet the new conditions. The needs are, compared

* The German potato crop averages 40,000,000 to 50,000,000 tons.

with last year, more wheat and more fodder. The easiest and most abundant crop of fodder that can be raised is potatoes. Every effort is being made to attain these objects. Only 60 per cent of the normal area devoted to sugar beets is being sown for beets. It is estimated that this will supply the home sugar demand. The remaining 40 per cent of the former beet area was planted with wheat and potatoes. Soil has been sown which under normal conditions was not worth cultivating. Moorlands in Brandenburg, Pomerania, Schleswig-Holstein, Hanover and West-phalia have been drained and planted. We read of potatoes growing on former tennis courts and front lawns.

The occupied regions of Belgium, France and (to a lesser degree) Poland have been planted, and while they will not contribute to the feeding of the civilian population of Germany, they will help feed the 4,000,000 soldiers quartered upon them. Early in the war, large food supplies were found in such centers as Antwerp, and these were available for feeding the German army in the West. The Russian invasions of East Prussia, which produced about 60,000,000 bushels of Germany's wheat, were less destructive to the wheat than to the homes, farm buildings and implements of the owners. The Russian army sweeps clean. However, great efforts have been made to rebuild East Prussia, and certainly a large part of its normal harvest will be gathered.

So many farm laborers were drafted into the army that during the last harvest a shortage of hands

was feared.   But volunteer helpers nearly swamped
the farmers.   In addition, this year there are nearly
two million prisoners to help gather the harvest and
most of these prisoners are Russians, farmers by
profession.   The supply of farm horses will be 40 per
cent less than in peace time.   This lack will be met by
a large use of colts, oxen and cows, and also by an
increase in the employment of motor plows using
benzol as fuel.

Finally, Germany in this crucial year has been
helped through by a smuggling trade of large pro-
portions.   Probably the smaller part of this trade
was in American breadstuffs and provisions moving
into Germany via adjacent neutrals.   No doubt there
has been a considerable volume of this business.   No
doubt it will continue, no matter how stringent the
"blockade."   Once goods are in the free channels of
commerce in Scandinavia, the sharpest laws and the
most industrious British supervision cannot prevent
them from being drawn over the borders into Germany by the magnet of high prices.   And there can
be no scarcity in Germany that is not reflected in
attractive prices for imported food, which is exempted
from the government grain monopoly and the government's price maxima.

Yet the largest smuggling trade has been from
Roumania and Russia.   Roumania is normally a
heavy exporter of grain.   In the fall of 1914, before
her exports were marketed, the Dardanelles were
closed.   Austria and Germany both had wheat defi-
cits, and were paying high prices for imported wheat.

What else could Roumania do with its grain than sell to the Teutonic Allies? It sold them so much that before the first of 1915 the Roumanian Government put an embargo upon fúrther exportation, and in the spring of 1915 that country was even buying wheat to carry its population through to the summer harvest.

Roumania, having marketed its own grain, turned dealer for Russia. Russia has always been dependent upon her exportation of grain to pay for her imports of other things and the interest on her enormous foreign debts. Her grain crop, harvested, found the Dardanelles closed by the Turks and the Baltic exit held by the Germans. Exportation to western Europe via Vladivostok and the Suez Canal was out of the question, partly by reason of the high freights and partly because of the deterioration due to transportation through the tropics.

Moreover, Russian grain cannot be indefinitely stored, as ours can. That country has few grain elevators like those of the United States and western Europe. Russian grain is usually sacked and stored on the open shipping platform of the country railroad station, covered only with a tarpaulin. At best it is put into an unheated shed. There is no capacity at the Russian seaboard for the storage of any quantity of grain. The successful marketing of the cereal depends upon an unhindered movement from ports like Odessa. Restrict that movement, and the grain backs up on the station platforms and in the farmers' shacks.

The dealers in this grain are mostly Jews. They have no especial love for Russia. They had advanced money to the farmers for which the grain served as security. They could get their money back only by selling the grain. The only countries they could reach, and which wanted to buy grain, were Germany and Austria.

Therefore they sold to Germany and Austria, not direct but via Sweden and Roumania. The early Russian embargo on grain exportation was universal, but this changed to an embargo on exports to Russia's enemies. The New York *Journal of Commerce* of February 18 contained a despatch from St. Petersburg, in which the Russian Ministry of Commerce and Industry was reported as believing that quantities of foodstuffs were reaching Germany from Russia through Finland and Sweden. The attention of the Russian authorities had been called to unusual shipments which had resulted in flooding Finland with frozen meat, flour, grain, butter and eggs. An inquiry was said to have revealed that Swedish commission merchants, who bought from the Finns, in most cases represented houses in Hamburg. The extraordinary demand for the Russian ruble in coin or in bills—a demand existing in both Sweden and Denmark—and the high prices offered for produce in Finland, were considered clear signs of this illegal trade.

The Russian Government itself must have winked at this trade. It was the only means of letting the Jew dealers make money, so that they would be avail-

able for taxation. The February 18 "discovery" of
the Russian Ministry of Commerce and Industry may
be attributed to pressure exerted on Russia by England to support the British starvation plan. There
is plenty of evidence that the Russian trade did not
cease on February 18. If the Dardanelles still hold
out when the Russian 1915 harvest is gathered, we
may expect to see another flood of foodstuffs into
Germany, if Germany is in the market. The chances
are that the latter country will have far less use for
imported food during the coming year.

With respect to Germany's measures for increasing agricultural production, one difficulty has existed
of a kind not yet mentioned. This is the loss of
foreign supply of fertilizer. The large German agricultural production, on an area only equal in size to
the state of Texas, is only possible by a liberal use
of fertilizer. Commercial fertilizer is made from
potash, lime, nitrogen and phosphoric acid. Germany has the necessary potash and lime. Nitrate
has been imported in the form of Chili saltpeter, of
which 800,000 tons annually are brought from South
America. Some nitrogen has been procured at home
from ammonium sulphate, a by-product of coal-
tar distillation. Phosphoric acid has come from
abroad in the form of phosphate rock. A million
tons are annually imported: 400,000 from the United
States and 600,000 from Algiers and Tunis.

The oversea supply of nitrate and phosphate was
cut with the opening of the war. Fertilizer could
not be made without them. If fertilizer could

not be made, there was the prospect of a decrease of 25 per cent in the production of German agriculture. One of the German triumphs has been in the meeting of this situation.

The foreign phosphate supply was replaced by reclaiming the phosphate waste in the slag of iron ore smelted in Lorraine from the "minette" ore. The foreign nitrate supply was replaced partly by a larger quota of ammoniates from the coal-tar distilleries, but principally by the extraction of nitrogen from the air. This process had been developed— largely by German capital—in Norway, because there existed in Norway the cheap water power which alone made it commercially possible to produce this artificial nitrate in competition with the natural product of Chili. After the outbreak of the war, five such nitrate factories were established in Germany.—So the fertilizer difficulty has been met.

The new supply of nitrate also solved the powder question for Germany. Chili saltpeter was cut off by England's sea power, and a nitrate is necessary for powder. In ignorance of this substitute Sir John French in May gave an interview to the Havas Agency saying that the Germans were getting chary of ammunition and not wasting shells as before "because the failing supply of nitrates necessary for high explosives is making itself felt in Germany."

So much for the prospect of starving Germany in the matter of foods. How is it with regard to the necessary raw materials of industry? The situation has been considered at other points with respect to cotton, copper, rubber and wool. It was not hard to show that Germany's supply of each of these, or of substitutes for them, is such that there is no prospect of Britain's interference with the oversea supply affecting the duration or outcome of the war.

This applies also as to oil. Germany annually imports 750,000 tons of petroleum, over two-thirds of it from the United States. In the fiscal year 1914, ending June 30, we sold Germany $20,000,000 worth of petroleum or its products. Petroleum was made absolute contraband by Britain on October 29. There is no more flagrant abuse of British manipulation of the contraband list than is afforded by petroleum. Absolute contraband means articles so suited for warlike use that their destination for the military must be assumed. Such articles are guns and powder. But petroleum is used primarily for light, and, moreover, used by the poorer classes. The next largest use of it is in the form of gasoline, for motors. Some motors are mounted in automobiles, and some automobiles are used by the military. Can petroleum, by any stretch of the imagination, be conceived of as conforming to the definition of absolute contraband of war; namely, *obviously warlike nature, use and destination?* In the Declaration of London petroleum was not even on the conditional contraband list.

As has been the case with much of England's procedure in "starving" Germany, so with oil. The pressure has been heavier on the United States than on Germany. The Germans have found a substitute for the oil they could no longer import from us. The

Americans thrown out of work by an enforced decrease in our production and refining of oil were less
able to find substitute work in a depressed labor
market.

To a considerable extent, gas and electricity have
been used to replace petroleum. Moreover, the Germans have a substitute for gasoline as a motor fuel
in benzol, a product of the great coking industry
which produces coke and coal-tar. From the coal-
tar are distilled the various products that are bases
for the dyestuff industry, including benzol, which
also has other uses. Benzol is an acceptable substitute for gasoline for all motor purposes, except such
special uses as submarine and aeroplane engines. For
these uses Germany will hardly starve for gasoline.
The stock on hand at the opening of the war was
80,000 tons, and in May, 1915, the German forces
drove Russia out of the great Galician oil fields.

If we stand aside much longer and see Germany
compelled to find substitutes for American products
which Britain—according to our interpretation of
international law—illegally bars from Germany, it
is not impossible that we may force Germany so to
develop her substitutes that our old markets will be
permanently gone.

We should not be pleased, at the end of the war, to
find that Germany had developed a benzol that was a
perfect substitute for gasoline, and that she had pipe
lines from Galicia to supply such gasoline as she
continued to buy. The phosphate rock producers
would not be happy if Thomas slag proved a per-

manent substitute for our Florida rock. The copper miners would suffer if Germany, the largest user of copper, found the new soft steel suitable for many of the old uses of copper. Our farmers may not rejoice to find that we have aided in forcing Germany to raise at home the wheat and meat that we annually sold her in the past. May not Britain be asking us to drive German genius farther than our interests can follow?

Because of the sacrifices which Germany has laid upon herself, because of the genius which devised substitutes for what could not be imported, and because of the skill with which she has thrown her whole industrial organization into the new lines demanded by the state of war, her industries have worked on with perhaps less disturbance than is apparent in any other of the fighting countries. The English themselves admit this. For example, a writer in the March *British Technical Journal of Engineering* writes:

"In examining into the reasons why German industry has not only escaped being brought to a standstill by the war, but has even worked on with an imposing certainty without any suspicion of nervousness, it becomes clear that the most potent factor is that the German army aided in carrying the war into foreign countries. In addition to this, the industrial and financial authorities succeeded by wise measures in establishing confidence in the power of resistance of the German industrial organization, which in its turn rested upon military success.

"The causes of the uniform continuity in German industrial growth, however, in the last instance, ought to be found in the fact that German development more than that of any other country has grown systematically and shows no gaps of any moment in the manufacturing process. Germany produces herself all her half-finished goods, and she utilizes the residuary products of her industrial processes for the manufacture of valuable auxiliary commodities, with such financial results that no other industrial nation in the world even approaches her in this respect. What these auxiliary products mean to Germany at the present time is more especially demonstrated by sulphate of ammonium (nitrate) and benzol (fuel). The industrial expansion of Germany, although it is much newer than that of England, has been laid out on more systematic lines and in such a way as to render the country more nearly independent of foreign aid. Under the difficult and strenuous conditions of war are demonstrated the extreme value of system and method and the advantages which they confer on a nation when it is cut off from countries from which it draws raw material."

There is no indication of any industrial collapse in Germany, due to "economic pressure." Unemployment is no greater than in peace times. The freight earnings of the state railways, the surest measure of the movement of business, are nearly normal. There has been a decrease in foreign trade with oversea countries, not with all countries. Adjacent neutrals are still supplied by Germany, some of them in higher degree than ever before. The decrease in foreign trade is compensated, so far as industry in general is concerned, by the vast increase in production for the military.

One of England's mistakes in the war has been the willingness to sit still so long, and to await the silent action of the irresistible "economic pressure" which the siren voice of Winston Churchill told them would defeat Germany as certainly as winter struck the leaves from the trees. Whether Churchill's country can now regain the ground which Germany won while England was lulled by the siren, is the question of the outcome of the great European War.

How the war comes out is none of a neutral's affairs. Our business as a nation is to look after our own interests. If there has been any lurking belief that we could serve those interests by silently aiding Britain's economic pressure and so shortening the war and the period of our sacrifices, knowledge of the facts and the prospects must dissipate the illusion. The war will be shortened by military victory, in which we, as neutrals, cannot be participants.

Our interests dictate a resumption of our peaceful trade with Germany. Our interests speak the same language as our rights, our duty to treat belligerents alike and our need for maintaining precedents under which our children can live.

CHAPTER XV

WAR ORDERS AND THE POWER THEY PLACE IN OUR HANDS

Of all our exports, the most attention has fallen to the export of war munitions. We have heard a great deal of the moral and legal question as to whether a neutral should or may send abroad weapons for killing citizens of a nation with whom we are at peace. Such exportation is said to be more unjustified, because circumstances are such that only one of the belligerents, the Allies, can get supplies from us, while Germany cannot. On this ground we are charged with being unneutral as well as inhuman and false to our professions of being haters of war. The question is perplexing millions of Americans. No quick judgment can be passed upon it. Nor can any one person judge for another. Each decides for himself according to the combination which his own mind makes of such conflicting elements as humanity, our rights, our obligations, our precedents, our future and our material interests.

Before this war had been many months under way, it became apparent that it was to be largely a matter of ammunition. It is an artillery war. Under the hail of German shells the fall of Liège, Namur, Antwerp and Maubeuge was a matter of days. Then

Von Kluck was stopped in his rush for Paris partly because of a lack of ammunition. All winter the armies lay facing each other, inactive except for sporadic attacks, while Krupp, Skoda, Vickers, Schneider, the Bethlehem Steel Company and the Japanese arms and ordnance works were rushing through their orders to make ready for the spring campaign. Kitchener's remark that he did not know when the war would end, but that it would begin in May, was typical for all the contestants. They were waiting less for the firm dry ground of May than for the spring crop of shells.

The May days were battles of artillery. It was the terrible bombardment of British guns that cleared the way for the advance at Neuve Chapelle. It was heavy German guns that tore Hill 60 like a volcanic eruption when the British tried to hold it. French Seventy-fives in May buried German trenches before they were captured. Przemysl was "sprayed" with Teutonic shells and the fortress which Russian infantry had besieged for months fell before German artillery in as many days. It was lack of ammunition that forced Russia—largely cut off from foreign supplies by the Dardanelles and German control of the Baltic and with Archangel long closed—to lose all Galicia, Bukowina and Poland in the summer months of 1915.

Under these conditions it was natural for the Allies, who controlled the seas and who alone could keep up communication with us, early to close contracts with our main ammunition, arms and ordnance factories. The ammunition people were booked full for a long period ahead. Some big guns have been ordered, mostly from Bethlehem Steel, but the Allies' factories were better able to turn out the guns. It was shells they needed, particularly shrapnel. The big guns and small arms that we exported have gone primarily to Russia, because Russia is short on factories for war materials, having relied on the French and German makers; and because Russia in her Masurian and Galician defeats, when whole armies were captured, suffered the loss of vast quantities of the tools of war.

Shells were the principal demand. Shrapnel shells can be made by anyone with a lathe who can get the steel to work with. This country has an unlimited supply of steel and a very large number of machine shops which, due to the slack times in our industrial situation at home, were glad to get the shell contracts that were sublet to them by great contractors for the foreign governments, like the Canadian Car and Foundry Company. There is no doubt that these shell orders have been of considerable financial aid to great industries like those which manufacture electrical supplies, to the railroad equipment companies which at the beginning of the war noted the disappearance of incipient railroad orders, and to many a small machine shop throughout the land.

Before the end of 1914 a very large number of our industrial concerns were interested, directly or indirectly, in manufacturing implements of war. We have a large population of German or Austrian extraction who were outraged at the prospect of our turning allies of the Allies; and the practical effect of the situation was, they claimed, nothing less than this. When Congress opened in the first week of December bills prohibiting the export of arms to belligerents were introduced in both the House and the Senate, the bill of Senator Hitchcock of Nebraska being the one to which most attention has been paid. It never got beyond the Committee of Foreign Affairs, to which it was referred; the same fate befell Senator Works' later bill and also the various House measures.

A great many American manufacturers were unwilling to embark upon the manufacture of munitions of war without knowing that this was approved by our State Department. Many letters were sent the Department on the matter and on October 15 it issued a statement of its position. It said that a citizen of the United States could sell to a belligerent government or its agents any article of commerce which he chose. The risk he ran was that the goods he shipped, if contraband, would be intercepted and confiscated, if possible, by the belligerent against whom they were to be used. A neutral government is not compelled by international law to interfere with contraband trade from its territory to the belligerents, nor is the President of the United States or any executive department of the government possessed of the power so to interfere. So the statement read.

Official complaints of the German Government were

at first directed not against our exportation of arms
and ammunition in general, but against our exportation of war implements which were forbidden by
international law. On December 8 Count Bernstorff
called the attention of the State Department to
alleged violations of international law by the British
army. It was stated that the British army was using
dum-dum bullets. It was claimed that Winchester
and the Union Metallic Cartridge Company were engaged in supplying illegal forms of arms and ammunition to the Allies. The State Department was
asked to investigate these charges.

On January 8 the State Department answered the
German Ambassador. It stated that, while it was
willing to take into consideration such assertions as
were made in the Ambassador's note, with regard to
the British use of dum-dum bullets, it would not
investigate such charges or make any comment upon
them. Regarding the charge that American companies had been making illegal sorts of ammunition,
the specific denial of Winchester and the Union Metallic Cartridge Company was communicated to the
Ambassador.

About the middle of December it came to the
knowledge of the administration that the president
of the Bethlehem Steel Company, C. M. Schwab, had
contracted to deliver twenty submarines to Great
Britain during the war. The submarines were to be
delivered to Britain in parts, which were to be
assembled across the water. The Bethlehem Steel
Company apparently figured that this measure

would avoid the Hague Convention prohibition which forbids neutrals to construct war vessels for a belligerent. The State Department thought differently and Mr. Schwab, it was reported, agreed to desist.

The other case in which the administration was called upon to decide the legality of the exportation of war supplies was with regard to hydro-aeroplanes.

On January 19 the German Ambassador at Washing wrote the Secretary of State complaining that hydro-aeroplanes were being constructed in the United States and shipped to the Allies. He stated that hydro-aeroplanes were war vessels whose delivery to belligerent states by neutrals should be stopped under Article 8 of the Thirteenth Convention of the Second Hague Conference of October 18, 1907. The answer of the Secretary of State was a nugget of gold in the dry pages of diplomatic correspondence.

Its essential part reads:

"As to the assertion of the character of hydro-aeroplanes, I submit the following comments: The fact that a hydro-aeroplane is fitted with apparatus to rise from and alight upon the sea does not, in my opinion, give it the character of a vessel any more than the wheels attached to an aeroplane fitting it to rise from and alight upon land give the latter the character of a land vehicle."

Presumably, if conditions were reversed and the British were protesting hydro-aeroplanes which were being shipped to Germany, the ingenious German Ambassador would contend that the machines had asbestos fittings on their wings and hence were to be classed as fireflies.

In January the American Government had a second occasion to state its position regarding the exportation of war implements in general. On January 8 Senator Stone of Missouri wrote a letter to the Secretary of State. In this letter he summarized the complaints that he had received from sympathizers with Germany and Austria, regarding the manner in which we had been guarding our neutrality in the war. Complaint No. 9 was that we had exercised "no interference with the sale to Great Britain and her Allies of arms, ammunition, horses, uniforms and other munitions of war, although such sales prolonged the war."

In the answer of the Secretary of State, two weeks later, it was stated that the President of the United States had no power to prevent the sale of ammunition to the belligerents. It was said that it is not the duty of a neutral to restrict trade in munitions of war, and such had never been the policy of this government except in cases of civil strife in neighboring American republics. Germany herself, the answer continued, had been an enormous shipper of arms and ammunition to belligerents; for example, during the Russo-Japanese War. Moreover, Mr. Bryan said, on December 15 the German Ambassador presented a memorandum of his government specifically stating that under international law no exception can be taken to neutral states letting war material go to Germany's enemies. Finally, the answer read, these principles had been laid down by the United States Government in the October 15 proclamation of the Department of State, entitled "Neutrality and the trade in contraband."

The German Government, apparently encouraged by the agitation in this country regarding the export of ammunition, included a reference to it in its first formal note to us: the note of February 16, answering our protest regarding the German War Zone. In this note, the Germans pointed out "very particularly and with the greatest emphasis" that a trade in arms estimated at many hundred million marks had arisen between American manufacturers and Germany's enemies. It was admitted that no formal breach of neutrality could be charged but both the German Government and the German people felt themselves placed at a great disadvantage in that neutrals achieved no success in the assertion of their legal right to innocent trade with Germany while they persisted in their contraband trade with Great Britain.—The words were less a protest against our export of arms on principle than against our export of arms to England when we refused to insist upon our right to send food and raw materials to Germany.

This passage in the note of the German Government required no answer. The same cannot be said of an unusual communication from the German Ambassador to the State Department, dated April 4, a short note enclosing a memorandum of the Ambassador on the subject of our arms exports.

The memorandum stated that, because of the

British Orders in Council, neutral trade with Germany had been strangled. The Wilhelmina, the first food ship for Germany, had been held up for two months. Such a delay, the Ambassador continued, was equivalent to a denial of the American right to trade. The Imperial Embassy must, therefore, assume that the United States Government acquiesced in the violations of international law by Great Britain. It was claimed that all previous policies of shipping arms to neutrals were inapplicable in this war. The United States was said to be the only neutral nation furnishing war material to belligerents and an entirely new industry was being created in America for this purpose. It was pointed out that the industry was delivering goods only to the enemies of Germany. The least that America could do, the Ambassador said, was to utilize its supplying of arms to England for the purpose of protecting its legitimate trade with Germany, especially in foodstuffs.

Moreover, the memorandum went on, for the United States to put an embargo on the export of arms to belligerents in Europe would be similar to President Wilson's reason for putting an embargo on the exportation of arms in Mexico; namely, in President Wilson's words:

"Because Carranza had no ports, while Huerta had them and was able to import these materials, it was our duty as a nation to treat Carranza and Huerta upon an equality if we wished to observe the true spirit of neutrality as compared with mere paper neutrality."

The German Ambassador then asserted that this principle, if applied in the present case, would lead to an embargo on the exportation of arms.

On April 21 Mr. Bryan sent to the German Ambassador an answer which the President of the United States had written. It was a proper answer to the memorandum of Count von Bernstorff. It suggested that the relations between the United States and England were not a proper subject of discussion for the German Ambassador. It was assumed that the Ambassador did not intend the clear implication in his note that the United States had not in good faith been performing its duties as a neutral. As a matter of fact, the answer continued, the United States had acquiesced in no violation of its neutral rights. It was shown that this was evidenced by our notes of protest to England. Our impartiality, said the President, was evident by our suggestion to Great Britain and Germany that they should return to the fold of international law. It was denied that the United States Government had the choice of stopping the sale and exportation of arms by its citizens. It was affirmed that under international law, if a country is to maintain its neutrality, it may not during the progress of the war alter its own rules of neutrality. The President said that the placing of an embargo on the trade in arms at the present time would be a direct violation of our neutrality.

In July, 1915, the Austrian Government formally protested our ammunition exports. An answer was sent Austria early in August, similar to the answer

sent Count von Bernstorff. The Germans alleged
the presence of ammunition on the Lusitania as their
justification for torpedoing her. The crux of the
present diplomatic correspondence with Germany is
the question whether passengers can sail on munitions
ships and protect those ships from sudden attack by
submarines.

As a matter of fact, the German Government
cannot well call upon either international law or its
own practices to contest our right to ship arms to
belligerent nations. It was in the manufacture of war
materials delivered all over the world to nations both
at peace and at war that Krupp grew so great that
it can now supply most of the needs of the Teutonic
Allies, without outside aid. In Article 7, Convention
VII, and Article 7, Convention XII, of the Hague
Conference of 1907 the right of neutral citizens to
ship arms to belligerents is stated. These provisions
are but the crystallization of immemorial practice
among nations. Kriege, German delegate to that
Hague Conference, declared during the proceedings
that:

"Neutral states are not bound to forbid their subjects to engage in a commerce which from the point
of view of belligerents must be considered illicit."

As for our rights in the matter, they are not lessened by the fact that 20,000,000 or more of our
people are of German and Austrian descent, and that
all of the ammunition is being used against their
brothers in Europe. Our rights are not lessened, nor

our neutrality impaired by the circumstance that only one of the belligerents can get our supplies. We are willing to sell to both; but only England can send its ships to take away what it buys. England's advantage is an incident of its sea power and we are under no obligation to deprive it of the advantage which its sea power confers. We have repeatedly in the past refused to lay arms embargoes at the request of belligerents. who were suffering by our war exports. All our arms embargoes in the past have been at times of national peril when it was necessary to conserve our supplies for the home defense; or embargoes for the purpose of discouraging civil contentions in near-by Latin American countries, like Mexico and San Domingo. There is no doubt, the rights and the precedents in the matter are with us.

It is rather upon grounds of humanity that many American neutrals stand with the German sympathizers in this country in the demand that the arms export cease. They cannot reconcile our peace conferences and our peace propaganda with the creation of perhaps the greatest arms industry the world has ever seen. The war might have been over months ago if we had refused to send ammunition. To be sure, it might have been over to the advantage of the prepared Germans, but is it the business of a neutral to worry which side wins the war? Is not German preparedness an advantage which we are in no way obligated to compensate?

There are some features of this mushroom ammunition business that are not attractive. Hotels in New

York swarm with brokers soliciting orders from foreign buyers and native producers. Graft and bribery necessarily follow the huge profits in these contracts. We hear strange rumors of attempts to bribe government officials to sell at exorbitant prices discarded Krag-Jorgensen rifles. It is as if a new gold field were discovered.

Some of the up-to-date methods of booming the ammunition trade are less attractive than business-like. On May 6, 1915, the Cleveland Automatic Machine Company published a double page advertisement in the *American Machinist*. It announced a special lathe for making a high explosive shell. On one page was given a cut of the lathe and a cross-section of the shell that it made. On the other page is a description of the shell's peculiar properties.

"The material is high in tensile strength and Very Special and has a tendency to fracture into small pieces upon the explosion of the shell. The timing of the fuse for this shell is similar to the shrapnel shell, but it differs in that two explosive acids are used to explode the shell in the large cavity. The combination of these two acids causes terrific explosion, having more power than anything of its kind yet used. Fragments become coated with these acids in exploding and wounds caused by them mean death in terrible agony within four hours if not attended to immediately.

"From what we are able to learn of conditions in the trenches, it is not possible to get medical assistance to anyone in time to prevent fatal results. It is necessary immediately to cauterize the wound if in the body or head, or to amputate if in the limbs, as there seems to be no antidote that will counteract the poison.

"It can be seen from this that this shell is more effective than the regular shrapnel, since the wounds caused by shrapnel balls and fragments in the muscles are not as dangerous, as they have no poisonous element making prompt attention necessary."

It is easy to be shocked by this frank exposition of the death-dealing qualities of an American product. But, after all, this is a perfectly logical advertisement. People are buying shells to kill; therefore the killing qualities of the shells are the qualities to put forward. The advertisement is not directed to the general public, but to the makers and buyers of shells. Makers, if sensible, will make this type of shell. Buyers, if they are wise, will insist upon this Very Special product in their specifications.

Yet, in spite of all sentimental talk against the export of arms, our right to export them cannot be denied or even logically disputed. The pound of flesh is ours. What is more, the law of Venice not only allows us but compels us to take it. In the preamble to the 1907 Hague Convention we read:

"The rules impartially adopted by the neutral powers shall not be altered in principle during the course of the war by one of the neutrals, except in the case where experience shows the necessity for such action in order to safeguard the nation's rights."

It was this to which the President referred in his note to Ambassador Bernstorff, explaining that to place an arms embargo in the middle of the war would be a violation of our neutrality.

There are some tangible advantages that we shall gain from a continuation of the arms industry. Besides employing men in the machine shops who would otherwise be out of work, we are training a large number of mechanics in the rapid production of the weapons of war. They would be a great asset to us in any war in which we might have to engage in the future. Every war of the future will be still more an artillery war than the present. As a French senator says, "the problem is to industrialize war." We are industrializing war. The plants and the men we shall have, trained and ready at the end of this conflict, may be worth to us fifty army corps. They will be worth this to us not only in the unhappy event of war, but also a known reserve power with which to prevent war.

It is frequently said that we must continue our arms exports because we cannot afford to aid in establishing the principle that belligerents in war time shall not get arms from a neutral. Such a principle, it is said, would condemn to helplessness an unprepared nation attacked by a prepared aggressor. The unprepared would be unable to turn to neutrals for arms with which to defend itself.

The argument is sound on general lines, but it has no value when applied specifically to us. In any future war we need fear only a European or Asiatic aggressor, separated from us by a wide expanse of ocean. As a possible supplier of arms, we can think only of one of the nations of western Europe or Japan. No one else makes them. If we in that war cannot command the seas, obviously we shall get no arms or ammunition. If we in that war command the seas, we shall need no aid in arming ourselves. No one can reach us. Surely our former arms manufacturing facilities, expanded as they have been by the European War, will suffice to keep the navy and the coast defenses supplied with shells. If before the war breaks out we have not enough ammunition for the regular army to repel a surprise landing, we can hardly expect our opponent to politely wait until we go abroad and bring it back.

The real arguments for continuing the manufacture of arms for the Allies are that it is to our present commercial and military interest so to continue, and that it is our duty as a neutral to do so. England would justly accuse us of unneutrality, if without reason, in the midst of the war, we ceased the shipments of arms which our government had publicly approved and upon which, relying on the given word of our government, the Allies have become dependent. There is no doubt that, whatever our personal sentiments, our official actions up to this point have imposed upon us some obligations in the matter.

Upon only one condition can we withdraw from the fulfillment of those obligations, namely,

"In the case where experience shows the necessity for such action in order to safeguard a nation's rights."

If we are ever to learn by experience, we have learned that some action is necessary in order to safeguard our nation's rights. In two strong notes of protest to Great Britain, we stated her violations of our rights. She prevents us from shipping non-contraband to Germany and receiving any goods from Germany at all, in defiance of our right to enjoy such trade via neutral countries even if Britain were to establish that her blockade of German ports is effective. Britain has seriously deranged our trade with the little neutral nations of Europe upon the suspicion that some of the trade may be going through to Germany. We have seen in great detail how deeply these violations of our rights affect our material interests, how little submission to them would accord with our history or our rank as a leading neutral, and how dangerous is such submission for our future welfare.

Therefore, neither Great Britain nor any other nation of the world could blame us if we laid an embargo upon the exportation of arms for the purpose of enforcing our right to trade unhindered with Germany and the neutral nations of Europe, in all but contraband (as defined in a reasonable contraband list) with German destination. Our rights and the rights of neutral nations are that international law be observed, international law as codified and recognized by civilized people in the Declaration of London. Now, in the midst of the conflict, there is no time to frame a new code.

The Allies have placed with us somewhere between

$500,000,000 and $1,000,000,000 of arms and equipment orders. That is the precise measure of the power we have over them. If the United States had set out in October to secure a means to force belligerents to return to the realm of international law, it could not have proceeded more wisely than to publish its October 15 proclamation assuring this country and others of the legitimacy of our arms trade.

There need be no formal session of Congress to declare an arms embargo. The State Department need only intimate that the administration is prepared to call such a session, and the result will be attained. A word to the wise, from the wise and the powerful, is sufficient.

Should the impossible happen and should it be necessary to declare an arms embargo, the country would by no means be plunged into ruin. England could not fight us; that would mean to starve herself. In bringing our own armament up to date, our government could afford to employ the country's arms capacity whose contracts with the Allies would be broken.

That is more than impossible. England would know that an arms embargo might be followed by a food embargo, if necessary to attain our rights. These rights are so incontestable and this means of attaining them is so in accord with even the letter of international law, that a country which has pawned with us its military future would not think of losing so precious a pledge.

In every note that Germany has written she has

emphasized that the submarine campaign is a retaliation for the unlawful British measures in holding up food and raw materials for Germany. When both belligerents are breaking the law and each is claiming the acts of the other as justification, the pressure of neutrals must be applied to the one which refuses to join in a return to law and order. Our problem is to compel that joint acceptance of a compromise which we proposed in our note to the belligerents in February.—Germany is ready for acceptance; the pressure must be applied to England.

With the attainment of this end—the acceptance of the Declaration of London and its contraband list by England and Germany and the return by Germany to lawful use of her war vessels—both belligerents return to the limits of law. Neutral trade rights are recovered and established for all time. Our excuse for stopping the export of arms ceases. In unhindered access to the arms supplies of the oversea world, barred to Germany, England enjoys a great advantage from her sea power, the only advantage which she can be allowed to enjoy without destroying the rights of those who have had no part in making or prosecuting this war.

APPENDIX

PRESIDENT WILSON'S APPEAL FOR IMPARTIALITY AND RESTRAINT IN DISCUSSING THE WAR

My Fellow Countrymen: I suppose that every thoughtful man in America has asked himself during the last troubled weeks what influence the European War may exert upon the United States, and I take the liberty of addressing a few words to you in order to point out that it is entirely within our own choice what its effects upon us will be and to urge very earnestly upon you the sort of speech and conduct which will best safeguard the nation against distress and disaster.

The effect of the war upon the United States will depend upon what American citizens say or do. Every man who really loves America will act and speak in the true spirit of neutrality, which is the spirit of impartiality and fairness and friendliness to all concerned. The spirit of the nation in this critical matter will be determined largely by what individuals and society and those gathered in public meetings do and say, upon what newspapers and magazines contain, upon what our ministers utter in their pulpits and men proclaim as their opinions on the streets.

The people of the United States are drawn from many nations, and chiefly from the nations now at war. It is natural and inevitable that there should be the utmost variety of sympathy and desire among them with regard to the issues and circumstances of the conflict. Some will wish one nation, others another, to succeed in the momentous struggle. It will be easy to excite passion and difficult to allay it. Those responsible for exciting it will assume a heavy responsibility; responsibility for no less a thing than that the people of the United States, whose love of their country and whose loyalty to its government should unite them as Americans all, bound in honor and affection to think first of her and her interests, may be divided in camps of hostile opinions, hot against each other, involved in the war itself in impulse and opinion, if not in action. Such diversions among us would be fatal to our peace of mind and might seriously stand in the way of the proper performance of our duty as the one great nation at peace, the one people holding itself ready to play a part of impartial mediation and speak the counsels of peace and accommodation, not as a partisan, but as a friend.

I venture, therefore, my fellow countrymen, to speak a solemn word of warning to you against that deepest, most subtle, most essential breach of neutrality which may spring out of partisanship, out of passionately taking sides. The United States must be neutral in fact as well as in name during these days that are to try men's souls. We must be impartial in thought as well as in action, must put a curb upon our sentiments *as well as upon every transaction that might be construed as a preference of one party to the struggle before another.*

My thought is of America. I am speaking, I feel sure, the earnest wish and purpose of every thoughtful American that this great country of ours, which is, of course, the first in our thoughts and in our hearts, should show herself in this time of peculiar trial a nation fit beyond others to exhibit the fine poise of undisturbed judgment, the dignity of self-control, the efficiency of dispassionate action, a nation that neither sits in judgment upon others nor is disturbed in her own counsels and which keeps herself fit and free to do what is honest and disinterested and truly serviceable for the peace of the world.

Shall we not resolve to put upon ourselves the restraint which will bring to our people the happiness and the great and lasting influence for peace we covet for them?

WOODROW WILSON.

Washington, August 18, 1914.

BRITISH AUGUST 20 ORDER IN COUNCIL

Whereas during the present hostilities the naval forces of His Majesty will co-operate with the French and Russian naval forces; and

Whereas it is desirable that the naval operations of the allied forces so far as they affect neutral ships and commerce should be conducted on similar principles; and

Whereas the governments of France and Russia have informed His Majesty's government that during the present hostilities it is their intention to act in accordance with the provisions of the Convention known as the Declaration of London, signed on the 26th day of February, 1909, so far as may be practicable.

Now, therefore, His Majesty, by and with the advice of His Privy Council, is pleased to order, and it is hereby ordered, that during the present hostilities the Convention known as the Declaration of London shall, subject to the following additions and modifications, be adopted and put in force by His Majesty's government as if the same had been ratified by His Majesty:

The additions and modifications are as follows:

(1) The lists of absolute and conditional contraband contained in the Proclamation dated August 4, 1914, shall be substituted for the lists contained in Articles 22 and 24 of the said Declaration.

(2) A neutral vessel which succeeded in carrying contraband to the enemy with false papers may be detained for having carried such contraband if she is encountered before she has completed her return voyage.

(3) The destination referred to in Article 33 may be inferred from any sufficient evidence, and (in addition to the presumption laid down in Article 34) shall be presumed to exist if the goods are consigned to or for an agent of the enemy state or to or for a merchant or other person under the control of the authorities of the enemy state.

(4) The existence of a blockade shall be presumed to be known—

(a) to all ships which sailed from or touched at an enemy port a sufficient time after the notification of the blockade to the local authorities to have enabled the enemy government to make known the existence of the blockade;

(b) to all ships which sailed from or touched at a British or allied port after the publication of the declaration of blockade.

(5) Notwithstanding the provisions of Article 35 of the said Declaration, conditional contraband, if shown to have the destination referred to in Article 33, is liable to capture, to whatever port the vessel is bound and at whatever port the cargo is to be discharged.

(6) The General Report of the Drafting Committee on the said Declaration presented to the Naval Conference and adopted by the conference at the eleventh plenary meeting on February 25, 1909, shall be considered by all prize courts as an authoritative statement of the meaning and intention of the. said Declaration, and such courts shall construe and interpret the provisions of the said Declaration by the light of the commentary given therein.

The British October 29 Order in Council

1. During the present hostilities the provisions of the Convention known as the Declaration of London shall, subject to the exclusion of the lists of contraband and non-contraband, and to the modification hereinafter set out, be adopted and put in force by His Majesty's government. The modifications are as follows:

(I) A neutral vessel, with papers indicating a neutral destination, which notwithstanding the destination shown on the papers, proceeds to an enemy port, shall be liable to capture and condemnation if she is encountered before the end of her next voyage.

(II) The destination referred to in Article 33 of the said Declaration shall (in addition to the presumptions laid down in Article 34) be presumed to exist if the goods are consigned to or for an agent, of the enemy state.

(III) Notwithstanding the provisions of Article 35 of the said Declaration, conditional contraband shall be liable to capture on board a vessel bound for a neutral port if the goods are consigned "to order," or if the ship's papers do not show who is the consignee of the goods, or if they show a consignee of the goods in territory belonging to or occupied by the enemy.

(IV) In the cases covered by the preceding paragraph (III) it shall lie upon the owners of the goods to prove that their destination was innocent.

2. Where it is shown to the satisfaction of one of His Majesty's principal Secretaries of State that the enemy government is drawing supplies for its armed forces from or through a neutral country, he may direct that in respect of ships bound for a port in that country, Article 35 of the said Declaration shall not apply. Such direction shall be notified in the *London Gazette* and shall operate until the same is withdrawn. So long as such direction is in force, a vessel which is carrying conditional contraband to a port in that country shall not be immune from capture.

The British March 11 Order in Council

1. No merchant vessel which sailed from her port of departure after the first of March, 1915, shall be allowed to proceed on her voyage to any German port.

Unless the vessel receives a pass enabling her to proceed to some neutral or allied port to be named in the pass, goods on board any such vessel must be discharged in a British port and placed in the custody of the marshal of the prize court. Goods so discharged, not being contraband of war, shall, if not requisitioned for the use of His Majesty, be restored by order of the court, upon such terms as the court may in the circumstances deem to be just, to the person entitled thereto.

2. No merchant vessel which sailed from any German port after the first of March, 1915, shall be allowed to proceed on her voyage with any goods on board laden at such port.

All goods laden at such port must be discharged in a British or allied port. Goods so discharged in a British port shall be placed in the custody of the marshal of the prize court, and, if not requisitioned for the use of His Majesty, shall be detained or sold under the direction of the prize court. The proceeds of goods so sold shall be paid into court and dealt with in such a manner as the court may in the circumstances deem to be just.

Provided, that no proceeds of the sale of such goods shall be paid out of court until the conclusion of peace, except on the application of the proper officer of the crown, unless it be shown that the goods had become neutral property before the issue of this order.

Provided also, that nothing herein shall prevent the release of neutral property laden at such enemy port on the application of the proper officer of the crown.

3. Every merchant vessel which sailed from her port of departure after the first of March, 1915, on her way to a port, other than a German port, carrying goods with an enemy destination, or which are enemy property, may be required to discharge such goods in a British or allied port. Any goods so discharged in a British port shall be placed in the custody of the marshal of the prize court, and, unless they are contraband of war, shall, if not requisitioned for the use of His Majesty, be restored by order of the court, upon such terms as the court may in the circumstances deem to be just to the person entitled thereto.

Provided, that this article shall not apply in any case falling within Articles 2 or 4 of this order.

4. Every merchant vessel which sailed from a port other than a German port after the first of March, 1915, having on board goods which are of enemy origin or are enemy property may be required to discharge such goods in a British or allied port. Goods so discharged in a British port shall be placed in the custody of the marshal of the prize court, and if not requisitioned for the use of His Majesty shall be detained or sold under the direction of the prize court. The proceeds of goods so sold shall be paid into court and dealt with in such manner as the court may in the circumstances deem to be just.

Provided, that no proceeds of sale of such goods shall be paid out of court until the conclusion of peace except on the application of the proper officer of the crown, unless it be shown that the goods had become neutral property before the issue of this order.

Provided, also, that nothing herein shall prevent the release of neutral property of enemy origin on the application of the proper officer of the crown.

5. Any person claiming to be interested in, or to have any claim in respect of, any goods (not being contraband of war) placed in the custody of the marshal of the prize court under this order, or in the proceeds of such goods, may forthwith issue a writ in the prize court against the proper officer of the

crown and apply for an order that the goods should be restored to him, or that their proceeds should be paid to him, or for such other order as the circumstances of the case may require.

The practice and procedure of the prize court shall, so far as applicable, be followed mutatis mutandis in any proceedings consequential upon this order.

6. A merchant vessel which has cleared for a neutral port from a British or allied port, or which has been allowed to pass, having an ostensible destination to a neutral port, and proceeds to an enemy port, shall, if captured on any subsequent voyage, be liable to condemnation.

7. Nothing in this order shall be deemed to affect the liability of any vessel or goods to capture or condemnation independently of this order.

8. Nothing in this order shall prevent the relaxation of the provisions of this order in respect of the merchant vessels of any country which declares that no commerce intended for or originating in Germany or belonging to German subjects shall enjoy the protection of its flag.

Extract from British March 23 Order in Council, Revising Rule 29 of the Prize Court and empowering England to seize any Neutral Vessel

Where it is made to appear to the Judge, on the application of the proper officers of the court, that it is desired to requisition on behalf of His Majesty a ship in respect of which no final decree of condemnation has been made, he shall order that the ship shall be appraised, and that upon an undertaking being given in accordance with Rule 5 of this order, the ship shall be released and delivered to the crown.

United States Note presented jointly to Britain and Germany, February 20, suggesting Modifications in the Severity of their War at Sea

"In view of the correspondence which has passed between this government and Great Britain and Germany respectively relative to the declaration of a war zone by the German Admiralty, and the use of neutral flags by British merchant vessels, this government ventures to express the hope that the two belligerent governments may, through reciprocal concessions, find a basis for agreement which will relieve neutral vessels engaged in peaceful commerce from the great dangers which they will incur on the high seas adjacent to the coasts of the belligerents.

"The government of the United States respectfully suggests that an agreement in terms like the following might be entered into. This suggestion is not to be regarded as in any sense a proposal made by this government, for it of course fully recognizes that it is not its privilege to propose terms of agreement between Great Britain and Germany, even though the matter be one in which it and the people of the United States are directly and deeply interested. It is merely venturing to take the liberty which it hopes may be accorded a sincere friend desirous of embarrassing neither nation involved, and of serving, if it may, the common interests of humanity. The course outlined is offered in the hope that it may draw forth the views and elicit the suggestions of the British and German governments on a matter of capital interest to the whole world.

"Germany and Great Britain to agree:—

"First. That neither will sow any floating mines, whether upon the high seas or in territorial waters; that neither will plant on the high seas anchored mines except within cannon range of harbors for defensive purposes only; and that all mines shall bear the stamp of the government planting them, and be so constructed as to become harmless if separated from their moorings.

"Second. That neither will use submarines to attack merchant vessels of any nationality except to enforce the right of visit and search.

"Third. That each will require their respective merchant vessels not to use neutral flags for the purpose of disguise or *ruse de guerre*.

"Germany to agree:—

"That all importations of food or foodstuffs from the United States (and from such other neutral countries as may ask it) into Germany shall be consigned to agencies to be designated by the United States government; that these American agencies shall have entire charge and control, without interference on the part of the German government, of the receipt and distribution of such importations, and shall distribute them solely to retail dealers bearing licenses from the German government entitling them to receive and furnish such food and foodstuffs to non-combatants only; that any violation of the terms of the retailers' licenses shall work a forfeiture of their rights to receive such food and foodstuffs for this purpose; and that such food and foodstuffs will not be requisitioned by the German government for any purpose whatsoever or be diverted to the use of the armed forces of Germany.

"Great Britain to agree:—

"That food and foodstuffs will not be placed upon the absolute contraband list, and that shipments of such commodities will not be interfered with or detained by British authorities if consigned to agencies designated by the United States government in Germany for the receipt and distribution of such cargoes to licensed German retailers for distribution solely to the non-combatant population.

"In submitting this proposed basis of agreement this government does not wish to be understood as admitting or denying any belligerent or neutral right established by the principles of international law, but would consider the agreement, if acceptable to the interested Powers, a *modus vivendi*, based upon expediency rather than legal right, and as not binding upon the United States either in its present form or in a modified form until accepted by this government."

LETTER OF PRESIDENT JEFFERSON TO THOMAS PINCKNEY, UNITED STATES MINISTER TO ENGLAND, REGARDING ENGLAND'S STOPPAGE OF OUR FOOD SHIPMENTS TO FRANCE

Philadelphia, September 7, 1793.

Sir:—We have received, through a channel which cannot be considered as authentic, the copy of a paper, styled "Additional Instructions to the Commanders of His Majesty's Ships of War and Privateers," &c., dated at St. James, June 8, 1793. If this paper be authentic, I have little doubt but that you will have taken measures to forward it to me. But as your communication of it may miscarry, and time in the meanwhile will be lost, it has been thought better that it should be supposed authentic and that on that supposition I should notice to you its very exceptional nature, and the necessity of obtaining explanations on the subject from the British government; desiring at the same time that you will consider this letter as provisionally written only, and as if never written, in the event that the paper which is the occasion of it be not genuine.

The first article of it (the British Order) *permits all vessels laden wholly or in part with corn, flour, or meal, bound to any port in France to be stopped and sent into any British port, to be purchased by that government, or to be released only on the condition of security given by the master that he will proceed to dispose of his cargo in the ports of some country in amity with His Majesty.*

This article is so manifestly contrary to the law of nations that nothing more would seem necessary than to observe that it is so. Reason and usage have established that *when two nations go to war, those who choose to live in peace retain their natural right to pursue their agriculture, manufactures, and other ordinary vocations, to carry the produce of their industry for exchange to all nations, belligerent or neutral, as usual, to go and come freely without injury or molestation,* and, in short, that the war among others shall be for them as if it did not exist. One restriction on their natural rights has been submitted to by nations at peace; that is to say, that of not furnishing to either party *implements merely of war* for the annoyance of the other, nor anything whatever to a place blockaded by its enemy.

What these implements of war are has been so often agreed and is so well understood as to leave little question about them at this day. There does not exist, perhaps, a nation in our common hemisphere, which has not made a particular enumeration of them in some or all of their treaties, under the name of contraband. It suffices for the present occasion to say that corn, flour, and meal are not of the class of contraband, and, consequently, remain articles of free commerce. *A culture which, like that of the soil, gives employment to such a proportion of mankind, could never be suspended by the whole earth or interrupted for them, whenever any two nations should think proper to go to war.*

The state of war then existing between Great Britain and France furnishes no legitimate right either to interrupt the agriculture of the United States or the peaceable exchange of its produce with all nations, and consequently the assumption of it will be as lawful hereafter as now, in peace as in war. No ground, acknowledged by the common reason of mankind, authorizes this act now, and unacknowledged ground may be taken at any time and at all times.

We see then a practice begun to which no time, no circumstances, prescribe any limits, and which strikes at the root of our agriculture, that branch of industry which gives food, clothing, and comfort to the great mass of the inhabitants of these states. If any nation whatever has a right to shut up to our produce all the ports of the earth except her own and those of her friends she may shut up these also and so confine us within our own limits. No nation can subscribe to such pretensions; *no nation can agree, at the mere will or interest of another, to have its peaceable industry suspended and its citizens reduced to idleness and want.* The loss of our produce destined for foreign markets, or that loss which would result from an arbitrary restraint of our markets, is a tax too serious for us to acquiesce in. *It is not enough for a nation to say we and our friends will buy your produce. We have a right to answer that it suits us better to sell to their enemies as well as their friends.* Our ships do not go to France to return empty. They go to exchange the surplus of one produce which we can spare for surpluses of other kinds which they can spare and we want; which they furnish on better terms, and more to our mind, than Great Britain or her friends.

We have a right to judge for ourselves what market best suits us and they have none to forbid to us the enjoyment of the necessaries and comforts which we may obtain from any other independent country.

This act, too, tends directly to draw us from that state of peace in which we are wishing to remain. *It is an essential character of neutrality to furnish no aids (not stipulated by treaty) to one party which we are not equally ready to furnish to the other. If we permit corn to be sent to Great Britain and her friends, we are equally bound to permit it to France. To restrain it would be a partiality which might lead to a war with France, and between restraining it ourselves and permitting her enemies to restrain it unrightfully is not difference.* She would consider this as a mere pretext, of which she would not be the dupe; and on what honorable ground could we otherwise explain it? Thus we should see ourselves plunged by this unauthorized act of Great Britain into a war with which we meddle not, and which we wish to avoid if justice to all parties and from all parties will enable us to avoid it. In the case where we found ourselves obliged by treaty to withhold from the enemies of France the right of arming in our ports, we thought ourselves in justice bound to withhold the same right from France also, and we did it.

Were we to withhold from her (France) supplies of provisions, we should in like manner be bound to withhold them from her enemies also, and thus shut to ourselves all the ports of Europe where corn is in demand or make ourselves parties in the war. This is a dilemma which Great Britain has no right to force upon us, and for which no pretext can be found in any part of our conduct. She may, indeed, feel the desire of starving an enemy nation, but she can have no right of doing it at our loss nor of making us the instruments of it.

The President therefore desires that you will immediately enter into explanations on this subject with the British government. Lay before them in friendly and temperate terms all the demonstrations of the injury done us by this act, and endeavor to obtain a revocation of it and full indemnification to any citizens of these states who may have suffered by it in the meantime. Accompany your representations · by every assurance of our earnest desire to live on terms of the best friendship and harmony with them and to found our expectations of justice on their part on a strict observance of it on ours.

It is with concern, however, I am obliged to observe that so marked has been the inattention of the British court to every application which has been made to them on any subject by this government (not a single answer I believe having ever been given to one of them, except in the act of exchanging a minister), that it may become unavoidable, in certain cases, where an answer of some sort is necessary, to consider their silence as an answer. Perhaps this is their intention. Still, however, desirous of furnishing no color of offense, we do not wish you to name to them any term for giving an answer. Urge one as much as you can without commitment, and on the first day of December be so good as to give us information of the state in which this matter is, that it may be received during the session of Congress. . . .

Whether these explanations with the British government shall be verbal or in writing, is left to yourself. Verbal communications are very insecure; for it is only to deny them or to change their terms, in order to do away their effect at any time. Those in writing have as many and obvious advantages, and ought to be preferred, unless there be obstacles of which we are not apprized.

I have the honor to be, with great and sincere esteem, dear sir, your most obedient servant.

MINORITY REPORT OF THE COMMITTEE ON MERCHANT MARINE OF THE UNITED STATES CHAMBER OF COMMERCE, FAVORING THE SHIP PURCHASE BILL

I dissent from the views of the majority of this Committee, and approve of the Ship Purchase Bill now before Congress.

The emergency is such that the ordinary arguments against the government entering the field of private business do not apply.

The emergency is the re-establishment, or the maintenance, of our trade communication with neutral and belligerent European countries which are our chief markets and sources of supply.

I conceive that the chief task confronting us today is to

uphold, as against all belligerents, the rights of our merchants to the peaceful pursuit of commerce of all sorts, uninterrupted excepting for contraband of war sent to belligerents. This is the principle for which this country has fought successfully at recent international conferences.

This principle is being increasingly violated by belligerents in the present war. I apprehend that vessels owned by the United States Government will have a standing that will compel respect by all belligerents. There can be no question of the good faith in which they were purchased, no matter what the source. It can be guaranteed that they carry no contraband. All excuse for interfering with the commerce they carry will be removed.

As a theory, government ownership of merchant vessels is wrong. As a measure to meet the present economic emergency, it is justified and right.

(Signed) E. J. CLAPP.

February 1, 1915.

DECLARATION WHICH AMERICAN ASSOCIATE MEMBERS OF THE LIVERPOOL COTTON EXCHANGE WERE ASKED TO SIGN

DECLARATION

I,   of   , an Associate Member of the Liverpool Cotton Association, do solemnly and sincerely declare that neither I nor my firm nor any partner in the same nor any branch house or other firm or firms in which I or any one of my partners may be directly or indirectly pecuniarily interested will trade or have dealings with any person or a member or representative of any firm or person domiciled or carrying on business in any state at present at war with His Britannic Majesty until such time as peace may have been declared, and I further undertake when trading with subjects of neutral countries to make all necessary enquiries in order to satisfy myself as to the ultimate destination of the goods and that none of them are intended for consumption in or for transit through any state at war with His Majesty.

Declared this   *day of*

Witness

Address of Witness

Record of British Detentions of American Copper
Exports to Neutrals, Autumn, 1914

British Detentions of Copper Destined for Italy,
October to November, 1914

Ship	Nationality	Destina-tion	Sailed	Seized	Copper Cargo (tons)
Ascot	British	Italy	Oct. 10	Oct. 26	1340
Palermo	Italian	"	Oct. 20	Nov. 2	300
Regina d'Italia	"	"	Oct. 15	Oct. 26	1180
Italia	"	"	Oct. 24	Nov. 8	900
Kroonland	American	"	Oct. 15	Nov. 8	1300
San Giovanni	Italian	"	Oct. 14	Oct. 26	550
Duca di Genoa	"	"	Oct. 17	Nov. 8	300
Verona	"	"	Oct. 24	Nov. 8	325
Europa	"	"	Oct. 21	Nov. 8	300
San Guglielmo	"	"	Oct. 21	Nov. 8	700
Tabor	Norwegian	"	Oct. 26	Nov. 13	1020
Taurus	American	"	Nov. 1	Nov. 13	400
Perugia	British	"	Nov. 1	Nov. 13	515
Norheim	Norwegian	"	Oct. 17	Nov. 18	425

Total 9555

21,403,200 lbs.

British Detentions of Copper Destined to Sweden
(and Norway)

Ship	Nationality	Destina-tion	Sailed	Seized	Copper Cargo (tons)
Sif	———	Sweden	Oct. 31	Nov. 18	400
Sigrum	Norwegian	"	Nov. 8	Nov. 26	450
Ran	Swedish	"	Nov. 13	Dec. 1	650
Antones	Norwegian	"	Oct. 22	Nov. 14	650
Tyr	"	"	Oct. 29	Nov. 19	750
Francisco	British	"	Oct. 17	Nov. 2	200
Idaho	"	"	Oct. 24	Nov. 10	200
Toronto	"	"	Oct. 31	Nov. 15	200
Marengo	"	"	Oct. 10	Oct. 25	200
Galileo	"	"	Nov. 7	Nov. 26	200
New Sweden	Swedish	"	Dec. 6	Dec. 28	730
Soerland	Norwegian	"	Nov. 27	Dec. 28	600
Canton	Swedish	"	Nov. 12	Dec. 1	375

Total 5605

12,555,200 lbs.

Copper Agreement between United States Exporters and British Admiralty

Copper from United States of America to Neutral Countries

"Whilst His Majesty's Government are at present, so far as they are able, preventing any copper from reaching their enemies, they have no desire to interfere in any way with the sales of the United States copper producers to purchasers in neutral countries which are willing to guarantee that the copper which they import is for the consumption of those neutral countries.

"If the United States producers would be willing to co-operate, His Majesty's Government will not interfere with their copper shipments to those neutral countries which have placed copper on their prohibition list, and whose prohibitions of export are found to be effective.

"Whilst His Majesty's Government cannot abandon in any way their right to search vessels, they will be quite willing to allow to proceed to its destination all copper which is to be sold only to named consumers, and not to merchants, dealers or forwarding agents, in such neutral countries as have placed copper and articles manufactured mainly of copper on their list of prohibited exports, provided that a copy of the contract of sale is sent to the director of the Trade Division at the Admiralty, and it shall contain a clause to the effect that neither the copper itself nor any of its products shall be exported. Such copper upon arriving at its destination shall be put into warehouse, so that it cannot afterwards be declared in transit. The bill of lading must show clearly the name of the actual consumer, or of a recognized London merchant, or the name of a banker who shall be approved by His Majesty's Government.

"It is agreed that the undersigned will not export copper to Sweden, Norway, Denmark or Italy, except in compliance with, and subject to, the conditions of Article 3 hereof, and that it (the undersigned company) will not export copper to other neutral countries except subject to permit of British Admiralty.

"Shipments of copper to Great Britain or her allies may be made without restriction.

"All sale contracts for neutral countries to be forwarded to the British Admiralty, either through its London representatives or through His Britannic Majesty's Consul at the port of New York.

"Shipments of copper against contracts entered into previous to the signing of this agreement and any existing f. o. b. contracts are exempt from its provisions.

"We will be prepared to conform to the different provisions

set forth in the above regulations of the Admiralty as regards shipments of copper from the U. S. A. to neutral countries, and we assent to the terms of the letter of January 2, 1915, from Richard Webb, Director of Trade Division, to Messrs. C. S. Henry & Company, Ltd., a copy of which letter, marked Exhibit 'A', is attached hereto."

Blank Company . . . .

STATEMENT ISSUED BY BRITISH EMBASSY AT WASHINGTON, MAY 3, 1915, TELLING AMERICAN SHIPPERS HOW TO EXPORT TO EUROPEAN NEUTRAL COUNTRIES

"The British Embassy have received since the issue of the Order in Council of March 11 numerous applications from shippers of American produce for information and advice on general lines as to the steps which ought to be taken by them to facilitate the quicker expedition and passage of consignments of goods to neutral designations for neutral consumption.

"The British Embassy can give no assurance as to the immunity from visit and search or detention of any particular shipments, but with regard to consignments of non-contraband articles as well as of articles of conditional contraband, they are authorized to state that in cases where adequate information is furnished by consignors to show that the goods shipped are neutral property and are to be used exclusively for consumption in neutral countries or by the Allies, this will be taken into consideration by the authorities charged with the execution of the Order in Council. This will also apply to shipments of certain descriptions of goods listed as absolute contraband. Such goods are, however, usually subjected to closer scrutiny and control, and in some cases to special arrangements.

"It would greatly facilitate and expedite the work of clearing vessels bound to neutral ports, which call at or are brought into British ports for examination of their papers, if shipping houses or their agents would give British consular officers a duplicate of the final manifest of the vessel immediately on its departure for Europe in order that, if possible, it may be transmitted to the British authorities in London in time for it to be received and considered before the vessel arrives.

"To further accelerate proceedings, manifests and bills of lading should disclose the exact nature of the goods and wherever it is possible the name and full business address of the ultimate consignee as well as the name and address of the consignor.

"Shippers would avoid the use of generic descriptions such as hardware, dry salteries, machinery, &c., which are capable of being employed to conceal the real identity of goods classed as contraband. An exact definition of the specific character of consignments will save delay in their examination. It will also facilitate their identification with the articles comprised in the export embargo—lists of the country to which the goods are consigned. For example, in the case of lubricating oils, it should always be stated whether the oil is vegetable or mineral. The precise nature of animal and vegetable fats and oils should also be indicated. The term 'lard,' alone, for instance, is not adequate without some closer definition, because the lists of prohibited exports of certain neutral countries differentiate between various preparations and compounds of this article.

"It should be clearly understood that the forwarding of goods to a neutral port is not proof that they are destined for neutral consumption. Consignors should always endeavor to procure and exhibit complete information as to the final destination of the goods. Shipments manifested 'to order' or 'in transit,' or with bills of lading addressed to a branch or agency of the consignors, or to 'commission agents,' 'banks' or 'forwarding houses' for account of an unnamed consignee, afford no evidence as to their ultimate destination. Wherever it is practicable, the full name and address of the ultimate consignee should figure in the documents relative to the goods concerned, and metals should, so far as possible, be addressed to the actual consumers and not to dealers.

"In connection with the establishment of proof of ultimate destination, it may be observed that if goods definitely addressed to a neutral consignee can be clearly identified as being comprised in the export embargo list of the country to which they are consigned, this will be taken into consideration as corroborative evidence of their destinations for neutral consumption. Precision in describing goods will accordingly accelerate comparison with the lists of prohibited exports of neutral countries, and in the case of shipments to Sweden it would further hasten proceedings if the corresponding number of articles in the British tariff were always given in addition to the description of the goods. Certificates of final destination issued by the official representatives of the country concerned will be accepted as collateral evidence that the goods are for neutral use.

"In all arrangements which may be made for shipments of goods under the supervision of British Consular authorities, it should be clearly understood that the right of visit and search or detention is not waived, but that the operations of verification which may be called for by the proximity of the countries of destination to Germany is simplified and expedited if consular supervision has taken place and if full details are furnished.

"With regard to shipments to the Netherlands, wheat and wheat flour and meal destined for consumption in that country should be consigned to the Netherlands government, and all other articles on the British contraband lists, as well as cocoa, coffee and tobacco, destined for consumption in that country, should be consigned to the Netherlands Overseas Trust.

"Information as to the description of goods included in the British lists of absolute and conditional contraband will be furnished on application to any British Consul.

"The foregoing recommendations are offered for the assistance of shippers, and compliance with them will materially hasten the expedition and passage of cargoes in cases where there is no further information at the disposal of the authorities of a nature to throw doubt on the neutral character of the goods or their neutral destination."

CIRCULAR LETTER SENT TO AMERICAN IMPORTERS IN APRIL BY FOREIGN TRADE ADVISERS OF THE STATE DEPARTMENT, EXPLAINING THAT THE FOREIGN TRADE ADVISERS WILL PRESENT TO THE BRITISH AMBASSADOR REQUESTS FROM UNITED STATES IMPORTERS TO LET THEIR GOODS PASS THE BRITISH BLOCKADE, ON THE GROUND THAT THE GOODS WERE BOUGHT AND PAID FOR BEFORE MARCH 1

The following note has been received from the British Embassy at this capital relative to the movement of American-owned goods now in Germany to this country:

"The British Embassy are authorized to state that in cases where a merchant vessel sails from a port other than a German port carrying goods of enemy origin for which American importers claim to have made payment prior to March 1, 1915, proofs that such goods were paid for before March 1 may be submitted for examination to the Embassy. If such proofs are presented at a sufficiently early stage to enable the report thereon to be communicated in time to the British authorities, the results of the investigation will be taken into account and due weight attached to them in deciding whether the goods concerned should be discharged under the provisions of Article IV of the Order in Council of March 11."

On March 30, 1915, the government of the United States replied to the British Orders in Council assuming that the

British government will not deny the rule that innocent shipments may be freely transported to and from the United States through neutral countries to belligerent territory without being subject to the penalties of contraband traffic or breach of blockade, much less to detention, requisition or confiscation, and that this would of course include all outward-bound traffic from the neutral country and all inward-bound traffic to the neutral country except contraband in transit to the enemy.

While the government of the United States cannot in any way lend its aid in an official and formal manner to procuring American-owned goods now in Germany for the importers of the United States which would in the slightest degree amount to a recognition of the position of Great Britain in respect to non-contraband goods, especially from neutral ports, the Office of the Foreign Trade Advisers of the Department will aid informally American importers who desire to present proof of ownership of American goods in Germany for which American importers claim to have made payment prior to March 1, 1915.

You are therefore advised that if you desire to submit proofs of your ownership of goods, paid for before March 1, for examination by the British Embassy, you may forward such evidence as you have to the Foreign Trade Advisers of the Department of State. In doing so, it is suggested that you incorporate with the evidence of ownership and payment information in the following order:

1. A history of the case, showing dates of payment, nature of the goods bought, location of goods at the present, date when they reached their present location, name of steamer on which it is desired to ship such goods, date of sailing of such steamer and all further information pertaining to origin, payment, and shipment of goods in your possession.

2. Original bank drafts or evidence of transfer of money from this country to belligerent country, verified by bank officials if possible.

3. (Paragraph cancelled.)

4. Invoices of goods and such other evidence as will prove the identity of the goods with those actually paid for.

5. Such other and further information in regard to the shipment of goods and payment therefor as will be pertinent and corroborative.

This evidence will be collated and presented to the British Embassy for communication to the British authorities. In presenting this evidence the Foreign .Trade Advisers will act unofficially as your representatives and with the understanding that in so doing the Department does not recognize the position of the British government under Article IV of the Order in Council of March 11 or any other article contained in the

Orders in Council, but the unofficial aid of the Foreign Trade Advisers is given merely to facilitate the shipments of American-owned goods of belligerent origin.

Very truly yours,

ROBERT F. ROSE,
WILLIAM B. FLEMING,
Foreign Trade Advisers.

INDEX

Printed for the Yale University Press
by E. L. Hildreth